# THE NEW GUARD

LITERARY REVIEW

P.O. Box 5101
Hanover, NH 03755
www.newguardreview.com
www.writershotel.com

*Supporting writers in practice and in print.*
*We are writers for writers' sake.*

Cover painting: *Independence* 46 x 60", oil on wood panel © 2015 Marilyn Kalish

Cover art photograph by Michael Kalish, 2015


For book orders, please visit www.newguardreview.com
ISBN: 978-0-692-52629-3
Volume IV

$20

*In loving memory of Sara Patton*

## CONTENTS

# EDITOR'S NOTE

Writing an editor's note is an honor, in service of the authors appearing in this book. It's also in service of team *TNG*. We've all given of ourselves and pulled deep to make this anthology happen. An editor's note is a gesture of appreciation, one last moment to celebrate the rare opportunity to publish admired writers. Still, issuing an editor's note smacks of pomp and commotion. Like putting a mustache on the Mona Lisa. A certain absurdity of tone. I'd maybe like to weigh politics, let out my truth, or even go on about how "Editor's Note" is the name of a thoroughbred racehorse foaled in Kentucky in 1993. But in this context, talking about the severity of our difficult times, a profoundly serious matter, rings hollow. I'm going to keep it short. These stories and poems will see clear to those farthest reaches from where we are, in the liminal space between writers and readers. Perhaps the editor's note should be more like hanging a hat on a doorknob, if what's past that metaphorical door and threshold is the full florid universe.

Debut and established writers, who sent us their entries from all over the world, are presented between these covers. No doubt we will watch these writers broaden in art and scope over the coming years. Here, they've given us pieces that sing and strut and jump, pieces that sorrow and fight as their insistent voices come to find the light. Our poetry judge, Tim Seibles, selected *Seven and Seven Is*, by Jose Padua, a powerful poem that turns on a microcosmic childhood street and arches its narrative over America. Fiction judge Joe Wenderoth chose *Ghost Deer* by Micah Perks, a poignant fragmented narrative told by four family members, who tell stories in the spirit of Passover; stories that range from a petting zoo to Chile to Egypt. Alissa Paige Joseph is our Featured Writer, and her resonant story, *Nachlaot*, centers on a woman going to mikvah in Jerusalem as she has many times before, hoping and yearning for children. Throughout this volume are stunning stories and poems, all operating in concert to form an unforgettable anthology.

And with that, I'll take back my hat. Here's me waving to all of you readers before I take my exit. Here's me, blowing a kiss to my fellow writers, working hard and dreaming harder, laying your best words down hard, and never, never, never giving up. See? The door is open.

*—Shanna McNair, 2015*

*Roger Bonair-Agard*

# LETTER TO THE FUTURE

*Ave Maria, gratia plena...*
*Et benedictus fructus ventris*
Ave Maria

Dear Future:

I'm in love with ruin—the half-overgrown lots next to warehouses, the office chair on three wheels abandoned in it. I'm in love with the memory of industry, and the way rust captures sunlight and amplifies it toward the evening. I will not live in your afterglow. I've spent too many hours learning the names of flowers, and memorizing the flight patterns of starlings to recall when my sight leaves. Dear Future: my daughter will have more to do with you than I, but I'm casting spells to make her stomach muscled against attack, to enrich the precision of her kata, to make her supplication to you wholly unnecessary. It is not that you aren't beautiful. It is that you are made of ephemeral things: foreign cities, unbuilt houses, skills to be learned, paintings to be framed. I have spent too much of my life on you, and so I'm learning in my old age to stand time up—to grind it slow. For instance, yesterday: the wolves came to my door. They growled with your scent. Have you ever heard the low moan a smell can make? That's how I knew you had sent them. I went outside. I let them come while I listened to the cicadas, who just then amplified their chorus. How do they know such unison? To call and answer in so precise an *Ave* that the whole boulevard swells at exactly the same skipped engine. The trick, Dear Future, is to pay no attention to how deeply you need that song, and the song rescues you from the question in your throat, from your own weeping, from the seductive edge of the hunting knife on your nightstand. The trick is to pretend not to know that this is a love song the body contracts to bellow out through the hollow of its own drum, not to know that this is an aggregate ballad that may or may not be requited. Whatever—the tiny beasts canopying the trees with choir have come to say *listen to what is now; that you're alive to make a song*, no matter what's yet undone, no matter who's marching with other plans toward you.

*Adeeba Afshan Rana*

# GRADIENT

There will be pain,
white-hot heat, red flashes, and pink panic.
Learn to be colorblind until everything throbs violet.

The rainbow between agony and distress endures.
Find the weight of each color in your palm,
taste their flavor, commit them to memory.

Learn to say *No* when it matters,
learn to say *Yes* when it matters more.
Wield color like a kaleidoscope made from bone and sinew,
a bright chorus, a cacophony of will.

You are okay.
The fast animal of your body will heal,
curving into itself until you are round as a rubber wheel.
Become a bowstring, an arrow,
supple and pliable as a reed.

Your eyes will become deep pools,
your shadow, a dark, tangible mass.
Weave light into your crown.
Your smile is a sharp thing now, beautiful even.

*Erica Vega*

# DEAR ERICA

Erica,

We are not here to tell you there is anything wrong with the ways in which you walk into prayer, but we are here to show you an error of perception.

See, you spent 2014 talking to some Born Agains, listening to Evangelical pastors, emailing questions to Aramaic scholars, participating in group meditations, mediumship classes, and sound healing. Researched chakras and crystals, the Egyptian Pantheon, an etymology of a new word every day, went mad in ambient music. When your friend handed you a flier advertising a week of lectures promising to be the last self-help tools you'd ever need, you laughed, *How did this happen? How did my life get like this?*

It was nearing one in the morning and you'd been exercising in the oppressive June, no air conditioner, a small fan in the windowsill, gasping for breath. You collapsed onto the hardwood floor, pled for benediction, *God, take it away, take it all away.*

The prayer took off its shoes & wandered your home barefoot and wild.

Next day, you woke up and no longer smoked. Another, you transformed small talk into communion: Frank, who hated the weather, had been at the mechanic's four hours, and they were overcharging him. Said he recently moved back to Illinois from Florida. *Why?* Family is here and home is home no matter how you feel about it.

Another day your boyfriend dumped you, saying, *I can't accept you. Don't take it personally.*

Suddenly, you were jobless, out of cash, and moving back into your parents' basement.

You lived with spiders and millipedes, all those disgusting legs and still you prayed take it away, take it all away. And then came the headaches and nightmares, the ghost-boy in the basement, who your parents swear is not there, a sprained left ankle, an injury from decades ago, reappearing.

Your dad asked if you were eating again. You were. He said, *But you just ate yesterday*, and laughed as he passed by. It sounded so mean in your head so you tried to change your head; said you'll reprogram this carbon-based memory, attack the body-mind-spirit like a scientist.

You thought you went three steps back, *How did this happen?* Months before, you had it all. You had nothing. You had it all and it was nothing.

Nothing and nowhere.
No where and now here.

In the basement, looking into a mirror. You see a face and you think it is *you.* You see the eyes and you think you are looking at you.

That is not you that sees you. What is looking is what you have prayed to. All the images, they must come and they must go. Even your face.

We are breathing you. Here is where you must continuously create home.

Eternally,
Erica

*Benjamin R. Turner*

## LAMENTATION FOR TOMORROW

I write to you from today because I remember seeing your skies covered in black like the pall of all our stillborn tomorrows.

Because together, we could have made something later still, the day *after* tomorrow, that world we barely see over the lip of your horizon, something even more beautiful than you were supposed to be. I hate you for not being beautiful enough to shake us out of hopelessness—or at least into attention. Time has been a lullaby.

We sleep, we stumble, we struggle—but always hypnotized.

We have watched impotent with apathy as soot gathers in the creases between bricks, like tears running down the lines in old faces that have seen it all before, like the primordial canals on the moons of the other worlds, filled dusty with the detritus of species who tried and failed to do all this before we were born.

We are looking for salvation on those strange lands, but they are already graveyards. And we write our epitaphs on stone with bullets, pay the ferryman in spent brass.

We cared only for ourselves—but it worked, didn't it? You're reading this, aren't you?

Aren't you?

Writing to the future is liberating; it won't matter. I don't believe you're there to read this, future-person. And that's the problem. It's too late for letters from today. There were plenty of letters from yesterday to tomorrow that hadn't arrived by the time tomorrow became today. We need letters written from tomorrow to yesterday. Maybe then there would be time enough, and they would have credence enough. Or would we have treated the letters like textbooks, suspect for being written by the victors—like novels full of warnings, suspect for being written by liars?

What do you have for me, Tomorrow? Bang? Whimper? Ice? Fire?

I never planned to be alive to see your arrival. But you've hastened your approach. Perhaps I will see you, after all. I pray that I won't. Seeing how you shape yourself, I will send no children to see you, to fight in your wars.

Though we have gone forth, and multiplied, we have not grown enough to live in this world. Our reach exceeded us yesterday—and instead of resting, we made tools too big for our womb-fat hands to handle, and they crash down on us. We hummed hymns to our virtuous victories while baking bricks for our greatest failures. Slaughter spun for lebensraum on a twisted loom. The spinning of a broken wheel.

Entropy is written on the hearts and hands of men and women. There is no point in writing to tomorrow. Something inside us wants tomorrow to be empty—quieted of our noise.

Tomorrow, we are the dust choking your lungs, parching your throat against cries to our forebears. We deafen ourselves to your warnings with the bacchanal of living, of *now*. Out of this orgy will rise more children pressed to fight before they learn to yearn beyond the simplest answers. Their bodies, arms, trigger fingers, their dribbling blood, their blinded eyes and blinding thoughts will be the hammer strokes at the forge, at the bell. I will send no children to fight in your wars, to make you and to suffer your weight.

*Chill* is the sound of that bell, ringing above the gray swath. What empty acolytes will be there to sound our requiem? Some choir of angels who ran out of tears before Creation, mourning for its spoil to come, turned now to living stone, their eyes lined with grit as they watch the cosmic wind spin our dust and ash into filigree, a few illuminated pen strokes before the suns expand for their final meals, like spiders finished waiting in their webs.

Yesterday, we read our dooms writ long ago. Today, we watch our hands moving the pen, and move only to finish the sentence.

*James Patrick Kelly*

# DEAR FUTURE

Dear Future,

Okay, I admit it. I've been chasing you for forty years now, writing my little scenarios of what you would bring—and they were mostly all wrong. We've dodged nuclear war so far, which makes all my fallout nightmares published during the Reagan years seem quaint. Most of us aren't going to space anytime soon, so there go a couple of my early novels. Meanwhile, no *Star Trek* or *Star Wars* in my lifetime—but then again, no *Alien*, *Aliens* or *Alien Resurrection.* Thanks for that! My predictions about politics? Not so great. I've got stories in my backlist, *really good* stories, that reference the Soviet Union in the Twenty-first Century. Back when Bill Clinton signed the ridiculous Defense of Marriage Act in the middle of the night in 1996, did I imagine that my gay friends would be getting married in less than twenty years? Nope. And even close to home, in my chosen profession of writing and publishing, I just didn't Get It. I never saw Amazon coming until it stomped on my local bookstore like a capitalist Godzilla on a rampage. I thought the internet would be all about personal communications: email and bulletin boards and maybe telepresence. Not self-publishing, ezines and Netflix originals. I mean, I didn't even understand about the phones. Do you realize how many species of plot your mobile phones have driven to extinction?

Some futurist I am. At least I have the bitter satisfaction of knowing that the professional futurists, the guys who got paid the big bucks to look into their statistical crystal balls, got it wrong too. We all chase you, but nobody catches the future. Even if we managed to clutch at your sleeve, you twist out of our grasp and dodge in a different direction.

Deep down, I knew it would be like this. But in order to get the stories written, I had to pretend that maybe, just maybe, I could anticipate where you were going. I needed that act of intellectual gymnastics to suspend my disbelief in order to convince myself that the work was important because it could *really happen.* Now I know that if the work was in fact important (and heaven help me, I still believe some of it was) it wasn't because it was some flavor of future history, or even that it was plausible, but because it was about people dealing with some very odd situations.

Which is the human condition here in 2015. You are more unknowable than you've ever been because you keep going faster and faster. The half-life of a science fiction story used to be measured in decades; now it's five, maybe ten years. Then it decays into fantasy. *2001: A Space Odyssey,* that most famous of science fiction novels and movies? It is, as we sometimes say in my genre, *counterfactual.* Alternate history. The real 2001 was much stranger than Stanley Kubrick and Arthur C. Clarke could have imagined. And 2015 is even stranger. So yeah, future, the one thing I know with absolute certainty about you is your acceleration, which means that you are going to be very peculiar indeed.

But don't you even think about slowing down! I'm still right behind you.

Regards,

Jim

*Jonathan Segol*

## DEAR FUTURE

Dear Future,

In the spirit of the time—this current time—I am communicating to all of you through g-chat. I downloaded it last week. My app-stenographer, it listens to me and transcribes what I say. This may sound primitive to you, but to me this is the cutting edge of communication. Before g-chat, I had to walk up and down my block, talking to myself, then run inside when I had a sentence to write down. I don't know how I got through school. This g-chat is one of the major inventions of my time, making this letter to you possible. My big hope is that you have apps that can cross over time. That is, you can read my letter in fifty years and one of you can write back to me and send it back to my time.

Even with my g-chat, the future is hard to imagine, so you will understand my recruiting help from my Great-Aunt Darcy, who also works as a psychic. She's here with me now, dressed in her work clothes, a purple robe and purple scarf. She's turned my stoop into her storefront. We've got scented candles at the top step, tarot cards and a ouja board one step down. Her incense sticks burn on the first step as their eucalyptus aroma drifts down my block. Say hello into the g-chat, Aunt Darcy.

"Hi kids."

I think you'd like Aunt Darcy. She's modernized her business, kept up with social media, she does fortune telling via Skype—do you still have Skype, and has it gotten any better?—yet she's still old school. She channels voices, goes into trances, and visits other spiritual dimensions if you pay extra. Travel expense, she says. She's staring at my palm right now, checking out the cracks in my skin. She might channel one of you folks if it would make today's operation more efficient. Aunt Darcy's got something else to say:

"I see struggle in the future."

I wait for her to elaborate but she falls silent. She frowns at the bottom of the stoop as she holds my wine glass in both hands. It was my own dumb idea to serve Aunt Darcy wine when she got here. I forget how she gets after one glass. Aunt Darcy, could you tell your listeners more about this struggle?

"It will be a time of great change in the world. Focus on the immediate. Your neighbors. Those close to you. They will give you strength during this time of transition." Aunt Darcy stops for a moment. She leans in for another suggestion, "Maybe you want to ask *them* about the future?"

Maybe I do. Is school just as boring? Did they fix it up? Make video games that teach you science and history? Or did they keep it the same, and only use the technology to hit you with tests every day?

Have they fixed up the cars? Do you even drive them? I hear that soon all we'll have to do is punch in the address and sit back. And the cars will sense other objects and stop. No more car accidents. Did they do that? And are they solar-powered, electric, or is it still gas?

And what about work? Did people make work a little more interesting? Or did it make everybody unemployed and miserable?

What about the music? Do people still have bands? Or do you press the computer for a certain jam and that's it? And does anybody dance to this stuff? If your app lets you write back to me fifty years in the past, if you could include a few clips of your music, I'd like that a whole lot.

Aunt Darcy. Could you talk more about big changes?

"Honey, I could keep talking like a fortune cookie or I could say it straight out. Most of you will be too ignorant to know you're struggling. And the schools are only getting worse so I can hardly blame you. Even the gifted programs are going to be about learning code or whatever task can make you an "unpaid intern" or whatever glorified term gets your employer around the minimum wage rules if they still exist. Form unions for whatever dumb thing they've turned you into—form an internship gofers union. Will you know enough to do this? If I hadn't left my crystal ball in the shop I'd give that one a shot."

Aunt Darcy, are you in a psychic's union?

"Don't get cute with me or I'll pack up my stuff. My nephew and his friends all think it's normal to use over half your money to pay for rent. I'm afraid to think what rip-offs have been devised for you. If I was my nephew's age, I'd team up with a locksmith and move into one of these Manhattan condos that the owner doesn't bother to visit, held by some high-flier from another continent using the title to launder money, selling it back and forth with his brother before the cash comes back to St. Petersburg or Wilmington, Delaware, clean enough to spend again."

Aunt Darcy's got a point. I try not to think about it. I lost my job last week, so I might have to think a little harder. Excuse me, I'll be right back.

"Hey kids, this is Aunt Darcy again. My nephew crossed the street to pick a fight with two hipster-boys that moved into the neighborhood. Those boys probably designed this g-hole I'm speaking into. If those boys did move here, my nephew won't be able to afford to stay on this block even if he gets another job. What kind of job was it anyway? I know, this is coming from a storefront tarot-card shuffler. He typed paper files into a computer. I told him, work in slow motion like they do up in Albany in the state offices. You've got nothing to prove, and your job can last another half year. Do your job successfully and your job disappears. And don't buy a fancy phone the day they lay you off. Just kidding, even a psychic couldn't see that last part coming.

"If your app lets you text my nephew back—fifty years back that is—please do. If you want to field some of his questions, great. More importantly, can you give him some idea as to what profession he should get some training in? Kids his age are learning to code for things that might not even exist in five years. Which codes, I couldn't tell you. I've got thousand-year-old equipment burning on the stoop here. Maybe you can give my nephew some pointers.

"And me! I'm sure your app has already identified my voice to you and given you my phone number, which is great. I'm getting old, I can't channel voices every day. Why should I have to depend on my crystal ball when you folks have my number? A callback from you could be a terrific feature in my business. Let's get in touch. Peace."

*Jody Hadlock*

# Bessie Moore Rothschild's Letter to the Future

*Jefferson, Texas, January 21, 1902*

Today marks the twenty-fifth anniversary of my death. It wasn't due to old age, illness, or even childbirth. My husband killed me. I was only twenty-four, too young to die. Every year on this date, I visit the site in the piney woods of northeast Texas, to remind me why I'm still here.

We had only been married eleven days, but it was a tumultuous relationship almost from the first time we met in Hot Springs, Arkansas, the year before he committed the deed. I was a prostitute and had traveled from New Orleans to spend part of the winter in Hot Springs. Veterans from the war flocked there, to heal their wounds, both physical and mental, in the warmth of the springs and in the soothing arms of a woman.

Abe Rothschild was a traveling salesman, but he preferred to spend his time drinking and gambling. He was never a customer like the other men. I liked to think we loved each other and that I would be able to leave my life of "service," as we demimondaines call it. But Abe loved something more than me. You see, I had acquired a number of valuable diamonds from my lovers, which earned me the sobriquet Diamond Bessie. I was killed over something material, and yet at the same time, so immaterial. In hindsight, I realize that our relationship was doomed, but I never would have thought that it would mean *my* doom.

Even though I knew Abe could never introduce a prostitute to his family—he was the son of a prominent Cincinnati merchant—I still had harbored some hope deep inside that being married to him would make me respectable enough to overcome my reputation. How wrong I was.

The reasons I've stayed earthbound have changed over the years. At first, I waited for my murder to be avenged, to see Abe hanged. My dear friend in the afterlife, Edla Vines, warned me that my quest for revenge would be painful. She was right. I didn't count on a congressman, who was also the best criminal defense lawyer in Texas, defending my husband, or the madam of my brothel in Cincinnati betraying me. For years there have been rumors about thousand-dollar bills floating through the ceiling to the jury room, and grand pianos supposedly showing up in every juror's home after they let Abe walk free. They're untrue, but it is true that Abe's father spent a small fortune on the team of lawyers he hired to defend his son.

When Abe was acquitted, he became somewhat of a celebrity. Newspapers across the country had reported on my murder and Abe's two trials, and he became a news item wherever he traveled for his father's company. Reporters noted his "long-suffered imprisonment," and referred to me as a "notorious female." Abe thought he was invincible—he had gotten away with murder—and soon he slid right back into his swindling ways, becoming a wanted criminal again.

I've endured his escapades, waiting for him to hopefully make a mistake that will finally send him to the gallows. The swindles did catch up to Abe, and he's been imprisoned the last several years, first in Missouri, now in Texas, but he won't hang. Once again, he gets to live, while I don't.

In a few months, Abe will be released from the Huntsville prison. Will he come to my grave and finally express remorse for what he did? Will he continue to live a life of crime, or will he finally see the error of his ways? These are the questions I want answered, and so I stay.

There's one more reason as well. Many people still think I was another murdered prostitute, Annie Stone, from Watertown, New York. How I grew sick of being referred to as her! Annie was a brothel whore. I was a sought-after prostitute, as skilled in the art of conversation as the art of seduction, and worked in the most fashionable "houses" from Cincinnati to Chicago to New Orleans.

I want the truth to be known. I am not Annie Stone. I am Bessie Moore Rothschild, daughter of Irish immigrants who fled Ireland during the Great Hunger. My family crossed the Atlantic to Canada, before settling just across the border in the Catholic enclave of Canton, New York.

I didn't intend to become a prostitute. My father died when I was just a young child, and my mother could only find solace in her grief. I was left to raise myself and then sent to female seminary. Looking back, I realize that I was always searching for a father figure. I was too young and naïve to foresee the severe consequences of allowing a man to seduce me. Society can be harsh and ruthless. I had brought shame to my family and had to leave Canton.

I learned that making a bad choice usually begets more bad choices, but did that mean I had to pay for them with my life? I was blinded by love, or what I thought was love, and married a man who would stop at nothing to gain possession of my diamonds, even if it meant killing me. But fear was the real reason I married Abe. Fear of being alone, fear of not being able to provide for myself. I saw the women around me. They were all younger than I.

Soon I would be past my prime and forced into a less desirable place and then onto the street where opium and morphine would be my only friends. I lived under false hope, a dream that didn't really exist, that I could somehow have a traditional life.

These days I feel I've been all but forgotten. There's a nice young man who tends my plot, but mostly I am alone. I wait for the answers I seek, and hope that someday someone will tell my story. I wasn't just a prostitute. I was a person, and all I wanted was to be loved.

—Bessie Moore Rothschild

*Keith Hill*

# A Letter from the Future

Dear Señor Jorge Luis Borges,

I write to you on the day that celebrates your birth, in a gesture as much filled by contrition as it is an expression of flamboyance. My father would only support an education that had practical application. Accordingly, I studied the law. Lacking the self-confident acumen of my fellow students, who after graduation flooded the offices of major firms, I subsided into a small office in a company dedicated to conveyancing. I later found my professional level as a notary public. My father applauded an occupation that allowed me to buy a house, marry and raise children. But this same occupation caused me, year by year, to shrink inside. Accordingly, this gesture of writing to you—from a future that you never described, but that you may very well have imagined—could be said to be inconsistent with the life I have lived. Yet it reflects a deep desire circumstances never gave me the opportunity to pursue.

The young are not so naturally cowed. At university I had pretensions to literary prowess. However, my ambition and my writing style proved to be of a piece: both possessed insufficient power to propel my work into the literary yearbook, let alone beyond. You wrote of the literary Borges who was your close companion, a parallel identity with whom you shared tastes and interests, even if you each used what you mutually absorbed to different ends. As I stood at the bus stop one morning two years after graduation, one year after marriage—I need to make clear, to a woman I have ever dearly loved—with the weight of a mortgage hanging Damocles-like over me and our first child due in two months, I felt a shudder pass through me. Appearing like a wavering figure in a mirage, I watched my ambition detach itself from me and walk away up the street. I was certainly willing to discuss a possible future accommodation. But it failed to acknowledge my existence, let alone turn and engage. That was the last I ever saw of it.

I think of your work as that of a mid-wife, a Socratic enquirer into the mysteries of human existence, who brings forth dreams of what was and is, and weaves labyrinthine marvels that might be. In contrast, as a notary I deal not with dreams but fears, constructing legal documents that my clients hope will protect them from feared future calamities. This fear's children clamor for papers they clutch to their breasts in a vain delusion legal process can provide protection against despair. I am not embarrassed to admit I have built a house and raised a family on the bent backs of those quivering children.

All this is by way of a preamble, a defining of the terms of communication as it were, to my real purpose: to write to you, living in 1949, before your eyes lose their power to read, from one hundred and fifty years in your future. In describing the situation so baldly, now I *am* embarrassed, because given everything we know today, all the information you would assuredly find valuable for your own as-yet-unwritten work, especially given the millioned astonishing events and gadgets I could describe, what I have to narrate exists at a level far below those thrilling possibilities. This is one of the few occasions in my adult life when the absence of my ambition is telling because, like an errant schoolboy addressing a demanding teacher, the events I have chosen to recount to you consist of … what I did during my holiday.

My dear wife and I recently travelled to New York, going there to fulfil a vow we made, in the year of our fortieth birthdays, that we would one day visit that renowned city. The vow was spurred by friends' stories of all the rebuilding that had been undertaken there. I can honestly state it was the most memorable Thanksgiving holiday of my life.

The aircraft landed at the newly completed Newark Airport. The passenger terminus had only opened three weeks before, being specially designed to cater to the burgeoning numbers of tourist who travel from all over the world to look at the newly relaunched New York. You will no doubt be pleased to know that traditional American ingenuity and enterprise have not diminished. Within thirty minutes of landing, as luggage handlers collected our bags, we were standing on a moving walkway that took us in just a few minutes from the terminus to the pier, where we boarded a delightful old-styled riverboat called *Mark Twain*, complete with canvas canopies, a Dixie jazz band, and a huge wheel frothing the ocean at the stern. The cruise across the Hudson Harbor felt leisurely, but we must have been pushed by an incoming tide, because Manhattan's downtown skyscrapers soon loomed before us, their bare upper floors rising stiffly from the surging waters.

This last statement, no doubt, will surprise you. The world's oceans have risen over fifty feet since your day. I will not describe the Arctic ice melt, the dissolving of Siberian tundra, or the collapse of first the Western then the Eastern Antarctic ice shelves. Neither shall I recount the disbelief, denials, blame, and excuses that followed—you are living through sufficiently turbulent political times to appreciate how calamities are publically processed.

We, of course, had come precisely to witness the striking cityscape nature has resculptured. By degrees, we began to discern which buildings had once been office blocks, which apartments, and in a medley of voices those around us recounted where distant family and friends had once lived and worked, and others avidly added tales of their own. Then a curious occurrence followed. As the slapping wheel took us past shell after shell, the voices gradually died away. A group of Irish visitors at the end of the boat had been talking loudly in their distinctive lilting accents. It was only when they too fell silent that I realised the band had launched into *Danny Boy*. We all watched with wet eyes as the riverboat motored between concrete pillars, collapsing facades, and corroded steel ribs, all slapped by the choppy tide.

Naturally, everyone has seen images of waves mounting skyscrapers, and witnessed the damage storms have dealt to the metal peaks of twentieth-century civilization. Nonetheless, as we stood in an uneasy line along the steamboat's rails, with the jazz band pumping solemnly behind us, being confronted in the flesh by the twisted skeletal carcasses of what had once been vibrant monuments to our nation's storied success placed this moment among the most disconcerting experiences of my life.

The passengers' chatter only restarted as we approached the Flat Iron Building. The top floors are now home to alligators that followed the warmer waters north as the Florida coast became inundated. Someone told a story about a visitor in a small speedboat leaning out too far and being snatched, a tale that generated hollow hilarity, the type that disguises a deeper lurking anxiety. A deckhand threw chunks of meat off the prow and relieved chatter started as we jostled to get video of ourselves with the snapping reptiles in the background.

Our first stop was the Empire State Building. It looks as magnificent as in your day. We made a big circle around it for everyone to take photographs, then pulled up to a floating dock moored at what used to be the tenth floor. The entire building is now surrounded by massive concrete placements that rise to the fifteenth floor, stabilizing the structure and protecting it against storm surges.

We rode the lift to the observatory deck on the eighty-sixth floor and looked down to see the waters' impact. Photos and maps hung on the nearby walls showed where the water level had been before inundation and where it is now. All lower Manhattan is under water, and what was once the Hudson River has flooded well inland, forming the Hudson Harbor. The same has happened west, with the two sets of pylons of the Williamsburg Bridge standing alone above the East Harbor, which stretches almost a mile before reaching the new coastline of Queens and Brooklyn.

From the observation deck we could also see our next destination, the newly launched Macy's floating department store. The therapeutic virtues of shopping are well-known. After this stark confrontation with reality, the talk as we descended in the elevator indicated everyone was primed for a soft landing among the world's leading luxury goods.

*  *  *

Hiya Mr Borges!

I'm writing this cos Pop is in the kitchen, preparing dinner. I gotta tell you I've read a set of your stories, you know with these out there characters who trip into the wildest places and do all these weird things. I read it cos at school we had to write a report on a book by a South American writer and *The Aleph* is one of Pop's favourites. It turned out cool because now with Pop deciding to write you this message I get a chance to tell you how wow your writing is. I had to look up a lot of the references especially Homer and Roman history and all but doing it impressed my teacher enough to give me an "A" so a big ups to you Mr Borges!

Course we do have majors over you. You have telephones that plug into walls and have to send long distance messages by telegrams and stuff. That's so primitive! Today we have i-TAGS plugged right into our cortex. It's great cos to launch my media stuff I just hold the thought and it reads my brain waves. Parents think its cool too, cos they get nervous when their kids are out and an i-Tag app automatically tracks them, so they'll never go missing on the way home from school. That's how the advertising goes anyway. The best is that my progged stores autosend me whatever's on sale so I won't miss out.

I just read what Pop wrote about his trip with Mom to New York. It was actually to celebrate their wedding anniversary. He didn't write that, I guess he's way too modest. But you can tell he's super smart. He's says the country runs much better since the corporations took over. And all that palaver about elections—that's how Pop calls it, palaver—hasn't happened for the last ten years which means we'll never have dictators like in your time—I know cos I studied that too. So hang in there. One hundred and fifty years on the world gets way sorted!

Another thing I'm envious of is how much you travelled, lecturing all over. When I graduate I'll get work travelling. I tried boarding a bus headed to the Catskills last summer to visit friends but my i-TAG lit up the driver's dash and I had to get off cos he wouldn't drive with me on board. Like Pop said, you never know who is on public buses. But I would've liked to have gone there at least for a day and just done stuff with my friends. Anyhoo luv your stories. And it's great to be able to tell you like this. Kisses an all.

—Suze

* * *

Dear Mr Borges,

Pop is still in the kitchen, and my sister has sent you her message, so I'm picking it up now. I figure you'll want to know more about how things are so far after your time, so I'll start by telling you bodies have no future. The life force triggered by conception that reads DNA and shapes cells of undifferentiated tissue into arms, legs, ears, nerves, plus the biological momentum that has given us a brain containing enough processing power to translate ephemeral sense data into knowledge about the world—all of it is on the verge of being replaced by something else, something … well, it's not really describable yet. But it's on the way. My generation is changing everything in the biggest advance since relativity!

I know because right now I'm on a holiday break from studying quantum consciousness at MIT. The big breakthrough was made in 2071. It's what has made this message from us possible—although communication is only one way for now. But that will change. It all happened via the Large Hadron Collider in Switzerland. It's a particle accelerator launched in 2010 to find the fundamental building blocks of matter. After a fifth major refit quadrupled its power and speed, in 2079 scientists discovered the first traces of dark energy. Twenty years on we're only at the first stage of understanding what dark energy is and how we can use it. Given your own work's relationship to science fiction—which is what my explanation will sound like—I'm sure you'll find it fascinating.

The best way of describing what we've discovered is to think of spacetime as a stream. In theory time has no direction and can flow into either the future or the past. That's what quantum mechanics assumes. But in practice we experience time like a stream that incessantly flows towards the ocean of the future. We can't stop time flowing, although psychologically we can feel it speed up or slow down. However, all the matter and energy caught up in streaming spacetime only constitutes a small part of the universe, at most 4%. The rest of the universe, the 96% we can't see, is dark energy and dark matter.

So if spacetime is the stream of visible matter and energy that always flows in one direction, think of dark energy as the banks that constrain the stream.

As I stated, we naturally float in the stream of spacetime as it takes us towards the future. But if we jump out of the water and onto the bank, we escape the flow and are free to walk on the bank in either direction, up or down the stream. That's what tapping into dark energy enables us to do: jump out of spacetime and travel into either the past or future. Right now we only have the knowhow to upload digital data as dark energy and send it to a digital destination, such as the telegraph machine that will deliver this to you. Learning how to do that has taken years. But researchers are already working on how to digitize awareness. When we can do that, we'll no longer be limited to spacetime at all!

That's why I started off by writing the human body has no future. Biological momentum takes bodies in one direction, towards the inevitable future dissolution of their component molecules. But once we're able to use dark energy fully, we'll be able to jump out of spacetime and go anywhere and anytime we want. Instead of biological consciousness, we'll have quantum consciousness. It's exciting days, Mr Borges!

Anyway, Pop's calling us to dinner. There's a lot more to fill you in on. Using dark energy for intergalactic travel, for one thing. Dark energy jumps us right out of the paradigms of classical physics—no more Newtonian action-reaction, no more thermodynamics or entropy. It's a blast. But that's for next time. For now, it's been an honor, sir.

—Louis signing off.

*   *   *

Mr Borges,

I trust my children were stimulating companions in my absence. The energy allocation for this communication is nearing its maximum, so I need to complete my account of what happened during my holiday. I was writing of Macy's new floating store. It is a marvel of entrepreneurship. Everyone agrees the shopping is stupendous. But I had not selected this tour to shop. What excited me was the opportunity to explore the old Macy's.

We entered mini-submarines that held groups of six. As we sank, headlights revealed the roof of the old Macy's building, a hole cut into which gave us access to the top floor. This was empty, all the goods having been removed before it was abandoned to the rising water. The subs descended by following the rails of escalators. Windows in the sub's glass floor and sides allowed us to see the escalators' permanently stilled metal steps as we glided silently down them. On the next floor, lights had been set up. Seaweed growing on the central pillars cast undulating shadows on the building's floor and walls as the sub's wake disturbed them. We cruised forwards, and the headlights next picked out a row of mannequins still dressed in the fashions of 2083, the year now designated The Great Submergence. It sounds so flamboyantly final. Even unnecessarily melodramatic. Like *The Lost Decade*. And *The Crack-Up*. I know you are an admirer of F. Scott Fitzgerald. I could picture Scott in 1933 walking across this same floor, head snapping frantically from side to side, calling out as he trotted past the lines of mannequins sporting lingerie, and to his overwhelming relief finding Zelda sobbing her heart out, curled up on the floor between the new season's blouses and business-like skirt suits.

That thought returned to me the following afternoon, on the *Mark Twain*, as we chugged through the skeletal skyscrapers on the return journey to the Newark airport. Most of the passengers were downstairs in the bar, listening to the band. I went to the stern, stood to one side of the churning wheel, took the urn I had brought with me out of my bag, unscrewed the lid, and gently poured its contents into the foaming water. A dark gray smear briefly hovered in the water, trailing towards Manhattan's ghostly remains, then sank out of view.

Señor Borges, I, Xavier Williams, wish you well in coping with the darkness that we both know will soon prove all-devouring. I end this missive with an account of a dream I unexpectedly woke remembering this morning.

I was alone in the submarine, descending the escalator in the underwater Macy's. But instead of finding the open floor, the sub slid between two narrow walls. Fortunately, the width was just sufficient for the sub to progress. As I negotiated one corner, then another, I realised I was in a labyrinth. Turn followed turn, and I was propelled through a seemingly endless maze of narrow passages. I started to panic. On the brink of falling over the precipice of feeling utterly trapped and lost, the sub emerged from the labyrinth and its headlights picked out a long line of mannequins. As we drifted past them one by one, I looked out through the submarine's window and saw that each wore a paper mask portraying my wife's face. The corners of the masks undulated in the water as I silently passed. Finally, the line came to an end. The submarine kept travelling into the darkness, its headlights useless now because there was nothing but water to pick out. Through the eyes of the last mannequin, I watched myself looking back through the submarine's rear window. Soon I was too small to make out. Then the vessel itself was but a tiny speck of light. Presently, it blinked out forever.

—Yours from the future, Xavier Williams

*Natasha Arnold*

# Toynbee Idea

TOBLERONE AND I ARE SITTING ON THE BEACH behind our condo building when I tell him that last night my Nana said I shouldn't hang around with him anymore.

He says, Cause I'm twenty-five, right?

I nod and say, She thinks you shouldn't wanna be friends with a sixth grader. She thinks it's weird.

I decide not to tell him that she called me a little boy again too. I'm not a little boy. I'm eleven. I'm in middle school. Little boys are in elementary school. Nana has to know that. She wouldn't let me stay home alone while she plays bridge with her friends like right now if she didn't. I wonder if she let my dad stay home by himself when he was my age, way back before he met my mom and had me and then both of them left me with Nana and went away forever.

It's not weird, Toblerone says. He turns so his face points ahead, the pointed tip of his nose lining up with the stripe where the sky and the ocean meet, way far out. His sunglasses hide his eyes but I know he watches the water in front of us. He says, It ain't like I'm tryin to touch on you.

Touch on me how, I ask.

His mouth crinkles downward. Like, in a gross way, he says. Not like how me and you just do a bro-hug sometimes. Like kissy-touching but worse. Then he shakes his head and stutters for a second like he doesn't like what he's saying until he pricks his head back up and says, Some people are nasty, man, I dunno. I ain't tryin to touch you, though, Silver. Promise.

I tell him, I know. But she was like I don't trust a man who calls himself a candy bar.

Man, forget that, I've been Toblerone since before I can remember.

And then she went why doesn't he have friends his own age.

I hang out with em at night, when they're off work. First time I met her I told her that. She didn't say you're not allowed to hang out with me, did she?

No, I say, and then I groan. I say, It's just Nana never wants me to be friends with anybody. Never likes my friends. Everyone's trouble or lazy or they smell or she thinks they're gonna steal and then they quit hangin out with me and now everyone at school calls me Nana's Boy.

He says, Their loss. I'll hang out with you.

Sometimes Toblerone makes me so happy that I start to ache all over and I feel like I'll come apart and float away in millions of pieces.

Toblerone moved in next to Nana and me back in February so this is the first May I've had with him. Usually in May I have the beach to myself. But almost every weekend since Toblerone and I met we come out here and hang out, feed the seagulls, walk around, get food, talk about weird stuff he reads online. Whatever we want. I've waited for May all this time. May is warm and I get the sand and the sea to myself and now I can show it to Toblerone. I've never gotten to show it to anyone, my May beach. And I don't want Nana to see. She'll say it's too cold and bring me back inside and then try to take me shopping with her and I love Nana but she does the same thing about everything. Whine, drag, leave. Sometimes I wonder if my dad would let me hang out with Toblerone without making a big deal out of it.

Sometimes I think this beach and Toblerone are all I have to myself.

Ahead the ocean glitters under the sun. Foamy freckles pop and fade along the shore. Toblerone drums his fingers on his thigh but the waves drown out the sound. Toblerone is the biggest person I've ever met, so tall and muscular that sometimes it surprises me that he fits through doorways. Nana told me she thinks he's too big. Scary big, she said, like one of those FUC CFC UFC what-do-you-call-em guys. When I think about Nana I start to wish I hadn't said anything about her to Toblerone.

So I ask him, What'd you read about lately?

Toynbee tiles, he says.

What's a Toynbee tile?

Legit insane is what, he says, smiling. He leans over and pulls a folded-up piece of paper from his back pocket, then unfolds it. Says, I been waitin' for you to ask.

When I take the paper and turn it right-side-up I see a photo of some crooked words inside a rectangle embedded into a road, a corner in the concrete. The words in the tile say:

TOYNBEE IDEA
IN MOVIE '2001'
RESURRECT DEAD
ON PLANET JUPITER

The heck, I say.

This crazy recluse dude up in Philadelphia, Toblerone says, goes around driving this car with no floorboards dropping these linoleum floor tiles into the streets in all these cities. He thinks there's some conspiracy between the FBI and the Russians and like newspaper guys trying to stop him from spreading this weirdo message of his.

What, I ask, to make dead people come back to life on Jupiter?

Yeah, he says. The tile guy thinks they talked about it in *2001: A Space Odyssey* and Arnold Toynbee was this philosopher. I dunno. It's so weird.

How's he gonna make dead people come back to life on Jupiter?

You're askin me.

I thought Jupiter was just made out of gas.

It is. The guy's just a nutcase is all. What do you think about it, Silver?

I stare at the photo. I think about how someone believes in this idea. I imagine a million ghosts floating around in the clouds on Jupiter, white wisps popping up between streaks of yellow and orange. That might not be how resurrection works, but it's all I can picture.

Toblerone works out of his condo, taking orders for this online flower company, so he's basically on the phone and the computer all day. He told me he looks up these weird things when nobody calls and he gets bored. Nana doesn't get it. She just thinks Toblerone spends too much time on the computer reading about these weird things. She calls them freakshows and thinks they're all about death because the only time I ever told her about one of them I told her about the Dyatlov Pass incident, when a group of people hiking up a mountain in Russia seemed like they went crazy and died and something radioactive might have gotten to them and even now nobody knows what happened. I told her I thought it was sad. I thought it was sad that those hikers died and no one remembered anything about them but their deaths. She said that if Toblerone wants to be any kind of role model for me like he says he does he should be teaching me how to play baseball. I don't like baseball.

The foam on the waves looks like the ghosts.

I hand Toblerone the picture of the Toynbee tile and he folds it back into his pocket. It's kind of sad, isn't it, I say.

A seagull appears from one side of the sky, squawks, and disappears into the other by the time Toblerone asks, What is?

That this one guy thinks he can bring everyone back to life on Jupiter. You can't even stand on Jupiter. And he's going around with these tiles.

A wave rises and crashes onto the beach. Toblerone says, Yeah. That is sad. Huh.

One time Toblerone told me about a sea monster corpse some fishermen dragged up from the ocean in Canada. The black-and-white picture he gave me showed the dead monster all raggedy from sea water, propped up on a wood bench, nothing left of it but a head attached to a snakelike body. I imagined standing by it. I told Toblerone I'd pet it. I'd put up with the foamy fishy smell if I could tell it that I at least loved it, even if the crabs or sharks didn't care about it enough to finish eating it. I couldn't stand the thought of something dying alone and then still being alone afterward. That was the same day I asked Toblerone why I couldn't come over when he was bored while he worked, if I wasn't in school, and he said he had to be alone just in case someone did call.

Do you like your job, if you gotta be alone for it, I asked him.

He said, Eh. It's only a few hours every day. Plus I talk to people enough that it doesn't feel like I'm totally alone. Even though I guess I am.

Ever since then I've wondered if that's why he comes over to at least say hi almost every day around four, when he's done working, if that's why he likes hanging out with me so much. I talk to him. I make him not feel alone, just like he does for me.

Toblerone stands up and taps me on the shoulder. Time is it?

I look at my watch and answer, Like five fifteen.

Your Nana'll be home soon, Toblerone says. I oughta get you back inside so she doesn't think I'm touchin on you.

I don't wanna go home yet, I tell him.

But I'm thinking about it and I don't want her to hate him more than she already does.

She hates him and I know it. Whenever she talks about him she scrunches up her face like his name tastes rotten in her mouth. Royce, she spits, or Mister Tobler. Never Toblerone.

She doesn't hate you, I say.

Toblerone breathes out my name in one long hiss. Silver.

Five more minutes.

Five more minutes, he answers. Ain't like the tide's comin in, I guess.

He keeps moving his hand back and forth between the sand next to him and his thigh. He has such long legs and they're so thick too that they remind me of a horse. I've seen art of creatures, half man and half horse, but I can't remember their names. Toblerone makes me think of them. He draws something in the sand between the rests he takes on his thigh. A rectangle.

When he takes another rest and looks out toward the water I write inside the rectangle with my finger. TOYNBEE IDEA, I write. Toblerone's hand falls on mine and he says, Oh sorry.

He probably wasn't paying attention so I tell him, It's okay. Our hands move, together, and rest one atop the other just below my Toynbee tile. He shakes.

This isn't the kind of touching, I start to ask, but Toblerone answers No before I finish.

He says, But your Nana'd get the wrong idea.

All the way to where the Chesapeake Bay Bridge-Tunnel sticks out against the water, the beach sits empty under the sun. We're alone, though, I say. She isn't even home.

Yeah, but I don't want her to come home and like go to the balcony and look down and see us, or like see us from the parking lot. She'll get the wrong idea.

Well, I ask. What's the right idea, then? The one she should have?

That me and you are buddies.

And I'm thinking, But we're touching right now. Our fingers are linked together. If he'd move his hand then I'd move mine but he stays right in place. Kissy-touching, he had said, that was the bad touching. I don't understand why it matters if we touch like this, then, when it isn't kissy-touching. What's the wrong idea?

Time is it? Toblerone asks.

Do you think Nana's the only one who'd think you're trying to touch on me? I ask.

Silver, he says. I'm twenty-five and you're eleven. I'm this big beefy blond dude and you're this teeny pale dark-haired fella, it ain't like we're gonna be mistaken for brothers. Probably anyone who sees us is gonna think I'm tryin to touch on you.

Anyone?

Anyone. If anyone were around right now. Anyone who might see us from their window.

That many people would get the wrong idea?

Yup. Cause they don't get it.

Why not?

Cause they barely ever see it. Grown-up man like me bein friends with someone your age. It's like seeing lights in the sky or something, you don't know what it actually is. You just decide it's whatever's closest to stuff you've seen before. Airplane, UFO, bird.

That's so sad, I say, and when I hang my head I find the tile I drew into the sand.

Toynbee Idea, I think. Resurrect dead on planet Jupiter. He got the idea from a historian and a movie. My hold on Toblerone's hand goes limp. Why is a wrong idea crazy when one person thinks it but if everyone thinks it we have to go along with it? Maybe the tile man is like me and Toblerone, I think, that he's one person who has the right idea. I want to find the tile man and tell him I believe his idea. I bet standing on Jupiter feels like wading in the ocean.

Behind me the sand shuffles. Before I can turn all the way around I hear, Hello chickadee, hello Royce, and Toblerone and I let go of each other's hands and Nana looms behind us, dangling her clogs in one hand, her lips wrinkled and pursed.

I tell her, We were just about to go home, Nana.

You boys have fun? she asks me, but looks into Toblerone's face. I can only see his black sunglasses, so I wonder how his eyes look at her.

Yeah, he and I reply together.

Silver, you didn't get hurt, did you, she asks. You were holding Mister Tobler's hand.

I'm fine, Nana.

You're sure, she asks.

I'm fine.

Toblerone says, He's fine. We were just sitting.

Nana glares at him and the sun glares on the lenses of her glasses. Well, she says. It's dinner time. Having crab cakes. And with that she sweeps her arm toward us to follow her inside, but when she moves while we get up and brush ourselves off Nana makes sure that she aims her side at Toblerone, not inviting him. I wish she would pretend she likes him, just once, for me.

We head inside the building together. We ride the elevator to the eighth floor together, Nana and Toblerone each pressing the button one after the other like they don't know they live on the same floor. We get out of the elevator together. We walk down the hall together. I keep my head down because at least that way I get to watch my feet as they move. My flip-flops pop and flap against the carpet, grains of sand rolling off the soles and my heels in a whisper, the only real noise in the hallway until at last, when Nana and I stop at our door and Toblerone keeps walking toward his, he takes his sunglasses off and turns and says, See you later, Silver.

Nana's keys jingle when she takes them out of her purse but she says hmph loud enough that I know she wants that later to never come. Toblerone looks at me over his shoulder. From this far away his eyes make me think of birds that soar over the ocean and then come sweep and land on the beach just a few feet ahead. I keep thinking he'll rush over before Nana opens the door. I want him to take me away, back outside to the waves and the sun and the salt, where nobody will call the things he finds freakshows and nobody will be there to get the wrong idea.

When he pulls his key out of his back pocket the folded-up Toynbee tile picture flutters down to the floor. He just stands there. I guess he hasn't noticed.

Nana, I say. Lemme go help Toblerone.

She lets herself halfway into our condo and breathes out, Don't keep him. She stands in the doorway all puckery while I go up to Toblerone.

Sup, he says. He leaves his key halfway turned in the knob while I grab the picture.

I hand it to him. You dropped this.

He hangs on to it, says, Thanks, then I guess thinks about the paper for a moment.

He says, All these weird things of mine always make you sad.

No they don't, I say. They make me happy.

I dunno if I should dig these sorts of things up for you anymore, man. You always find something sad about em. I don't want you bein sad.

They make me happy, Toblerone. I like hearing them.

I'm just sayin, he says. Always seems like you get sad about em. Like you go into em and yank out some part of em that I didn't even think about. Plus you're. He leaves off there.

I want to say but I like them, I want to beg it right into his ear, even though his sun-blond hair hangs in front of it to hide it, because I know what he'll say. Plus you're eleven. Plus you've got a Nana who doesn't want you hanging out with me cause she's wrong. I want to tell him I like the stories and I like him and I need him but he keeps looking over at Nana. I shake my head. Didn't you say you'd hang out with me, I want to say. Don't just stand there. Stay with me.

Nana says, Come on, Silver.

Toblerone taps his fingers on the doorknob. Rolls his weight on his heels forward. I see the inside of his condo the way I see pictures in a viewfinder, little slits of bigger things, right there in front of me but looking so far away. What about resurrecting the dead? I think. What about us being buddies? Who cares about the wrong idea if we have the right one?

But when Toblerone goes inside, saying Bye, Silver, I say Bye and it comes out like a whimper and I stay right there until Nana in her clogs clomps up the hallway to me. That huge outline of Toblerone that shouldn't fit in the doorway but does stays there when I blink. The next time I see him, I'm scared I'll see only that outline and not what's supposed to fill it.

In the echo of her steps Nana mutters, What a freak.

Her fingers tentacle around my arm and she starts leading me back toward our condo, yanking and dragging. I manage to tell her in a voice that sounds like a gasp that he's not a freak but she doesn't say anything back to me, just opens the door and nudges me in. He's not a freak, I say. You're just a mean old lady.

She shakes her head.

You're wrong, I say.

She bangs around in the kitchen, starting dinner. She must be wrong if she can still do something this normal while she moves like she's angry—she must be wrong if she thinks she's so right. She's got the same look on her face that she did when she called him a freak. I slide against the wall down to the floor where I sit while I tell her, He's my best friend, he's my best friend. You've got the wrong idea.

She stands at the counter mixing spices into crab meat as if I'm a ghost, silent and invisible even though I'm crying right in front of her. But every time I breathe in I think about Toblerone vanishing behind his door. You're wrong, I tell her.

But I'm thinking Toblerone is wrong for going inside and the people who remember the hikers' deaths are wrong and I'm wrong and everybody everywhere is wrong for not believing the tile man. I go limp in my brain and my body. Only Jupiter, I think, where billions of dead people can walk around on gas and dust, is right. If I keep going limp, shouting You're wrong until my voice turns into a puff of air that makes me float up like a balloon, I can make it there.

*Lana Austin*

# Scrambled Eggs

LINUS IS COOKING AGAIN. I love to watch him. He doesn't like it, but he can't see me because I'm standing outside the kitchen door. I wonder if he's cooking because he thinks I'm hungry or because he's cold and the stove is the only place he can get warm.

The clean laundry must've run out again. He's wearing panties and that's all. When he wears them, he wants me to call them underwear. But I don't think they're much different from mine. Just because his underwear has a little hole in front doesn't change anything. I know he's ten now, but he still looks like me. He doesn't have hairy legs like some of Mama's guests. Linus looks soft.

He sees me standing there as he turns to get a plate from the table. The table is small but I like it. I ask him if I can go to it. It's green and I like that color, but it's more of an old green, kind of faded, not grass green. But it's close. Linus says it's khaki and he knows it's so because that was the color of his father's pants in Nam. I don't know what Nam is. Linus won't talk about it or his father. I've never even seen Linus' father. I've never seen mine, either. I guess I don't have one.

I'm hungry, so I look at what's on the table. Linus leaves stuff there so I can get it by myself when he's gone. Linus buys it with the money he gets from Mama's purse when she's sleeping. He says it isn't stealing because she'd just buy shit with it anyway. He never takes me to the store with him. He says it's too far away. This week he got bread and butter and crackers. That's lots of food and it makes the table look crowded with all of it on there and the plates, too. We only have three plates, but they're all sitting out even though we mostly use one. We used to have another plate, but Mama broke it. Linus says they come in fours. I think that's a funny thing.

How do the people who make them know there are four people together? Usually it's just two in our house.

Linus wants me to go. He doesn't say anything, but he points to the door. I go to the room by the kitchen. It has just a TV on the floor. I like TV, but I've been watching for a long time. When Mama's sleeping and Linus is at school I watch it all day. Except when I have to pee. I don't like to get up to pee. Then I have to take off my blanket and it's cold. Sometimes I just pee on myself. Linus hates that. When he comes home I'm sitting on the floor, wrapped in my wet blanket. He says I'm too damn stubborn. He ends up staying home for a whole day after I pee to make sure I go to the bathroom. He says he can't miss any more school or they'll hold him back again. I don't want him to go to school, so a lot of times I pee on purpose.

I'm not in school yet. Pretty soon, Linus says, I'll be able to. I want to go with him, but he says five year olds are too little. Besides, he says, right now I'm too skinny. He's going to fatten me up, like those pigs on the Monroe farm. That's right next to us. Pigs are okay, but I don't feel skinny.

We live on a farm with a farmhouse, too. But we don't have any animals. The house is big but we never use most of the rooms. There is a door at the front of the house and two other rooms. The door is locked. Mama's friend, Bruce, took the key with him when he left. Once, when Mama was talking a lot, she said she wanted to get the lock changed so Bruce wouldn't come back but we didn't have enough money.

It doesn't matter if we use that door because no one's ever in those front rooms anyway. They don't have any furniture, so why should we use them, Linus says. If I'm downstairs, I'm in the room by the kitchen. I like the kitchen best, but Linus never wants me in there except to get some food from the green table. He says it's too dangerous.

There are more empty rooms upstairs, but we all stay in Mama's room because there's a bed in there and there's a bathroom next door. I like it when Mama's home and I can sleep with her, when she lets me. It's warmer than with just Linus and me.

I can smell what Linus is cooking now. It's eggs. That makes me happy. Eggs are warm. That means Mrs. Monroe must've stopped Linus and given them to him. Mrs. Monroe probably gave him some milk, too. I hope so. She stops him when he walks home from the school bus. I like her. I don't know why Mama yelled at her a couple of weeks ago. Mama said she'd slice Mrs. Monroe's throat if she bothered us or turned us in. Said it was none of her fucking business. I know that's not nice because Linus won't let me say that word. But Mrs. Monroe still gives Linus food. Linus says other people usually get eggs and milk from grocery stores. I've only been in a grocery store a couple of times that I can remember. Linus says that before Mama got sick we used to go all the time, but I was just a baby. He says grocery stores have lots of eggs and different kinds of bread, too. Some even have bread with raisins and cinnamon, but Linus just gets the white kind.

Linus told me eggs are baby chickens. I don't really understand it, but once, while I was peeking at Linus cooking, I saw him break the shell and pour the egg into the skillet. He just let it sit there. The yellow part never broke and he kind of slid it all onto my plate. It was still one piece. I didn't like it like that because I thought I could see a baby chicken. The yellow part was its big eye looking at me. Even though I was hungry I couldn't eat it. Linus said he would scramble it so I wouldn't know it was a chicken.

Linus brings in one plate with eggs and one glass of milk. We always share. Linus says that's easier for him. We're watching *Logan's Run*. Linus likes this show and says it sure beats the heck out of *The Brady Bunch*. I like all of the silver things. Everything's silver, even some of their clothes. Once, when I had crayons, I had a silver one. It was like Mama's ring before she sold it. But I don't understand the show like Linus does. He says they're looking for sanctuary. But he says it's kind of sad because if they find it then the show will be over.

I can hear the back door open. I get up, not caring that I'm cold without my blanket. I run to see Mama. She's laughing so hard she's snorting. There is someone with her. I grab her leg. She pulls my hair and tells me to get off. She's tired and has a guest. He doesn't say anything. He looks old and smells like licorice. I don't like licorice. It's too sweet.

They go upstairs to Mama's room. I want to go with them but Linus shakes his head no. He says she's sick again. I don't think she looks sick. He tries to tell me that being drunk is being sick. I still don't think Mama looks sick. We finish eating. Linus is watching a show about fishing. He says that he used to fish with Gramps when he was still alive. He said that if Gramps and Nanna hadn't died we could've lived with them. He said that they had Goo Goo Cluster things to eat. I don't know what they are but they sound good.

After we eat, Linus takes the plate to the kitchen. I sneak up the stairs and stand outside Mama's room. She must not mind me coming up because the door's still open. I stop. I can see Mama's head up on the pillow. Her eyes are closed. The man's head is between her legs. Mama looks up and sees me. She grunts and the man rolls over. I can't help but look at Mama. She doesn't have any panties on and her legs are open really wide. The hair where she pees is black. It's wet, too. I wonder if she's cold. I tell Mama that I'm cold but she says to get out. I just stand there until the man puts his face between Mama's legs again.

I go back downstairs and Linus is mad that I left. He tells me to sit back down on the floor. He shares the blanket with me. He says we can watch TV late tonight. He says we'll sleep down here.

It's morning now and I don't know where I am. Then I remember Mama upstairs. Linus must've already gone to school. I wish he was still here. I don't know why he goes. He says people tease him about his name. He says Mama named him that because she liked the *Peanuts*. He said that was before she got sick.

I go upstairs to see Mama. She's asleep. The man's gone. I try to wake her up but she won't move. She's breathing through her mouth and it stinks. I wonder if she brushes her teeth anymore. Linus makes me, even though we don't have toothpaste.

Someone is knocking on the door. I'm scared because I know it's the front door. Maybe it's Bruce. But he'd probably just let himself in because Mama never changed the locks.

I go downstairs and look through the glass in the front door. It's a lady. I point to the right so she'll go around that way to the back door. I go to the kitchen and she's already there. She asks me if there's a lock on that door. I tell her no.

She tells me her name is Mrs. Jenkins. She says she's from dee ess ess. I don't know where that is. She asks me if I'm Laura. I say yes. She asks me if Mama's home. I say yes but I can't get her up. I tell her Linus said she was sick again. She says Linus is a good brother.

She asks if Linus is at school. I say yes. She asks what I've eaten that day. I tell her nothing yet but I'm sure Linus left me some bread. I tell her I ate real good last night and even had milk. She says I look skinny. At least she doesn't mention pigs.

Mrs. Jenkins says she wants to see the house. Linus told me to not let anyone in the house, but Mrs. Jenkins isn't a man. Somehow I think Linus only meant men, so I don't feel too bad that I've been talking to her. Besides, she smells good. Kind of like honeysuckle in the spring. Real clean.

I tell her the kitchen and TV room are about it downstairs. She wants to see Mama but I tell her I can't let her because I don't want Mama to get sicker. Mrs. Jenkins asks why and I tell her that Mama gets really angry when I wake her up and then she switches me. I tell her Mama says she only does it because I make her sicker.

Mrs. Jenkins goes upstairs anyway and says something like hello, hello, can you hear me, can you wake up at all and then leaves Mama alone.

When we go back downstairs, Mrs. Jenkins says she's going to stay until Linus gets home. I tell her that's okay and she can watch TV with me after I eat my bread. *Captain Kangaroo* is really good but it's already off. We watch *As the World Turns*. I don't really like that show, but that's what Mama used to watch when she was up during the day. Mrs. Jenkins says I shouldn't be watching it. She pulls out some paper and starts writing. I ask her if I can draw. She lets me. I always lose the pencils that Linus brings home and he gets mad so he's stopped bringing any.

I draw for a long time. Mrs. Jenkins doesn't say anything and I'm not used to having anybody to talk to so I talk and talk while I draw and she lets me keep talking until Linus comes home. He walks into the room and says we're fine. I think that's funny because Mrs. Jenkins hasn't asked him how we are. Linus seems mad. She tells Linus she understands this is hard, but we're going to have to go with her. I don't know why. Linus says no.

Mrs. Jenkins says she is going to help us. Mrs. Jenkins asks if Linus really wants me to grow up like this. Linus says we don't need help. He says it's like the scrambled eggs. He says he takes care of things and I'm just fine. He's crying. I've never seen that before.

Mrs. Jenkins says I need to have more structure or something like that. Linus doesn't say anything. He picks the blanket up off the floor and gives it to Mrs. Jenkins. He says I like it. He looks at me a long time and says I'll like where they take me. I ask if he'll be with me. He says maybe.

As we walk out the door Linus asks about Mama. Mrs. Jenkins says someone will take care of her. She says they'll try to get Mama well so she can take care of us. When we get in Mrs. Jenkins' car I wonder where we're going. Mrs. Jenkins says we might go stay with a real family. I wonder what kind of bread they have.

MACHIGONNE FICTION CONTEST WINNER

*Micah Perks*

# GHOST DEER

"NOW IS THE TIME TO SPEAK OF NARROW PLACES," Daniel says. "Each person in the family must relate a story regarding a time of confinement. En este manera we can remember the Jews in Egypt, yes?"

Colin, Daniel's new stepson, groans softly.

They're sitting at a small table crowded with all the Passover accoutrements, Fiona and her son Colin jostling each other on one side, Daniel and his daughter Little My squished together on the other. Little My always insists on sitting next to Daniel. The table is actually a desk, which is what Daniel and Little My have eaten at for years. Since Fiona and Colin moved in buying a bigger table has been on their To Do list.

"Little My," Fiona says, "Why don't you go first. Show us how it's done." Little My's real name is Sara, but since she turned six she only answers to Little My, after a sly character in the *Moomintroll* books whose hair is always raked back in a vise-like ponytail. Sara/Little My wears her thick brown hair in the same way. When her father gathers her hair back every morning, she always demands, "Tighter, tighter." Sometimes the rubber band breaks. She won't let Fiona do it, says she doesn't pull tight enough.

"Why me?" Little My makes a sly stab at some charoses and stuffs it into her mouth.

"Because you've done this before," Daniel says. "This is Colin and Fiona's first Passover. Show them how. And it's not time to eat yet."

"En todo caso the charoses está muy seco," Little My says.

"What did she say about my charoses?" Fiona asks Daniel. "I Googled that recipe."

"What did she say?" Colin asks Daniel.

"Sara," Daniel says. "Little My, por favor."

"Like when I was stuck in Snufkin's pocket?"

"That's Little My in the book. What about you?"

Little My's Story:

"Okay, fine! The time I put my head between the bars at the petting zoo and it got stuck and the llama licked my face with its long stinkin' tongue."

"The same story as last year," Daniel smiles.

"I screamed gigantically." She jabs her fork at the charoses again.

"Not time to eat yet," Daniel says. "Let's do this in the right order."

"Then it's your turn, Papi," Little My says, eating. "Make it a new one."

Daniel's First Story:

Daniel stares at the candlelight playing over his white plate, adjusts his blue yarmulke over his bald head, adjusts his black plastic glasses, looks up and smiles at each person in turn. "Here is a story so Fiona will not think I am always so boring. This is in Santiago de Chile, long before I came here for my graduate work. They called a general protest against Pinochet." He looks at Colin. "Pinochet was a dictator—"

"I know who he was," Colin says.

"Excelente. So, my neighbor and I, we creeped out after curfew. We filled a tire with gasoline to set on fire in the middle of the calle. In this manner, when the police come, they couldn't get by, and everyone knows we are protesting for freedom. But the police come while we are still filling the tire with the gasoline."

Little My stands up on her chair: "You're so cool, Papi. Did you have hair then?"

"Long hair, like this," he says, tapping his shoulder. "We ran the block to return to the house. They were chasing us in the armored truck. In Santiago I lived in the end of a small alley and at the front of the alley we have a gate. We were able to lock the gate, then we ran to the end of the alley, hoping to reach my house at the very end. The police officers pushed their guns in the bars of the gate and shoot a tear gas at the front window."

"Whoa," Colin says.

"We ran into the house and kick the can from the front door, but then they shoot another one in. My mother was in the house. Smoke was all over us. My neighbor and I knew tear gas, we held lemons on our noses and didn't rub our eyes."

"Lemons!" Little My says.

"Sí, this helps, but my mother never experiences it. She no allow us to hold the lemon near to her face. She rubbed her burning eyes. She thought she can't breathe. She was choking and coughing, but we didn't dare to leave the house. We thought we won't escape that narrow place."

"Exciting," Fiona says, "but why did you run to your mother's?"

Daniel smiles. "Forgive me, mi amor. I was sixteen. A year older than Colin."

Fiona shrugs. Takes a gulp of the wine.

"It's not time to drink yet," Little My says.

"Sorry," Fiona says.

Daniel looks at the children. "Perhaps the moral of this story is that once you emerge from your narrow place, you should not try to go back onto it."

"Into it," Little My corrects. "But what happened, Papi?"

"The police finally left. Mama was fine. The dictatorship ended. I escaped my narrow place, came to America, and after various adventures, here we all are, together."

"I really appreciate that story, Daniel, really," Fiona says, "but since it's your tradition to talk about confinement and narrow places, how about what's happening right now, today, outside our personal peaceful little circle? What about the outrageous misery in Syria? Or Palestine? Are we allowed to talk about Palestine?"

"Here we go," Colin mumbles.

"Yes, of course, mi amor, we always talk about the plight of the Palestinians at Passover," Daniel says. "It just comes a little later in the Seder."

"Do you think the interminable length of the Seder is meant to represent the Jews' interminable slavery in Egypt?" Colin asks.

"If you're going to work for justice you have to start by respecting other people's traditions," Fiona says to Colin.

"I never said I wanted to work for justice. And anyways, you're always talking about peace and justice in this totally like unpeaceful way. Like a bully for justice."

"That's true," Fiona says. "I'm a bully for justice. I'm annoyed for peace."

"More like annoying for peace," Colin says.

"That's not even a story, Fiona," Little My says. "That's like a conversation or something. You have to tell a story. Tell us about jail. Papi says you beat up a submarine."

Fiona smiles. "That was twenty years ago, before I had Colin. I was being annoying for peace. We damaged a nuclear submarine. I was in jail for eighteen months."

"Fiona was very brave," Daniel says.

"What did you do in prison?" Little My asks.

"I read, I knit."

"Sorry, but that's not really a story either," Little My says.

"Maybe we should call you Little Dictator instead," Fiona says.

"Okay, okay, it's time to sing Dayenu now," Daniel says.

"But we haven't finished the stories. We're getting out of order," Little My says.

"Ilu hotzi, hotzi anu hotzi anu mi mitzrayim," Daniel sings cheerfully. He picks up the scallion by his plate and hits Little My on the head with it. "Everyone join in! Mi mitzrayim, hotzi anu, Dayenu!"

Little My takes up her scallion and smacks Colin on the cheek.

"What the fuck?" Colin says.

"Colin!" Fiona says.

"It's part of the Seder," Little My says.

Colin grins and smacks Little My with his scallion. She smacks back.

"Ilu hotzi, hotzi anu," Daniel sings, and Little My and Colin mumble-sing along with him as they whip at each other.

"Okay, that's enough now," Fiona says. "Too violent."

Colin whips Fiona on the back of the neck.

Little My shrieks and hits Fiona, too.

Daniel sings, "Day-e-nu" and scallions Fiona smartly on the forehead, once for each syllable. Everyone's laughing, except Fiona, who flings her wine at Daniel.

The wine Rorschachs across his green Oxford shirt.

Everyone goes silent.

"I can get that out," Fiona finally says.

Daniel slowly unbuttons his shirts and hands it to Fiona. She goes to the sink, grabs the kosher salt. Turns her narrow back to the table, turns on the cold water.

Daniel sits shirtless. He mops at his chest with a paper napkin. He's covered in a soft pelt, front to back with an extra coxcomb of frizz between his shoulders.

"Yowza, that's a lot of hair you got there, Dan," Colin says with a half smile.

"Dads are hairy," Little My says.

"Mine wasn't," Colin says.

"But your Dad's not dead like mi Mama," says Little My. "Where is he? Still in jail like Fiona?"

Colin mumbles something into his plate that ends in "deer."

"What's this about a deer?" Daniel says.

Colin's story:

"This happened before my Dad took off, like a long time ago." Colin's blinking a lot, because he just got contacts, and it makes his eyes look big and wet, plus with his reddish brown hair and brown freckles, and the fact that he's skittish and slim, he looks a lot like a deer himself.

Fiona turns from the sink and says over the rushing water, "What did you say about a deer?"

"Is this your Seder story?" Little My asks.

"It's just this deer, okay? One day Dad was like, 'Get your nose out of that video game, son, we're going hiking.'"

"He never called you son," Fiona says.

"Whatever. You know I hate hiking. So then we were walking in the gorge, like a long way up, up by Taughannock Falls, and no one else was there because it was like October and grey and cold and no one wanted to be there, obviously. Then we saw this deer. It was tiptoeing along the cliff edge above the falls. When we saw it we were all, 'Whoa, holy crap!' The deer heard us and freaked. It tried to turn around on the ledge or whatever. And it fell off the cliff. Like a long way." Colin's face is so pale now his freckles seem to pulse. His eyes blink.

"Are you serious?" Fiona says, turning off the faucet. Daniel's shirt floats winey, salty and abandoned in the sink. Fiona's standing by the table holding the kosher salt. "I thought deer were sure-footed, like cats."

"It was lying half in that pool at the bottom of the gorge and half on the like, gravel," Colin says. "Its back was broken or something. It couldn't move even when we got up close to it, except its eyes were rolling around. We realized if we left it there, the coyotes or dogs would get it."

"Did you call the cops?" Little My asks.

"We put it out of its misery," Colin says, "or whatever you call it."

"Coño," Daniel says. "When did you say this happen?"

"Nobody ever told me this," Fiona says. "What do you mean you put it out of its misery?"

"Dad was like, 'Son, you have to put this deer out of its misery.' And he handed me a big rock."

"Jesus," Fiona says, thumping down the salt.

"You should have taken it to the vet," Little My says angrily.

"I couldn't do it. I just stood there holding the rock. So Dad hit it, but it wouldn't die, so he hit it really hard, with both hands above his head, like five times. He was, like, foaming at the mouth. Dad."

Fiona sits down in her chair and pulls Little My onto her lap. She doesn't struggle. Fiona hooks her long leg and her long bare foot around Colin's leg.

Colin hasn't looked up from his plate.

Nobody says anything. Then Daniel reaches across the table and squeezes Colin's forearm. "That's an excellent Passover story," he says.

Colin's eyes dart over to Daniel. Fiona laughs like a surprised bark.

"No, in truth, I am not jesting, so many narrow places—for each one in the story, the deer, the father, the son."

"Aren't you glad you're not in that gorge anymore?" Little My says, wriggling off Fiona's lap.

Daniel's second story:

"I thought of a last story to tell," Daniel says.

"You can't tell two stories!" Little My says.

"Do you know this story Sleeping Beauty? So, this story is very much the same, except the sleeping beauty is a man, and he is not so much a beauty, but a research chemist. And he doesn't even know that he is asleep. Each day he makes his daughter's lunch, makes her very tight ponytail, spends the day in his lab, and he never realize he is sleep walking, until a beautiful immigration lawyer with quite a temper slashes her way through all the weeds and wakes him. And we cannot forget that she brings along a knight, Colin El Suave. And this man is so full of gratitude."

"What's suave?" Colin asks.

"Like this," Little My strokes her own cheek.

"Gentle," Daniel says.

"Colin The Gentle?" Colin says, interested but like it never occurred to him.

Fiona puts her hand over Daniel's hand.

"I have a story about a deer, too," she says and leans over and gives Colin a fierce kiss before he can flinch away. She runs her hand through her short, reddish brown hair. Fiona is reddish and freckled, too.

Fiona's story:

"When we broke into the nuclear facility at Seneca Falls it was the middle of the night. We cut through the fence, and the first thing we saw was a herd of albino deer, glowing in the moonlight. At Seneca Falls the deer that live inside the nuclear facility are all albino. I used to think it had to do with radiation, but really it's because of inbreeding. They can't get out, generations of them. Fenced in. The albino genetic tendency has taken over. They've lost all their color. During our whole action those white deer stood absolutely still and watched us with their big, pink-rimmed blue eyes. Like ghost deer."

"Did you let them out?" Colin asked.

"We tried. I tried. I pressed open the cut place in the fence so it would be big enough, and I tried to bully them through it, but they just stood there. Story of my life."

"Finally you told a story," Little My says.

"But, mi amor, that's not the story of your life," Daniel says. "Look at us, outside the fence, our little herd. Yes, perhaps haunted, but so full of color."

Fiona laughs and squeezes Daniel's hand. "You don't have to make use of every metaphor. Just let some of them sit there and be."

"No offense, but is this over now?" Colin asks.

"That's how it always is," Little My says. "You think it's over, but it never is."

*Marcia Popp*

# VISITING THE DEAD, THE ALMOST-LIVED, AND THE NEVER-LIVED

i

if i could spend a day with people i loved who slipped away too soon i would choose an evening listening to classical music with my grandfather before his final heart attack an afternoon flying with my father in his piper cub before it took him propeller-first into a cornfield a morning with my grandmother eating hot buttered toast covered with brown sugar and cinnamon washed down with strong black coffee while my grandmother asks does mother let you drink coffee darling and pours me a second cup

ii

it would be a daunting and sometimes sad task to bring everyone up to date on all that had happened since they left oh no she did what why on earth and oh too bad i'm sorry to hear it or that's wonderful i never would have expected it some might say they were glad to have left when they did as they were too sick or too old there would probably be good wishes on both sides please tell her i loved her i didn't get a chance or give him a hug for me

iii

it would also be enlightening to spend a day or even an hour with someone who had never lived perhaps a character imagined into life such as the thirteen-year-old boy i created in a story who went away to play drums in the civil war i would ask him why he stayed at war once he had seen what it was like i should know the answer as i spent years researching his historical context and gave him what seemed like a convincing motivation i suspect it is because although i was once thirteen and played the drums i never went to war myself obviously it is not something you can really imagine and once you have experienced it you probably do not want to remember or speak of it again iv

and then there are others i knew only through someone else like my mother's brother who would have been my uncle herschel tall funny gone to the cemetery just after his sixteenth birthday whose death ended my grandmother's interest in life her only activity after that time cutting flowers to cover his grave i would ask him what he had planned to be when he grew up and if he would have enlisted in the army or the navy during wwii as he had always been daring driving cars back and forth to Chicago for a local auto dealer when he was only thirteen and tall for his age

v

or lucy my father's great-grandmother whose husband tired of waiting for the war between the states to end and enlisted in the union army to help get it over with but instead went home in a box to some other widow by mistake so lucy buried the man sent to her and hoped someone else would give her own husband a decent burial i would ask her what she liked to read as she named her second son Orlando Lorenzo after someone she met in a book.

vi

and then there was great-grandmother alice who had a mind of her own left two husbands who she said did not treat her right made hats for a living and became the first policewoman in illinois; she was a terror i could imagine her well enough as her daughter my grandmother had a scalding tongue that took no prisoners in any verbal exchange i would ask her what she found intolerable in her husbands who still adored her even after she left them

vii

or alice's mother melvina called gran who pulled her family back together after the war between the states when the loss of everything brought them north to tenant farm and jesse her husband who fought in the southern cavalry and later built barracks to house the boys fighting together again in the spanish-american war i would ask her how she fed her family on dandelions and tree bark when there was nothing left on their farm to eat i would ask jesse what happened in the card game and why a sheriff from kentucky was looking for him as no one in the family ever knew while he was alive

viii

after all these visits i would like to spend a few hours with someone who almost made it into life and then slipped away before she could see a rainbow listen to my father play the trumpet or taste my grandmother's fried chicken i could tell my stillborn sister born five years before me many things about the family she did not join even though she was always a reality among us spoken of as the absent older sister whose birthday we noted every november 29th her ghostly presence acknowledged each year when my mother talked to her as we put flowers on her grave

ix

in not too many years when i become a distant memory will anyone in the family want to know more about the time my sister and i had to walk a mile home from the stalled school bus in a surprise april blizzard without coats or boots ask what i knew of wwii the mccarthy era the turn of the twenty-first century if i ever met eleanor roosevelt martin luther king, jr. saw the beatles perform in person what life was like before microwaves and computers will they be curious about the history of family ornaments on the christmas tree i wonder if someone will put me in a poem

*Lyn Di Iorio*

# The Girl with Translucent Skin

ON THE SECOND DAY OF THE HURRICANE, after the Christmas party, my cousin Ubén and his friends were so drunk that my aunt Graciela locked them up in the storage room next to the kitchen so they could sleep it off. Us girls knew it was because Titi Graciela wanted to keep Ubén out of trouble. He was twenty-two years old, lived at home, and was drunk or high most of the time. He was bad news, but Titi Graciela wouldn't acknowledge it because he was her boy, her only son.

Outside the house, the invisible giant recklessly flipped cars over, plucked trees up like yucca roots, and pounded the taped glass of the windows in Titi Graciela's room into a fascinating mosaic. The electricity was gone and with it the TV and internet. The howling wind unnerved the adults so much they let us drink all the anise we wanted. Over a plastic cup of the greenish syrup, Angelita, fourteen years old and the second oldest of Titi Graciela's three children, told the two of us that if we put candles in front of mirrors we would create portals into other worlds. Since most of the mirrors in the house were in the back, in Ubén's wreck of a room, the three of us went there to see if what Angelita said was true, still sipping from our cups of anise.

Angelita had wet-looking hair like Ubén's, and narrow shoulders that stooped when she unlocked Ubén's bedroom door with Titi Graciela's master key. Inside the room was silky with darkness and smelled musty with a hint of sea brine. We kept tripping on empty bottles and clothes bunched all over the floor. Mila, Titi Graciela's youngest at twelve, who smelled of pork *chicharrones*, and had an enormous lumpy behind, shined her small flashlight on something, picked it up from the floor, and held it in the air. I went up close to it. "It's Ubén's shit-stained underwear," I said and giggled as quietly as I could. The silence of the others made the large dark room seem like a mausoleum.

Angelita was the only one with a lit candle in its holder. She shushed us. Something was stirring in the back of the room near the closet, she said. In the cottony blackness, we couldn't tell what was fluttering over there, where the largest mirror was supposed to be. Angelita held the candle up high. The candle flickered in the mirror and then, suddenly, I saw three pairs of eyes at different heights. When Mila passed her small flashlight over the mirror a wrinkled shirt floated up from the mess on the floor. It was a child, a very skinny child, exactly Mila's height. In the bad light, it looked like the bones and arteries in the child's face and arms were shimmering through its skin. I screamed first, followed by the others.

We ran to get Titi Graciela who was in the kitchen counting out the cans of beans left to feed us all through the rest of the hurricane. She brought a big flashlight with her to Ubén's room and shined the light on the creature. There was just a baby's brown fuzz of hair on its head and a few teeth in its mouth. It looked like there were phosphorescent nematodes and blue flatworms traveling under the luminosity of its pale face and arms and over the spatulas of its bones.

When Titi Graciela asked the girl with translucent skin what she was doing there, the creature bit into Titi Graciela's hand, which Titi Graciela pulled back quickly with a soft cry. By that we concluded the creature was hungry, and I went running to the main part of the house to open a can of beans and get Titi Marta.

Titi Marta came back with me. Her white hair had started to go yellow on the edges like the pages of an old book. She had a tarot deck she liked to fool around with and, two times out of five, Titi Marta had foreseen the future in the cards. From the tarot cards in the big pocket of her black-and-white flowered dress, Titi Marta pulled out two cards, the eleven of swords and the falling tower.

"It's a ghost," Titi Marta said. "An avenging spirit. The storm woke her up and let her come through the mirror." Titi Marta took the can of Goya black beans and spoon that I had brought from the kitchen, offering them to the creature.

The phantom of a girl threw the spoon on the floor, but drank the can of beans chug-a-lug style. Afterward, she burped and sat down on the floor, her legs splayed out like noodles.

"What are you here for?" said Titi Marta.

The creature let out a weak mewl. Then she stood up and vomited mashed black beans mixed with green and orange flecks on Titi Marta's flowered dress.

Titi Marta examined the vomit splatter on her skirt as if she was reading her cards. "She's come back for her revenge, but can't quite remember what it was she's supposed to avenge."

Titi Marta suggested that we turn the creature out into the street so that the storm would fully wake her up into a sense of what she'd come back for.

Us girls, though, begged hard for our aunts to let her stay. Mila—who never said a lot, and just munched on her *chicharrones* while she watched TV—said more that day than she had all year. "Let her stay. Please. I feel bad for her."

"Where can we keep her? We have a full house because of the hurricane," Titi Graciela said.

"Keep Ubén and his friends in the storage room, and the ghost in Ubén's room," said Mila. Ubén was no favorite with us girls, but Mila in particular couldn't seem to bear him, and flinched whenever she saw him flinging his arms around and talking about how high the waves had been the day before when he was surfing on the western coast of our island.

Titi Graciela said we could do that, but only while Ubén and his friends were still hung over. When they were back to themselves she would have to let them out of the storage room and the ghost would have to go.

On the third day after the hurricane, the wind stopped slapping people back into their houses, and our neighbors soon learned that we were haunted. Several of them called to suggest that we have an exorcism. One of them said she thought it would make a great interview on the local television show hosted by the giant puppet, *La Comay*. By now, the sky was clear and even poinsettia trees that had lost branches in the storm were starting to sparkle with crimson leaves. Most of our extended family, who had been stuck in the storm, had gone to their own houses. When Titi Graciela let Ubén's three friends out from the storage room, Ubén was slouching against the shelves, drinking from a bottle of Bacardi, his hair looking like he'd just been for a swim. He was wearing only jeans, and no shirt, exposing his broad shoulders and a stomach as supple as a coiled snake that the sun had cured to a blood sausage color when he went surfing.

"Where did you get the rum?" Titi Graciela said. Ubén backhanded Titi Graciela in the face. She slammed the door shut, locked it against his curses, and burst into tears. That night, she refused to even feed him. By now it was just Titi Graciela, Angelita, Mila, and me.

Titi Graciela suggested that we kids take the ghost girl to the mango tree, play with her there, and then when it was time to come inside, leave her out there so she could fade away as ghosts were supposed to do.

We tried to pull her out of Ubén's room, but it was hard getting hold of her. Angelita put her hand on one the ghost girl's wrists, but the girl flicked it off, and Angelita then grabbed the ghost's shoulder but tripped and lost her grip. She shouted that she could feel only electrically charged currents of air where the girl's hand and shoulder were supposed to be. Whenever I tried to touch the ghost girl, I couldn't even get close to her. She seemed to jump back over to where the closet was. She was in front of us one moment, and out of sight the next, and letting out a slow creaky sound as if she was trying to clear out the rust deep inside her.

Eventually, though, she wanted another can of beans. Angelita held it out at the room's entrance like milk to tempt a cat, while Mila and I went in again. This time she stood still in front of us, a small little ghoul with a large head, pink-rimmed, sepia colored eyes, and black spindly claws on hands and feet. She growled and showed three yellow teeth that looked human enough. Mila growled right back and that made the ghost tip her head in surprise and, then, respond deep from her stomach, a kind of "mmmmmmm" sound. Mila mmmmmmmed, too, and they started to sound like a singing duo.

Her interest in humming made her follow Mila around. That was how we were able to get the ghost girl outside under the mango tree next to the old pool in the fenced-in patio. On one side of the patio was a neighbor's yard; on the other was a field of grass that led up to the steep side of a hill. There was a paved street next to the field. In the aftermath of the hurricane, we all breathed in deep the green sap smell of every plant in the world. The *coquí* frogs were chanting their endless song, neither happy nor sad, just holding to the rhythm of the steamy heat. In the olive light under the mango tree, next to the swampy water in the old pool, the ghost seemed more like a girl. It was clear now that her dress was just a man's tattered shirt. Mila and I wanted to stay the night there with her, but Angelita, like a miniature, scolding, adult, wouldn't let us. We left the ghost girl under the mango tree vomiting up yet again the can of beans she had just eaten.

Early the next day we found television reporters and camera people all lined up against the fence around the tree. They were filming the ghost girl who was wandering around the patio pulling up the tuberoses and rubbing their buds on her wrists and sniffing them with a half-grin, half-grimace. When Titi Graciela shouted at the reporters to leave, a tall, brown woman, in a pink suit spoke into her microphone, and said she was Viviana Marte from Telemundo. Did we have any sense of why we were being haunted? Before Titi Graciela could answer that, Viviana Marte offered to pay her for an exclusive interview with the ghost and the family.

By then, a crowd had gathered around the fence. Some thought the girl was not a ghost, only somebody left behind, to starve to death. Others wanted to count her mmmmmmms to see if there might be some numerological sign in them regarding the island's future. Viviana Marte, leaning into her microphone in front of her camera man, said, "To me, her translucent skin is a clear sign of her phantom nature. I believe that local scientists should study this creature to see if we can establish a clear link here to the world of spirits."

Father Alonso, the parish priest who was from Spain, with curly hair and the sculpted legs of a soccer player, arrived while Titi Graciela was talking to Viviana Marte. He led the spiritual retreats that Titi Graciela attended every weekend. Angelita and I took him into the patio where the tiny ghost girl was sheltering under the mango tree, her eyes closed against the brightness of the noonday sun. The priest noted that she looked more like a skeleton wrapped in spider webs than a wandering soul doing some purgatorial penance. Indifferent to her possible eventual stardom on the local television channels, the ghost girl squinted at Father Alonso while he intoned, "Ave Maria," three times in greeting. The ghost girl only yawned in response.

"Ghosts don't yawn," he said aloud, but Angelita had already moved away from him to the *marquesina*. Standing at the entrance to the patio, I could still hear and see what he was doing. The priest peered at the strange girl more closely. He reached out to touch the black claws on her hands and feet, but she ducked out of his reach. He was starting to notice, I thought, that her claws were nothing but dirty nails so overgrown they had curled into root tuber shapes. He covered his nose against her smell of urine, earthworms, and tuberoses and I could tell that what he saw through her skin was not another world but shrunken muscles, chicken bones and, right under her clavicle, the beginning of a very pink aorta. He spoke to her in five languages including Latin, and she only growled at him. When he tried to touch her hand, she snatched it back and mumbled something that sounded like, "Heh thuht meeh." The priest didn't appear to know what that meant. Finally, he approached the people standing outside the fence listening to Viviana Marte's interview of Titi Graciela, and started giving a sermon noting that only the priesthood of the Roman Catholic Church could distinguish spirits from flesh. He said that ghosts usually disappear into thin air when the Hail Mary is chanted three times in Latin, as he had just done, and he noted the unlikeliness of a ghost exhibiting the impropriety of a girl wearing nothing but a shirt to cover her body.

But let's face it, people on our island get a thrill out of ghosts. Spirits, flying saucers, and the *chupacabras* are more real most of the time than the platitudes of priests and, for a week, the story was news in all of the island's media. A rumor spread that even tapping the fence surrounding the patio would grant one wish for a sincere supplicant. That's when the carloads of people started arriving, turning Titi Graciela's yard into a makeshift concert stadium. By the next day, when us girls were tired of the shin splints we got from picking up so many soft drink cans, soggy diapers, and empty *platanutre* bags that the revelers had thrown away, Titi Graciela decided she would charge a dollar for letting people come up against the fence to see the ghost.

Students on vacation from colleges and high schools swarmed the house followed by loads of town dwellers arriving by *carro público* and tourists by taxi. Even one big busload of Japanese salsa dancers visiting the island for a contest came, and one of the dancers commented aloud in perfect Puerto Rican Spanish that our ghost was much more wild-eyed than any she'd seen in Asian horror films. For five dollars Titi Graciela would allow people to touch the ghost, which was only possible when Mila walked with the jittery creature up to the fence where people would stick a finger through the wire so they could hold one of her broom-handle wrists between a thumb and a forefinger. Some people thought that holding on to her would give them relief from health problems: a man with angry rash lines on his face that doctors had not been able to cure; a woman who had chronic daily headaches; and one of the Japanese dancers who always had sore ankles but didn't want to give up salsa. Most of those coming however were islanders who thought they'd be able to find jobs if only they could get a spirit to carry their petitions to the other world. During the constant parade of visitors and TV interviews, Titi Graciela, whose mouth was usually downturned, started smiling every day. She was making good money from the interviews, and she stopped taking sleeping pills. Mila told the ghost girl her recurring dream in which she walked alone. In the dream she saw no light, only visibly dark shapes, which she stabbed at many times, but couldn't kill. The ghost girl mmmmmmmed every time Mila told the dream. Angelita and I were just grateful that Ubén was locked up for a few days.

Only the ghost girl took no pleasure in her own gig. When Mila wasn't showcasing her at the fence, she flitted from the mango tree to the ironwork gate, back and forward constantly, pressing her webbed phalanges into the floating veins on her skull. It was as if she was preoccupied with some ghostly obsession, only stopping at night when the outdoor nightlight went on and she curled up under the mango tree, next to the pool filled with old rainwater and leaves. She groaned and held her lower stomach as if it ached. We tried to get her to eat salt, which according to Titi Marta and our favorite TV show, *Supernatural*, would make her vanish into thin air. There must have been some truth to it, because she screamed when we brought her bowls of pure salt. She wouldn't touch them, and if we added salt to the canned beans, she refused to eat them. Maybe it was the salt in the beans that made her throw up to begin with. But really, the only real supernatural power she seemed to have was her ability to tell if someone was coming up behind her, even if they were in the parking lot. That was how she was able to avoid being touched unless Mila coaxed her. The gentle, twenty-year-old feral cat, Alcibiades, made her scream if he approached her from behind, and she started sobbing in nervous anticipation right before the nightingales sang each morning. Even the soft trilling sound of the gray-winged *pitirres* was so intolerable to her that she *pitirred* right back at them in a rage until they simply stopped showing up in the patio. Only the chirping of the *coquís* at twilight seemed to soothe her vigilant pacing into a relatively calm seated posture under the tree, and then she would be quiet, biting into the chicken wing bones of her fingers.

Titi Graciela might have become rich off the TV interviews and visitors if it hadn't been for the death of the twenty-three-year-old old boxer Cristobal Parao in San Juan. His family held a public wake for him in a fake boxing ring in the Marín funeral home. The dead man stood in the far corner of the ring, wearing sunglasses, black satin shorts, and a black satin jacket with a yellow hood that covered his head. His boxing gloves were blue. The mortician was so skilled that not only did Parao's coffee-colored skin glow with more health than it had in life, but members of the public swore that when they went up to him, the man would say hello, and whisper how sorry he was to have gotten mixed up with the thugs who shot him to death. The boxer looked so golden skinned and penitent in death, and was so chatty and friendly, it was no surprise that people liked him much more than the standoffish ghost girl who couldn't even walk through a wall.

We couldn't really complain. Titi Graciela had made enough money from the TV interviews to buy some of the land next to the hill and build a pool as well as two new rooms so that Mila didn't have to sleep in the same bed as Angelita, and I could have my own room when I visited. Titi Graciela also joined a gym and started losing weight. And she bought herself a red-haired wig with a French braid, like the ones all the fashionable middle aged women were wearing that year, along with a whole set of embroidered cotton tunics to wear over her pants.

Eight days after the hurricane had hit—after the reporters and visitors had stopped hanging out outside the gate—Titi Graciela remembered that Ubén was still in the storage room. Not even Angelita had thought it worthwhile reminding her. When we opened the door, we saw him sitting on the floor without his jeans or any underwear. The storage room smelled of shit and piss. His hair still had that wet-looking shininess, and his skin hadn't yet lost the flame-edged brown color of a blood sausage. He looked up, his eyes as hard and hollow as *guanábana* seeds, and bared his teeth at us. He tried to get up, and knocked over some cans of Goya beans on a shelf, but he was too weak to slap Titi Graciela in the face, as he so often had done. Eventually, without bothering to pull on his pants, he limped to his room, his sex hanging like a mollusk on his hairy thighs. Angelita turned away, Mila touched her stomach and frowned, but I followed, curious to see what he would do.

When he saw that his always-locked door was ajar, he said, "Holy fucking, mother of shit and cunts and their hell holes." He kicked around in the mess of his room, and his curses against little *averiguadas puta* bitches were so loud that one of the stragglers still hanging outside the fenced-in patio shouted from the outside, "Is there a demon in your house now?"

But it was the ghost who surprised us. She heard Ubén's curses and started wailing in language we could finally understand, "No, please, no! No, no, no!"

Ubén went running towards the patio but before he could go to the mango tree, Mila shut the ironwork gate, and blocked him from the ghost with her pillowy body.

Ubén leapt on the ironwork trellis and clung to it. "How in hell did you get out, you little whore?" The girl stayed under the tree, wailed louder, and looked away from him.

Mila grabbed his hair, but her hand slipped off it, so she yanked one of his hands off the ironwork. "So you hurt her, too, *hijo de puta*?"

Ubén punched her in the face, and Mila held her face in her hands without crying out. "Get away from me, you fat sack of shit," he snarled. "You got too fat, I don't know what I ever saw in you."

Mila threw herself on him, and clutched his exposed balls, which to me looked like the pink, hairy, embryos of some unknown creature; she smiled slightly and squeezed them hard. A jagged yowl rent the air, the sound of a cat having its legs smashed by a door, but then Mila let him go, and he ran back to his room. He slammed the door of his room shut, and we could hear him throwing his dresser drawers against the wall and yelling that he was going to find the machete his dead father had left him and use it to decapitate all of the women in the world. I guess that meant us.

But that didn't happen. It was then that we started to suspect the truth that eventually led us to call the police. Weeks later, the girl, and Mila, too, would tell their stories. Years ago, when she still looked like a girl, Ubén had taken her from a house near the beach where he used to surf. He had gagged her, locked her up and raped her repeatedly in his bedroom where he pretended to be an underworld king. There she became a stranger to herself, watching her other self's skin turn translucent like a worm under a rock, watching a ghost trapped in the otherworld of the mirrors.

*Renia White*

# 36C

the first time a boy asked me about my breasts
we were on the front steps of Abyssinia Baptist
and those boys everybody knew wasn't saved,
just brothers, had rode in with us
on the vacation bible school van
with that heavy door you had to dislocate
your shoulder just to close.
and I can't say I wasn't intrigued
but something about the moment felt
like maybe girl, go prove you talk to God
like you know him, so I tattled
and my church uncle grabbed that boy,
just a brother, up by his ear with a twist
so hard I heard it pop like a knuckle.
and if I knew then those brothers
would remain as unsaved as before,
that no vestibule assault would
take his eyes off my sprouting,
that just 'cause you've got a ticket
doesn't mean you'll get in
I would've told him, *36C like grown women*
like I wanted, like it was some shame to know
all by myself so I had to let him in
and maybe he'd have saved me,
that boy, just a brother, all black and real
solid, real wiry, in on the joke so soon
he couldn't help himself

*Artress Bethany White*

# MISSISSIPPI IN JUNE

*On a June morning in 2011, James Craig Anderson was beaten and run over in Jackson, Mississippi by a group of white teenagers driving a utility vehicle. His death was ruled a hate crime. It was a June day in 1964 when the civil rights workers James Chaney, Michael Schwerner, and Andrew Goodman were gunned down near Philadelphia, Mississippi. Despite the nearly fifty years separating these crimes, there is still something about Mississippi in June…*

For school children
it is a first long word,
spelling Miss-iss-ippi over and over
like a state song committed to memory.
All kinds of things are passed
down to generations by rote,
the good and the bad,
but there is no rhyme to teach
how to mourn the death of a child
run down like road kill
for being black.

Slow down for a rabbit, raccoon,
or a fox by reflex, watch
the glassy eyes of the innocent
stare into headlights
a stunned moment
between life and death
before compassion
presses a foot to the brake.

Sunday school teaches
do unto others as you would
have them do unto you,
whether animal or man,
confirming that it was not
God's workmanship

that killed your boy.
Born in 1963,
he was still a lap baby
when Chaney, Schwerner, and Goodman
were found dead
near a town named Philadelphia
that had nothing to do with liberty.
On that day you leaned down to kiss
the top of his head,
baby-fine hair softly curling
under your lips,
believing in your heart
that this child would inherit a better life
than Mississippi in 1964.
You were wrong.

Today, watching the videotape
of your son's last seconds on earth
raw footage
black and white
cars, people, headlights
and him holding up hands
before the bumper
dragged him from view,
in these moments
you try to work up the meanest
curse you can think of
against the injustice of it all,
but the only word
that keeps coming to mind
is Mississippi.

**KNIGHTVILLE POETRY CONTEST WINNER**

*Jose Padua*

# SEVEN AND SEVEN IS

The young thug from my neighborhood who whipped my older
brother Tony with a car antenna outside our
house, and the man who was both former governor and
senator from Virginia, and whose 2006
campaign to regain his Senate seat was derailed when
he used a racial slur while speaking to an Indian-
American tracker from his opponent's camp, were

both named George Allen. This is not an attempt to point
out the oddities and ironies of life, this is
simply the way things happened. My brother was thirteen
and I was nine, and George Allen, the young neighborhood
thug, laughed maniacally as he whipped my brother
over and over with the shiny metal car
antenna. Later, I imagined that if I'd had

a baseball bat I could have snuck up from behind and
swung like Frank Howard, home run hitter for the Washington
Senators baseball team, and killed George Allen, but I
didn't have a bat, and I didn't have the home run
power, so I didn't kill him and when it was over
my brother slowly walked into the house crying
in pain and all I could do was yell or try to yell.

George Allen was the first and probably the only
person I ever really imagined killing, and
when I was young I didn't understand that killing
him would have changed my life in ways I can't imagine.
George Allen, candidate for the Senate, was the son
of George Allen the famous football coach, and went
to high school in Palos Verdes, California, drove

a Ford Mustang that had a front license plate holder
that was adorned with the Confederate flag, and wore
a pin of that flag for his official yearbook photo.
George Allen, California fan of the Confederacy,
went to the University of Virginia when
his father became the coach of the Washington
Redskins and stayed on there to get his law degree, and

got married, got divorced, got married again and had
three children and now lives in a wealthy neighborhood
near the first president of the United States George
Washington's Mt. Vernon estate. George Allen, neighborhood
thug, was black and didn't have a famous father and
didn't have a fancy car, and was a skinny, kind
of weird-looking guy who after he'd whipped my brother

would always laugh at us, and everyone in the neighborhood,
black or white or any other color, knew that one
day he would end up in jail, and when he did go to jail
for armed robbery we never saw him again,
never got whipped or laughed at or threatened by him
again and his story like so many others just
sort of ends, like a film with no plot, a film that ends

with a sudden cut to black. And there are so many
ways to react to getting beaten down like this, and
too many people would take the neighborhood thug and
anyone who looks like him and lump them all together
like horrible monsters, like the landlord I once talked
to on the phone about renting an apartment in
New York and who suddenly said he had nothing

available when I told him my name was Jose,
and I later found out that ever since a Puerto
Rican employee ripped him off he doesn't trust
anyone he thinks is Hispanic, like me with my
Hispanic-sounding name, and this doesn't make the landlord
a poor, sorry, fearful, and fragile guy whose apprehension
is understandable, it makes him an asshole goon.

My brother got beaten and got better and got over
it, and I try to imagine what it was that made
George Allen, asshole candidate for the Senate, give
so much glory to the Confederacy, what could
have filled him with so much backwards shit—did he learn it,
did it beat him within a sliver of the heart beneath
his bleeding white skin? When George Allen, thug, was beating

my brother I was full of fear and anger and revenge,
but when I saw George Allen, the candidate, so
casually use that word, that slur that was meant to lay
another man down to some lesser place, I just felt
helpless, like in a dream where you want to run but you
can't, where you want fight back, but your arms won't rise
to shelter the color in your face, and you can't cut to black.

*Robert McGuill*

# Requiem for a Bantamweight

YOU SEEN HIM, RIGHT? RICAN KID, Danny Santos? The dead boxer? Okay, so fuck *me*, but I didn't even know the little *caco* had snuffed it. Not 'til I came across his photo in yesterday's paper. There I am, stirring up a cup of instant, and when I turn to the sports section who do I see looking out at me from the front page but the man himself. *Standing* in a boxing ring. Staring at me from behind a pair of Ray-Bans—or would've been staring, anyway, if he was still alive and breathing, which he wasn't.

Photo was on page two, next to the box scores and blog highlights, right below the trades and transactions columns. Danny Santos, deceased, standing in the corner, back to the ropes, like he's waiting on instructions from some mythical ref who's gonna step into the ring and motion for the microphone to come drifting down out the smoke and haze.

Well, one thing's for sure. Mortician-dude, he must've thumbed every rack hanger and shelf at Big Five to put together the man's wardrobe, cause it covered the whole matrix of bad, baddest, and badass. Black trunks, gold robe, black shoes. Nothing left out. They even laced him up in a pair of sixteen-ounce gloves (hardly used, just like in real life) and cocked his hands like this, so it looked like he was ready to charge into the ring and do some serious banging (this, too, fiction).

Hell. I thought only white people pulled those kinds of half-assed stunts. Dressing up their kids in shoes and jerseys, and having them masquerade like the real thing. Handing them trophies. Pretending they've got what it takes to go *mano a mano* with a person of my caliber, a man who rides the bullet. But the pic, the pic itself said it all. Whoever was responsible for putting that *alcahuete* in the ring, posing him the way they did in those fancy clothes with that big Rican flag behind him, they didn't pull no punches. They did everything but drape the champion's belt over his shoulder.

Whole thing made me wanna puke. Made me wanna stroll over to the funeral home and cuff the stupid bitch, dead or not. I couldn't stop shaking my head when I saw him like that, all princely and full of himself. Everything deserted me, even my anger, and I just sat there, gawking like a moron. I mean, there he was, Danny Santos, the bum, pimped out like cashmoney, not a care in the world, and here I was, Spider Moses, sitting in a two-room ghettofied shithole, trying to figure out how I was gonna pay my bills, the purse I was counting on having flown out the window.

*Pendejo.*

They had us booked for an eight-rounder at the Paradise Theater. Undercard for the Junior Jones fight. Only now, with Danny dead and no chance of my manager, Little Boy Lyle, shaking any last-minute opponents out of the trees, I feel safe saying I got no immediate future myself, unless it's staring out the window watching the world go by.

Yeah. You can see me making that face, can't you? Cause you know what I'm talking about. And you probly know what I'm thinking, too. I'm thinking, Laugh it up, Danny—wherever the fuck you at—you winky little *pato*—cause this is your big moment, bro. This the only way your dumb ass is ever gonna turn my lights out.

That stupid picture had me hunched over the table half the morning. Staring at him all blinged out in his gold satin robe. Badass *gafas*. Unscuffed, red leather gloves. Then something else caught my attention, and I leaned in closer, cause I had to know it wasn't my eyes that were lying to me. It was his skin I was looking at. It seemed like it wasn't even real. Like it was made of clay or wax, or something smoother. Something ain't never had a glove laid on it. *Shit.* Danny Santos ate more leather than any boxer I've ever known. His face been tattooed more often than Lady Gaga's ass. But now, not a scar to show for it. (Look it up online, you don't believe me. See for yourself. His skin looks smooth as mocha ice cream, straight out the cup.) I don't know who done the makeup job, but man, whoever it was, dude oughta move out to L.A. Get himself a gig with Industrial Light and Magic, he's that good.

More I studied that photograph, the more it got inside my head. More it set me off, you know? All the training I'd done—all the sweat I'd wrung from my muscles, all the hurt I'd willed my mind to suffer through—it was for nothing now, a waste! Me and Danny Santos was sposed to be facing each other for the third time in eighteen months—the match to decide it all—only now, with his dumb ass killed, my future's a foregone conclusion—as in, I ain't got none.

When I couldn't take it no more, I pushed the paper away and picked up the phone. Called Bennie Steele, my trainer, over at the gym.

Joint was crazy with noise that morning—you could hear all kinds of shouting and banging going on in the background—and when Bennie picked up the line he didn't recognize it was me at first. So there I was unloading into the mouthpiece, *blakka-blakka-blakka*, when all the sudden, he cuts me off, demanding, "Who the fuck is this?"

"It's me, *Spider*," I tell him, and he says, "Jesus, motherfucker! You best dial it back, fore you give yourself a cardiogram."

Whatever.

"You hear about Danny Santos?" I said.

"Yeah," he said. "I heard."

"The fuck happened?"

"Somebody cooled him, that's what. Got hisself stabbed in the eye. With a pool cue."

*"Pool cue?"*

Bennie sighed, real hard, like he'd been explaining the situation to folks all morning. "I been saying it for years, Spider," he droned, using the tired old line he's used on every boxer he's ever trained, "they *all* go if you hit em right."

"Yeah," I said, shifting the phone from one ear to the other. "Yeah, I understand that. But what happens now, huh? How am I sposed to take care of my bills? We had a contract, me and the Santos camp. I had a payday coming."

Bennie listened real sympathetic for a while, and made with a few polite grunts. He even tried to smooth things over with a light salve of professional BS to stop the bleeding. "Little sympathy," he said. "Little compassion, my man. Dude didn't take no shank in the eye just to piss you off."

"Yeah, well," I said, "he gone pissed me off anyway. My mouth's been watering for this fight, Bennie. Now the whole deal's in the tank."

"Look," he lowered his voice. "Take a deep breath and release. Focus, all right? Let out the toxins. We mourning the loss of a fellow boxer here. Fellow warrior."

I told him, fuck that shit. Wasn't his lectricity whose plug they was gonna pull. Wasn't his ride the repo man was gonna come trolling down the alley for with a big-ass hook truck.

"Oh, I'm in mourning all right," I told him. "I'm grieving the loss of all them Benjamins sposed to be coming my way. Sorrowing over the big-ass dent I ain't gonna get to put in that motherfucker's head."

Bennie told me to calm the fuck down, but he knew what I was saying. He knew Danny Santos wasn't nothing but a bum, a pretender. Two times I kicked that *joyo's* ass, and both times Bennie was in my corner, laying into the ropes, cursing me on with bloodthirsty instructions. Grinning while I took that little tomato can apart, punch by punch.

"Ain't no need for tragedy here, Spider," he said, side-stepping the issue, working my inside like a pro. "We all one big family at this gym. You know that. You need an advance, I'll get you one. Front you enough to see you through the end of the month. Longer, if need be. Just say how much, and I'll go to work on it."

I slumped in the chair. Bennie knew it wasn't the money that was eating at me. He knew my bringing up the bills and waving them in his grill was just a stupid feint, something to cover my true intentions, and he slipped the move as easily as I used to slip Danny Santos' limp dick of a right hand.

"Come on, Spider," he said. "I ain't got all morning. How much you need?"

I said nothing because I had nothing. Instead, I backpedaled. Got on my bicycle and looked for a way out. "Screw the money," I said. "That ain't the point."

"Ain't the point?" I could hear him sigh. "What do you mean, it ain't the point? You just went and made it the point."

"Yeah, well," I said, "now I'm *unmaking* it."

He put his hand over the phone, yelled at somebody across the gym. *That a left hook, retard! You telling me you don't know how to slip a left hook and go to the body? Long as you been coming here? Go home, dude! Just go-the-fuck home! We through for the day!*

He came back on the line, said, "Look, man. Quit your worrying, all right? Lyle's gonna sign your uptight ass to another bout soon as he can. He upstairs in his office right now, working on it."

I felt my whole body cave. Crumbling in despair. A different fight wasn't gonna fix things, and Bennie knew it. What I wanted—what I *needed*—was Danny Santos.

I'd been training hard the last three months. Spent no time with friends. Did no partying. Messed with no women, easy as they come. I thought about nothing during that three-month stretch, except making myself strong. Forging my body into a weapon. I watched no TV. Answered no phones. Wished for nothing that couldn't be found within the ring. Prayed for nothing that couldn't be had by my own two fists. When I went to bed at night, I saw only Danny Santos in my dreams—saw him the way a monk sees God when all he does is pray.

"Danny Santos stole from me," I said. "He stole what I had coming, and now he's standing in the ring like the punk-ass bitch he is, pretending it was his all along."

Bennie listened, but left the words hanging there. Let the quiet fill up the phone so I could almost see him with his finger in his ear, back bent. Shaking his head.

"Danny Santos *dead*, Spider."

I closed my eyes. I couldn't listen to him. I bit my fucking tongue so hard it bled.

"Spider?"

I looked at the phone. Brought it back to my ear, and took a deep breath. "You saying I don't deserve the same as what you got? Huh, Bennie?"

Silence. He didn't like being reminded what this was really about.

"No," he grumbled, after a moment. "I ain't saying that. I ain't saying anything like that. I'm just saying step back, and hear what Lyle has to say. Give things a chance to settle."

I took another deep breath and released. Let out the toxins, just like he said. All I wanted was to see my name in the books. See my record go to ten and one. "I was gonna give Danny Santos the beatdown of his life," I told him. "I was gonna knock his ass out of the ring. Prove to everybody—for all time—that what happened before wasn't nothing but a *fluke*."

Bennie knew what I was talking about. Hell, he'd lived this life before I had, and he knew what it was like. A man chasing his shadow-self through slow, agonizing dreams of pain and humiliation. Trying to corner immortality. Capture it with his fists.

"You gotta keep slugging, man. Ain't nothing else you can do."

"That's it, huh? That's the best you got for me?"

"What else you want me to say, Spider? What you want me to say that's gonna make you feel better?"

I had no answer for him. I understood what he was telling me—that it was okay to deceive one another in the ring, but that outside the ropes, lies were a poison that would corrode your soul—only it didn't make me feel any better.

"This was sposed to be my shot, Bennie," I said. "This was sposed to be the match that put me in the record books."

Again, he said nothing. All I could hear were the noises in the gym.

"Guy like me?" I said. "We both know I ain't never gonna get no title shot. No big-name fight under the lights. I was a good amateur, and now I'm—what?—a journeyman with a journeyman's record. Nothing more, nothing less. So, see, Bennie—I *needed* this fight. I needed it to put things right. Cause when this is over, when my time's up as a boxer, guess what? I go back to being what I was before. Which was nothing. Spider the *nobody*."

Bennie let me rant a while, hoping I'd punch myself out. But it didn't stop me.

"It ain't fair, man," I said. "I brought the best out in that little *mamabicho*. The dude sucked except when he fought me. He was awful, a poseur. But I made his punk ass legit. I raised him up and made him look like he belonged in a ring wearing a gold robe and sunglasses. This here was it, man." I thumped my finger on the picture in the paper. "This here was my chance. My time. Settling the score with Danny Santos was gonna be my little sliver of immortality. It was gonna be written in black ink, where it couldn't never be erased."

I stopped talking, and after a second or two of silence, Bennie broke in, his voice full of road rash, like it'd been run over and dragged behind a taxi. "You talking like a crazy man, Spider. You know that, don't you? You talking like Danny Santos killed hisself just to spite you."

"How you know he didn't? Huh, Bennie?"

"Spider."

"I'm just saying. Some dudes, that's their way. They ain't got it in them to face the beast. Stand up and be a man. I'm cut from leather, motherfucker. I'm cut from *suede*. Danny Santos? That little bitch was scissored outta fairy-ass taffeta, and I wouldn't put nothing past him. Specially when it came to this fight—cause he knew I was gonna take him apart, and he just couldn't bear to let that happen."

Me and Danny Santos didn't like each other. Two times we fought, and both times I kicked his ass. First fight, I beat the hell out of him four straight rounds and shoulda walked away with a TKO. But two of the ringside judges were homies, so it ended in a split decision. Welcome to boxing, right? Boo hoo. Anyway, I was lucky to take the match on points, and Bennie said as much when he got me back to the locker room that afternoon. He said it was better than losing—better by a long shot—and I agreed. But even so, it left a real bad taste in my mouth.

I can still see that fight, you know? Still see the ref lifting my hand, me looking down at the judges, watching them cringe at how close they called it. Wondering if maybe they'd tried to give it to Danny all along, but somehow got their math unzipped. All I know is, they turned and eyed one another, hard. Real hard. Like they expected to maybe wake up the next morning and find their daughters raped and their dogs poisoned.

Second fight? Second fight I won, too, even though they handed it to the little prick in the fifth round. Long and short of it, I was robbed. They had me ahead on the cards, then DQ'd me on a technicality—a head butt. It was a good call, except for one very important detail. It was Danny Santos who banged into me, opening that gash over his eye. But hey, no point pissing and moaning right? Water under the bridge is water under the bridge. All I got to say about the subject anymore is, you want justice in this life, don't expect nobody to hand it to you. Go out and grab it. Kick it in the balls, bitch slap it 'til it cries, and drag it home behind you by the short hairs.

Shit, someday when I hang up my gloves and I'm lounging, poolside with a drink in my hand, I'll write a book about my fights with Danny Santos. Put the whole weepy episode on paper. That way, anybody who wants can pass the Kleenex box around, maybe take up a collection and commission some sensitive fuck with a guitar to make up a sad song about me.

I'd looked at the photo again, long and hard. Danny Santos, absolved of his mortality. Danny Santos, beatified. Danny Santos, dead as Grover Cleveland but dressed like he'd just taken the bantamweight title. I don't know. Maybe I'm old fashioned. But hoping to make yourself into something you ain't by stealing a bunch of cheap publicity on the way out—man, that's lower level, in my book. The bottomest of the bottom.

Look at him there. It's his last stop on this side of the dirt, and he's dressed in a satin robe with two hot-looking chica peeps standing back on either side of the ring apron waiting to have their pictures taken with him. Like he was Arturo Gato, or somebody.

Photographer's there, too, over on the left, almost out of frame, and you can see the camera in his hands, flashbulb waiting to pop, imagine him yelling, *"No, no. Closer in! Right! Eyes just a little lower—yes! Yes, just like that!"*

Pictures? *Seriously?* Who the fuck poses with a corpse?

Story under the photo said his people were looking to honor his love of boxing, dressing him up in a robe and trunks. I laughed out loud when I read that! You fucking kidding me? Dude owned a punk-ass three and sixteen record. *He was a stiff before he was a stiff!* Shit. If he wanted to honor the sport of boxing, he shoulda tried doing a little roadwork once in a while. Or better yet, forget the address to his gym and take up something more his speed. You know, like synchronized swimming.

Look, everything is not for everybody, all right? Danny Santos ain't the first piece of shit to walk into a gym, hoping to feel like a man at the end of the day. But that said, he wasn't nothing but a ball-scratching miscreant. And dead or not, dressing him up that way disrespected the profession and everybody in it—myself included, first and foremost.

Danny Santos didn't have the talent to bring the title home on his own. So he tried to steal it with this numb-nut bit of bullshit at the funeral parlor. Only it isn't gonna work. I ain't gonna let it. I'm gonna find some way to take back what was mine. What I had coming.

"If the funeral home wanted to pose the dude proper," I told Bennie, "they should've saved time and money by having the janitor chuck his bitch ass on the canvas. Just toss it down, center ring, and let it lie there where it fell. Be a nice natural look for him."

"Spider," Bennie sighed when I said this.

"What?"

"Go easy, brother. You being rude now."

"Rude?"

"We talking about the departed here. Man who can't defend hisself."

*Defend himself!* Ha! As if that was something new! I shook my head and hung up when Bennie said that. Pitched the phone, skating across the countertop, and went to fix myself another cup of coffee. I couldn't listen no more about poor Danny Santos, not without going crazy. Not without wanting to punch a hole in the wall.

So I looked at the photo one last time, thinking, enjoy the moment you little prick. Live it the fuck up, cause it ain't gonna last. Remember how you used to talk about yourself when you thought someone was listening? Way you used to swear you were gonna win a championship someday? Hold that jeweled belt over your head, corner men jostling you round the ring on their shoulders? Clapping you on the back? Remember how you said you used to see the whole spectacle happening in slow-motion? Like in the movies? Big teary music in the background, your punk-ass body glorified under the ring-lights? Well, look at yourself now, pal. Look at yourself now. You could've rode my coattails into history. But instead, this what you got. A pool stick in the eye, and a goofy-ass picture in the newspaper.

Palooka.

Fucking *chapusero*.

*Kay Merkel Boruff*

# THE FUNERAL

*Ubermensch awakens and leaves, without turning back, burns his text, erases his steps: His laughter bursts out.*
—NIETZSCHE

*June, 1968 Bangkok*

I dragged my old red American Tourister suitcase from the back of the closet, sat on the floor, reading letters with two addresses—Air America, Box 60, Bangkok, Thailand, and Air America, Box 150, Sai-Gon, Viêt-Nam—searching for details.

I can't write sensibly about the war. It was fun. It was scary. It was pain. It was pride. It was death. It was devastation. It was none of these things if you weren't there. Writing about the war, Ford Madox Ford says, gets the sights of it out of your head. He's wrong. The sights hang on the black squiggles, in addition to floating on the inside of your fucking head.

Jeff wrote thirty-three letters, numbered in perfect sequential order, the printing perfect, all in caps written on small business-size sheets. I wrote thirteen, numbers out of order, three different writing styles, three different types of stationery—cramped cursive elementary penmanship on large air mail stationery from the Okura, a four-star hotel in Tokyo, where Air America bedded us and tried to entice us to fall in love with the Orient; artistic calligraphy, with stylized serifs on the letterhead from the Kent Hotel, a military hotel in Taipei where we roomed for a week next door to GIs and their prostitute "short timers"; and finally depressed illegible scratching on inexpensive paper from the local market in Bangkok, a pale blue transparent paper with words scarcely visible. Our letters, like paper dragon burnt offerings, crossed in the mail.

Jeff's letter from Sai-Gon arrived first. It was numbered and dated and filled with information to make me want to follow him to Sai-Gon—a description of the boarding house run by an Air American pilot:

> *#1 living arrangement, meals and laundry and maids.*

He knew how to persuade me. Then, of course, he made reference to his normal sexual state—horny. And finally the PS—sign the enclosed ID card and return it to the Company. At the time, I was too naïve to identify the same pattern in all Jeff's letters—romantic pandering, then Germanic directives.

My first letter from Bangkok was filled with lists of expenses, military jargon, daily bitching, and the long ramblings of a homesick bride too young to be alone. The ideas ran together as though I had only one speed, rampant hysterics:

> *My neighbor's maid bought 4 cokes for 5 baht for me and returns the bottles. I'm washing sheets by hand in the bathtub to save money. This must be punishment for past sins. Mailing your letters is epic: DPT 1200, walked to Sukhumvit. No samlar. Save 4 baht. Catch #45 green bus for .75 baht. Walk 3 blocks in the heat. Pick up the mail. Mail my letters. Repeat the process to RTN at 1400 in the rain.*

My rambling rantings—no matter how incoherent they were on the page—were important, a link to a resemblance of normalcy. In the states, secretly married to Jeff, I taught school one semester and lived with an aunt. My sole responsibility had been to my teaching, not to managing a house, and now I was living alone in a city where I spoke less than ten Thai words and I was unemployed:

> *I messed up on my Ortho Novum. Mai pen lai, no big deal, as the locals say.*

I tended to approach life verbally with that attitude when in reality I was crumbling behind the façade of my rose-colored glasses. Neither of the two Thai schools where I applied to teach had offered me a job. The real point of my letter, however, was buried in the middle of the ramblings:

> *Kind of scary when I go to bed. I stay up late so I'll fall asleep quickly.*

Counting every baht, living alone, waiting for *kamoys* to burglarize my apartment had reduced me to the point that I could barely function. That message of fear was lost to Jeff. The red flag to him was rather the PS:

> *I wrote my father for $50.00.*

Jeff wrote back instructing me *never* to write my father for money. He could take care of his wife. I wasn't so sure. After reading my thirteen letters filled with schizophrenic dribble, he should have had grounds for divorce or reason to lock me away.

Bits of Jeff's job and the war filtered in among his expenses and movies and wine lists:

> *Flew some USAID people out to an island thirty miles off the coast for a Sunday afternoon outing on the beach. A number of ugly tomatoes were in the crowd. It was a long tiring day.*

USAID mismanaged funds in Viêt-Nam, in all wars I assume. Interestingly enough, a year later I went with a girlfriend and a group of Air America pilots and wives to the same beach on Con Son Island, where the POW tiger cages were located. Not until *Apocalypse Now* was filmed did I see the juxtaposition of my existence—champagne and torture, bombs and caviar, red, white, and blue body bags and fetish flashbacks:

> *Happy Fourth of July. No fireworks in these parts although some have been expected. Nothing but the usual B-52s dropping bombs twenty or thirty miles from here on VC positions. Sounds like the rolling distant thunder of a summer rainstorm.*

Another letter continued:

> *I delivered food in Da Nang to some people whose homes and crops had been burned by the VC.*

A final letter referred to the rumor that denied our existence until former CIA director William Casey acknowledged the fact in Dallas in 1987:

> *We were working for some spooks who are reported to be CIA. The troops were wearing black pajamas. I never ask any questions.*

When I moved to Sai-Gon, Jeff stopped talking about his work. His letters to me in Bangkok, however, continued to beg and berate me to join him:

> *To have you far away is unbearable. I need you to be close to me as much as possible. We need each other too much to be separated like this.*

I knew Jeff didn't stay home every night. One letter mentioned a fellow pilot and his excursion to the short time houses to price the merchandise:

> *$5 S.T. and $15 all night. Better laughs or looks I could have had elsewhere. After a few rounds of my wondering 'What the fuck am I doing here? I must have better things to do' I finally headed back to the Nautique. Prices at the bar are unreal. Drinks are $1. We just can't afford it.*

The fact Jeff was pricing merchandise didn't infuriate me as much as the fact he had a life other than riding the bus, washing sheets, job hunting, and writing letters.

Another letter quoted our finances as further bait. He had detailed his salary with base pay, project pay, and overtime when he finally made captain. In a perfectly drawn chart, he calculated that if we stayed in Southeast Asia ten years and waited three years to start our family, we could return to the states and retire. Jeff didn't mention how dangerous the flying was, or how many of the wives became alcoholics or went crazy.

Then the final argument came. He sent seven pages of detailed instructions for me to fly to Sai-Gon and visit him, how to manage the paperwork, how to get to the embassy, how to get to the airport, how to call him in Sai-Gon. He briefly mentioned he was pissed that he hadn't been able to fly one day and another time his boss made him do remedial practice for a poor landing. Of course, he added:

> *It's very rough going without you. We don't really need to be separated. Come soon, my love.*

By that time I was entrenched in a routine of desperation in Bangkok and couldn't see my way to the airport, much less find the strength to fly into a war zone. My anger over the situation in Bangkok—hand washing my single sheet and three dishes, sweeping hardwood floors with an eighteen-inch Thai broom, riding buses with no air conditioning, shopping at the local market, having little contact with anyone who spoke English, while Jeff lived with maids, had his meals cooked and his laundry done, and enjoyed a social life—came to a head. I chewed his ass out and threatened to fly home to Texas and accused him of only thinking of his goddamn sex life and, of course, added a stinger:

> *Maybe I'll spend our $300 in my bank account since you don't want me to have a signature on your Virginia bank account.*

The last sentence held the vortex of my anger. Not content with one letter, however, I mailed a second one the next day. I mentioned my burned hand, a cut finger, ants in a new box of seventeen-baht raisins, weevils in a new eight-baht bag of flour, knowing the details drove him crazy. The sink had stopped up in the middle of baking muffins. Dirty dishes were piled up. Water was everywhere on my waxed floor. The *Time-Life* people sent six books and one damaged copy to Sai-Gon, not Bangkok. The sun had not shone in three days. And no, I hadn't talked to Hazel Kelly about Sai-Gon, reminding him that I hated to talk to strangers. It was the same type of dialogue I now listen to daily from my sixth-grade students, and eventually when I tire of their complaints, I tell them to grow up and get a life. Nowadays I would simply tell Jeff to fuck off. Forty years ago, I didn't know the words or the attitude.

Jeff responded in the manner which made me fall in love with him:

> *Reading your letter, I was so depressed I cried. I could not believe that you could say those things to me. I wasn't even sure you had written them, and then I noticed the letter was not even signed. I'm not sure what it was that could upset you so, but I surmise it was the insurmountable tasks outlined in the instructions, compounded by the cut finger, burnt hand, and broken sink. Some things I have no control over. I always try to do my best for you, for you are all I have to cling to, all that is important to me, all that I strive for.*

Until Jeff was dead, and I'd analyzed every facet of our relationship, I'd thought he was the problem. Two years before Jeff and I married I was hospitalized for a nervous breakdown, caused mostly from stress, and loss, and obsessive-compulsive behavior. My world shifted, platelets broke away. Subsequently, I lived with a barrier, a protection, like a broken leg you continue to favor with a slight limp even after the cast is off and the pins are out. Following a year of marriage, I still couldn't commit myself completely to loving him. Then if he left me, it wouldn't hurt so much. The problem wasn't Jeff. It would have been anyone who tried to love me.

Nonetheless, Jeff wore me down. I did go to Sai-Gon. I buried a husband. I survived. Jeff was a male chauvinist. He taught me to fight.

I'd forgotten most of my life in Bangkok until I read the letters. One incident, however, remained clear in my mind. As though mentioned almost in passing, embedded in prattling prosaic details—riding the bus, washing sheets, preparing meals—the heat, the rain, the dirt, the depression:

> *Toi came by. I'm going Sunday to see the cremation of her brother-in-law.*

The incident was filled with answers.

Toi was the Thai leasing agent who found my apartment. When she called, she explained that her brother-in-law died in a motorcycle accident going to visit his mother. She said that although his death was a tragic loss, karma governs all lives. That if, in a man's final moments he recalls a good deed he performed in this life, his good karma will take effect, and he will be born again into better circumstances. I thought of Jeff's death and his last thoughts. He always came home distraught yet strangely aroused after flying in a dangerous battle.

Toi said, since her brother-in-law was on his way to visit his mother, his death was good karma. So he would be born under better circumstances, unless he was thinking about some previous bad deed. Then he'd be born under worse conditions. I thought of the polio my brother contracted when he was ten. What had he done in a previous life? To understand the riddle of life, she said, required lifelong study and meditation.

After a short hot bus ride, Toi and I arrived at Wat Aroon, the Pagoda of Dawn. Red and gold roofs in seven tiers dipped and peaked above the fifteen-foot wall surrounding the Buddhist edifice. We entered the open courtyard. A huge cathedral-size temple on the right dominated the clear sky. Toi presented me to her family. I bowed my head and folded my hands in the traditional sign of peace, palms together, close to my breasts, fingers pointing up. I remembered not to touch the children on their heads, which invites their spirits to leave, and not to meet anyone's eyes directly.

A temple bell clanged. Yellow-robed monks led the procession into the courtyard. The sun shone overhead. Yet it seemed not oppressively hot. Miniature bells hanging from each of the roof peaks tinkled in the breeze.

The higher status a family has, Toi said, the longer the waiting period before the funeral. Her brother-in-law had been dead only three months. The King or Queen would lie in state for a year. Why was that? I said, thinking, horrified, *This man's body*—I assumed unembalmed—*in the heat*. I thought of the funerals of my great-grandmother and my nephew and began to feel panicked. I hated funerals. What the hell was I doing here? I seemed to float through life, untethered to emotions, passively allowing anyone, other than myself, to make decisions, or maybe allowing fate to decide.

Toi said that when the body and soul die, it takes time for the spirit to leave. The spirit is either quiescent or chooses to reincarnate. This facet of Buddhism was difficult for me to accept. I knew matter had to go somewhere. Matter and the soul. When a Christian died, I knew he was with those whom he loved.

I watched the other American guest, camera in hand, climb the narrow steps to the top of the temple. Two tall columns flanked a small level area. Near him stood a young Thai girl dressed in Western clothes.

The monks led the funeral cortege, the family members following slowly up the steps. I turned sideways, the steps too narrow for my sandals, and marched behind Toi. I concentrated on my balance, my leg muscles firm from climbing the stairs to the apartment. After a laborious ascent, I reached the top and faced the ornately carved red- and gold-lacquered casket. Beside it stood a huge bronze candlestick with a pale green candle. The monks handed me a bundle of sticks, then motioned for me to leave the area down the steep steps on the left side of the temple. Nervous yet excited, I was eye-level with the red tile roof of the smaller building. I counted seven tiers, the seven limbs of yoga sutras, and began the descent.

In the dirt courtyard I clutched the bundle of sticks and looked up at the American. His Minolta was the only foreign sound. The camera's clicking comforted me. I thought of Jeff's camera, clicking, continuously clicking moments of our lives from the present permanently into the future. The young Thai girl still stood beside the American. Four monks walked to the casket and lifted off the elaborate top to reveal a plain wooden box holding the man's body. The girl, who was taller than the monks, peered at the dead man's remains. The stench of the three-month-old decaying flesh flashed out at the surroundings. The girl screamed and fainted. The American caught her before she plummeted down the steps. He pulled a handkerchief from his pocket and covered his nose and mouth as he knelt down, holding the girl.

Ignoring the girl, the monks continued the ritual. They placed the wrapped body in an opening in the back wall of the temple, atop more bundles of sticks. With small candles, they lit the bundles of sticks underneath the man's body. The retinue again processed. The widow climbed the stairs and lit her offering from the tall candle and tossed her bundle into the flames. One of the priests cut a lock of her hair and threw it into the fire, symbolizing the ancient *suttee*, immolation of the wife with her dead husband. Then each family member followed her path. I guessed burning this man's body would be my first *chöd*, a Tantric teaching I studied requiring followers to overcome fear by embracing it. My fear was death, Jeff's and mine.

I followed Toi up the stairs. Thoughts as a child of three surfaced. I stared up at the smooth grey casket in my great-grandmother's parlor. My aunt lifted me off the floor. My small hands clung to the casket. I peered into the pink-lined box. Eyes closed, the elderly woman lay sleeping, her face powdered, white hair loosely curled on top of her head. She smelled of White Shoulders. I guessed my Mamsey was tired. I wanted to touch her. A pink net was stretched over the strange box. Why wouldn't Mamsey get up and play with me? My father stood beside me. He was crying. I reached over to pat the tears on his cheeks, to make him feel better, then put my fingers in my mouth. They were salty. He took me in his arms and hugged me. I felt warm and safe.

I slipped on the last step but regained my balance as I reached the top. The sound of car horns and bicycle bells drifted over the wall. Life on the other side was locked out, life on this side was cradled in. The monastery, insulated from reality and negative karma, was a womb for saffron souls. The temple bells' tintinnabulation in the breeze mingled with the gold leaf's refraction in the sun. I raised my offering to the candle's flame towering above my head and walked the remaining steps to the fire. It was frightening to be so close to death, to be included in this young man's funeral pyre, to know his body was being consumed by fire, his rotting flesh burning away, cleansing earthly ties, removing any sin he encountered during his life, severing his *sutratma*, his life thread, to leave weightless energy: truth: to repeat the cycle again. I watched the fire burn his body. Strips of white silk that had bound the body fell from the fire, flesh consumed, turbid smoke now etiolated from grey offal to a calcimine ash offering. The wind changed direction. I fought the urge to be ill at the smell. Tossing the burning sticks onto the center of the fire, I forced myself to pray, *May you live in light and find eternal peace*. Energy surged from the fire.

I walked away, folding my hands in the traditional sign of peace. Focusing on the monks attending the large green candle, light-headed from the sun, I bowed.

At the top of the stairs, two family members stood, handing out good luck mementos—to remember the dead man's journey. The widow approached me. I bowed, received the gift, and began the descent down the right side, now completing a final loop. I clutched the object.

At the bottom, I looked closer at the material. A small black and white print handkerchief had been perfumed in jasmine, then pleated with a narrow, black ribbon into a fan-shaped heart, like a lotus blossom unfolding. A calm hovered over the courtyard. No one was crying. People didn't seem sad. I looked at the crowd of black-haired Thais and felt isolated.

I said goodbye to Toi and her family and the American and got on my bus. I asked the driver to signal when we neared Soi Ha Sib Ha and moved through the crowd of Thais to the middle of the bus. Noise of the incomprehensible language was deafening after the quiet of the temple, then it became a buzz in my ear. The image of the burning body was replaced with that of my week-old nephew. In the small casket lay Ray's bloated body, nothing like the thin whisper of a child I had never allowed myself to hold. My brother Eric's arm around me, myself a week out of the hospital, heavily medicated, rail-thin. People on the bus crowded around me. I thought of the grief process. Denial. Anger. Acceptance. You work through the denial and the anger, and accept the loss, experience another loss, and the process begins again. The spiral continues, never complete. You place one foot in front of the other, continue on the path. The bus turned the corner by the market where I shopped. I continued to think about walking up the steps of the temple. The path was familiar, walking up, then circling down. It was like walking up the aisle to communion and circling back. The Eucharist invites us to remember Christ and those before Christ, like Buddha, to remember the priest's communion. Though you are dead so shall you live. I ran my fingers over the black and white cloth, the narrow black ribbon. In my mind, my fingers lace around my Buddhist prayer *hara*, tiny beads click between my palms, locust wings shirring in the humid heat. Silent chanting.

The bus driver waved. I got off at my *soi* and started walking down the dusty road. Children were playing in the muddy *klong* water. I approached the apartment, and the smell of coriander and allium greeted me. The maids were preparing their dinner.

I climbed the stairs and felt exhausted. Depleted. An empty vessel ready for manna. Yet in the exhaustion I felt peace for the first time since I left the states.

I unlocked the door and inspected the priest's markings. The six white dots above the door were arranged in three rows—at the top a single thumb print of ashes, followed by a second row of two, and a third of three, forming a triad: the shadow of an Egyptian pyramid: the illusion of an inverted cross.

*Jeanie Tomasko*

# IRONING, A LITANY

*"To do this ministry one needs to have a washer, ironing board and steam iron."*
HOLY CROSS BULLETIN, MAY 2014

Blessed be those who have

Blessed be their coffee and cream their smell of steam behind the scene work of women their clean
white kitchens their all manners of clotheslines

Blessed be the unhurried and the ironing

Blessed be the Online History of Ironing (see: Ironing, 1950s, drudgery)

Blessed be the Treatise on Domestic Economy, 1842, the *bosom board on which to iron shirt bosoms…*
*one foot and a half long and nine inches wide, and covered with white flannel*

Blessed be as soon as school was out in summer 1967, iron/fold/iron/fold/iron now the size of your
father's pocket quarter-fold stack a week's supply and the *I've been saving these for you for a month* and
the *but why do they need to be flat when they'll just get messed up again*

Blessed be the reasons why

Blessed be Permanent Press
No-Iron
Wash 'n' Wear
Durable Easy-Care
Wrinkle-Resistant
Blessed be Dacron & Polyester
and the mysteries of Brooksweave

## Ironing, A Litany

Blessed be learning to sew and iron open the seams and me on the chair my mother with pins in her mouth
asking how short and pinning 3 inches longer than I said anyway

Blessed be the smell of steam and scorch and starch and press

Blessed be Mary ironing in order for next day church pressing first buttonhole placket sleeve length
smooth yoke side seams shirttail collar last

Blessed be Christina of Virginia who survived a Black and Decker Digital and wrote (without punctuation)
*I was ironing yesterday I walked out of the room I heard a popping at the first I thought it was normal I*
*came back to the room the iron was fire all the handle and inside melted I unplugged*

Blessed be the buttoning up
buttoning down
unbuttoning of
the holy and crisp
unwrinkled white Oxford

Blessed be My Perpetual Birthday List:
Full Size Ironing Board
Rowenta Model #D9080 Steam Iron for $175
(but make it last for more than a year)
Cotton Clothes
White Blouse
More Time

Blessed be the Chosen Catholic Ironers of the Holy Cross and the un-Chosen un-Catholic who want
to take the *Purificator* and the *Corporal* home and would convert to smooth them out on a Full Size

Blessed be the pile to be done

Blessed be all who iron and blessed be their prayer for the world to be flat once more

*S. M. Decker*

## SIN

It wasn't the apple that blossomed with sex. No, if she desired knowledge, only peaches would do. Soft hairs, unshaven, rubbed smooth in puffs with the ball of the palm. Thin peel of skin held tender in the other hand.

> Gushing juice—smearing chin, lips, and the tips to creases of fingers. Tart tasted pulp, soaking teeth and tongue. Devouring meat like water until grinded by the core. Sucking veined branches from tunneled caves—wasting none. Flushed lips dry, licking fingers. Wanting more.

No,

sex was not the sin.
Twisted already in the winged will of Lilith. The struggle, mere corporal; taken under the muscled thighs. Turned over and demanding she wrestled for the right, clawed and dug deeper, bruising the flesh.

But,

side by side with Adam
bisected from the core, Eve helped herself.
She did not sit yawning under the tree, but bled the bark to reach the top and shake the bough before her. Elevated, wrapped around the limbs—her sight was stronger. Mother of Living, beguiled by vision, determined only to level eyes with

God.

She reached higher. So much taken in a curious bite. Sticking with sap and tasting the salt of her wounds, she breathed the life of her own lungs; feeling the eerie ecstasy of a fleeting single breath.

Yes,

Eve knew peaches—
savored them in fact.

*Benjamin Busch*

# QUI VIVE

Here is the barricade,
the corners filled with flashlights
and the cupboards stocked with batteries,
illumination the last defense of the visionary,
mad with wild knowledge of swamps
and riverbeds. The one
who bound the trees with sentences
and kept the forest from attacking,
spread his arms in the wind,
his beard gone leafless,
and held the floods away from the house.
This was his life;
to protect us from self-inflicted wounds
foreseen at breakfast.
Such was his love, this morning worry,
snow tires, rope, and aspirin on hand,
watching the weather from behind a typewriter,
pounding words to change the fate of nations,
forbidding loss by shifting stories.
It was here he made his stand for us,
legs planted wide beside his dog,
both of them barking their warnings at the shadows,
more afraid than anyone
of what they could imagine was near.

*Alissa Paige Joseph*

# NACHLAOT

I SCURRY ALONG TO THE RITUAL BATH, not wanting to be seen. Bright stars light my way. The smell of Passover food fans out to the courtyards where I walk. Salted chicken, carrot tsimmis with flanken, plain potato kugel. Bland food, nothing like the holiday food of my people. Our chicken is spiced Moroccan style with preserved lemons and turmeric. Cinnamon and cumin flavor our meats. Unlike our Ashkenazi brothers and sisters, we Sephardim are permitted to eat rice on Passover, which we crisp with saffron in pots with no handles.

The Jerusalem Marketplace is dead now. The booths and produce carts are empty in the shuk. I continue on Agripas Road before taking a right on Eilat Ave, a quick left on HaCarmel. Minyans of men file into thin doorways. They walk past me on their way to shul.

I pull my arms around myself and look at the stone beneath. Embarrassed. A woman walking alone on the night of a holiday is a giveaway for the mikvah, this most private and holy bath. Everyone who passes me will know that I've been separated from my husband for about two weeks and that tonight is our reunion. My shoes click in a rhythm I like against the stone. I pretend I'm a ghost, a childish thing. The air in Jerusalem tonight is warm and dry. I walk fast, breaking a sweat beneath my headscarf.

I have not been lucky. Faithfully, I've gone to the mikvah every month for the past seven years. Eighty-four immersions in all since the day I was married. I'm childless.

Two men in dark fedoras pass. I don't give a nod to another man I'm almost sure has been my parents' next-door neighbor for the past fifteen years. Mr. Friedman averts his eyes, too. Later when he gets home he won't tell his wife that he has seen me. Because he knows to mention it is to say that I'll be having relations with my husband later tonight.

The next time I see him, Mr. Friedman, he won't let his face betray me. He'll ask for my parents, my husband Ari in the same methodical way he always has, with a kindly nod and a thoughtful glance that seems to go nowhere except to the ground in front of him. That's what Mr. Friedman will do. This much I know.

My husband Ari and I have not touched since my period started twelve days ago. We follow the rules and sleep in separate beds. There's no kissing or touching at all during the five unclean days or for the seven clean days that must follow for my immersion to be kosher. We're not even allowed to so much as pass a cup between each other. I guess the Rabbis feared for the charge it could bring. I keep pace. Two hippies in long jeans wander by, meandering the narrow street in front of me. Three-story limestone housing stacks up on both sides. In the morning when the sun comes, the buildings will shine Jerusalem gold.

I try and imagine how he'll do it. How my husband will approach me tonight after the mikvah. It's always a surprise. When we're alone and it's just us he might come up from behind with a hug. Sometimes he runs across the living room and lifts me up into the air. It's tricky because we'll first see each other tonight at my parents' home. We're there for the holiday meal. Maybe he'll find a way to hold my hand under the table when no one is looking. Or with a wink he'll pass my mother's delicate corn salad, brushing my hand as he passes the bowl. Who could know but us what passing a bit of corn could do?

Ari was a paratrooper in the Israeli army. He and twenty-four other men were sent on a mission to Lebanon. Only Ari and his sergeant returned. He knows his way out of trouble. I once asked him how he made it through Lebanon. He slid his hand through the air and told me when he saw an open door, he walked through it.

Through the next archway, I'll see Fraha. Her terrace looks out to the courtyard below. I'll most certainly have to put up with her comments. Most days into night, Fraha sits out on her modest balcony to be away from her husband, Shlomo, who won't work since he got out of the army, and has comments to make about Fraha's weight and the way she keeps their home. Fraha was heavy in high school and has gained even more weight since her marriage a few years back.

"What is a skinny chicken like you doing out?" she calls down from her perch, as if she doesn't know where I'm going.

I put my pointer finger over my mouth to shush her as I walk through her courtyard. She's wearing a sequined black scarf to cover her hair. Her black robe passes to just below her knees, but because of her weight and the sitting position, it rides up to where it shouldn't. She's eating a chicken leg. Her makeup, as always, is over the top. Her pink lipstick crosses over the borders of her mouth as she chews. Her black eyeliner is smudged and she looks like the harlot she most certainly is not. Her only company is a chair opposite her, which is where I usually sit on Shabbat afternoon to hear her talk about the nudnik, as she has come to call Shlomo.

Fraha stands and cups her hands around her mouth with the chicken kicking up on one side and sings an old song in a whisper, "When I get that feeling, I need sexual healing."

I stop in my tracks and look up at her. She smiles in a way that tells me she knows she has gone too far. I also know she won't leave it alone. It's not in her nature to.

"You're so skinny, how does he even find you? If you were up here and seasoned, I'd eat you after I finish this." She waves her drumstick in a circle. I bow my head trying not to give her the satisfaction of my laughter.

Since she was small, Fraha's laughter has been high pitched and contagious. She leans over her mir'peset, shaking her chin at me.

"Nehama, Nehama," she says as if she pities me. She's talked to me this way since we were five and in gan, trading my boreka for her Bamba snack.

My name, Nehama—*comfort*—has always made sense to anyone who knows me. I'm the friend who will listen and I usually find a kind word, because most people deserve so much more than the few kind words I find for them. My middle name has always stumped me though. *Shira* means *song*. I have no song in the barrel. When I do make an attempt, I sound like a wounded little bird, as Fraha likes to point out. My father says that all people have to eventually find the meaning and peace in their names.

Fraha and me—what a twosome, complete opposites. Like all old friends, we have found the place of connection, the place of no words. We sit for hours together on her balcony watching tour groups come through on the Sabbath. We don't feel the weight of time together or the burden of having to fill it up. Fraha eats most everything she buys and I throw away so much of what I buy because my husband and I can't seem to get to the food, too busy with our jobs and the chores of our home and those of our parents' homes. I am the oldest daughter of my parents. I have two older brothers and eight younger siblings. All together, the Ben-Simon children number eleven.

When I was eighteen and in high school, it didn't occur to me that infertility would be my issue. I thought it would be money. Money was always an inch or so out of reach. It still is. But babies? Everywhere, in every nook, behind every doorway of the home I grew up in. Children were never scarce.

I have been twice for in vitro fertilization. Fraha asks me what the worst part is. I tell her without hesitation, the waiting room. Sitting next to woman after woman, comparing notes on how to stick a needle into an already bruised hip. We speak nicely to one another, but when our names are called to go in to inseminate, extract or retrieve, we freeze and stop the talk immediately. My face closes up, turns inward, and this other woman seems like a complete stranger to me as I collect my belongings. I hardly even feel the need to acknowledge her as I leave. For that moment, the moment I am called and she is not, I'm the chosen one, the one who might be blessed to get the baby behind the next door. And she, this other innocent, somehow becomes dust.

Fraha puts her thick leg into a slit between two black steel bars on the terrace.

"Nehama, tell Lipa I'm eating fifty carbs tonight because it's Yom Tov." Lipa is Fraha's aunt and one of the attendants at the Nachlaot mikvah.

Lipa and her cronies pity me. I can tell by the way they boom the word *kosher* while I dunk under the water. As if they were giving a wakeup call, a clue to the almighty that he should take up my petition and grant me a child.

I wave goodbye to Fraha and dip under an archway made of modern pavers and stones as old as the Romans. I can hear her calling after me into the alley, a thin corridor between two homes. "Come to me tomorrow, Nehama. I'm here all day. Not going anywhere. Us nudniks don't have any plans. We never do. Come to me, skinny bird."

Just out of the corridor, the view opens up. I've never gotten used to, or grown tired of, the hills that make up Jerusalem; on every hill, cranes point to the sky. The Jews are building. I move quickly. I don't want to be late for the mikvah because then I'll be the last one in at my parents' home for the meal. How sweet it might have been, to be young again, chasing a stray ball through the passageway to this view. Or to emerge from under the archway with a collection of my younger siblings in tow on an errand to the markolet for that last ingredient that our organized mother somehow forgot. I could stay here forever watching these hills. I couldn't say why it gives me such satisfaction.

I make my way. The road turns. I weave invisibly around the groups of men just starting home. I dash around a corner. The next street is deserted. I'm spooked, as if someone is following me. I often have this thought when I walk alone at night. A harsh floodlight shines down from atop a stone wall. A kitten stumbles out from under a shirt hanging on a standing clothing line. He's black. My Abba, that's my father, says the thousands of stray cats that populate Israel are really reincarnated Nazis. Their fate is to follow after Jewish garbage for eternity.

I steal my way into the second-to-last courtyard before the mikvah. Dark folded clouds sink down in the sky in front of me. I hear an argument from a gray stone apartment building behind me. The argument is more guttural and Arabic sounding than Hebrew. I turn, a window shade flattens; I keep close to a brick wall that opens up to the mikvah's courtyard. Fraha's aunt Lipa stands fiddling with the lock on the front door.

"Come in, Nehama. Why so late? I almost locked you out." Lipa is an obese diabetic woman, which Fraha fears is her fate.

"Why lock the door?" I ask. "Won't other ladies be coming?"

Lipa eyes the courtyard, "For safety, Nehama: the natives are restless." Lipa means the Arabs. "Anyway no one else will come at this time of night. After sunset?" She looks at me as if my calculations are crazy. Lipa coughs into her fist; she's a smoker and her voice is husky because of it. She is wearing her typical garb: a black head covering, housecoat, and slipper scuffs.

"You're last." she shrugs, "There are four before you."

I take a seat in the mikvah's waiting area beside a middle-aged woman. She's in from the States visiting a sister who lives in Jerusalem. She's excited to be in the Holy Land for Passover and tells me that she visited the Kotel today and laid her head on the Wailing Wall, praying that her oldest son doesn't go off the path, and become *fry*, a Yiddish word that means *not religious*. I tell her that it's not likely he will leave or leave for long because he knows what it is to grow up in a home of Torah, and he'll never find that warmth anywhere else. She lowers her brown-wigged head and tells me mistakes were made. I try not to look at her.

"Even with mistakes" I say, "we have something no one else does."

"You," Lipa barks, pointing to the American next to me. "Philadelphia." Lipa often does this, calls a foreigner by their country or state. It always seems so disrespectful the way she does it. Though I know she really wishes to make a connection. Her way is to belittle, a family trait. I shake my head. Lipa sees this.

"You're next, skinny bird." I nod my beak. Like all Sephardim, I am dark. My face is my Abba's. Happy eyes followed by a large, slightly crooked nose. At family occasions, my lips are painted candy red by my over-eager cousins, yet most days it isn't so easy to find my lips; they appear like more skin. I'm rather plain. A plain woman who somehow found love with a good man who people say is my twin. Even if I am infertile, there's the fact of my marriage.

Philadelphia goes to the mikvah and emerges fifteen minutes later. Her face seems to have deflated. She wishes me a good Yom Tov, and adjusts her wig more securely on her head, shoving stray wet pieces back underneath. I whisper that everything will work out with her son. "Just give it time," I say.

"Come, Nehama," Lipa calls.

I go first to a bathroom to take my clothes off. I put on a white terry cloth robe, as is the routine. Then I meet Lipa in another completely tiled room with a small deep pool the size of a Jacuzzi, the mikvah itself.

In silence Lipa checks my fingernails and toenails to make sure they're cut. She nods and I turn my back to her. She gently eases off my robe and holds it in the air in front of her so I can descend the stairs of the mikvah without her seeing my naked body. The water gently plays at my chest. Lipa puts the robe down on a steel banister that runs the width of the mikvah. I say a prayer and dunk my whole body under the water, holding my arms out in front of me. I spread my fingers apart so that every bit of me is touched by the water, including my open eyes. I try with all my spirit to imagine a baby, my baby.

"Kosher," Lipa almost screams. I come up. I dunk again. *G-d if not for me then at least make Ari a father.* I cry while I'm under the water. A sound escapes my lips, bubbles rise. My swallowed singing voice, my middle name, Shira. I have no song in me, no baby. Nothing's working out. When I surface, Lipa makes a *tsk tsk* noise.

"We all have trouble, bird. You think you have tzarot, you should hear Philadelphia tell it." I wipe my eyes and try not to speak. Lipa puts her arm around me and walks me to the bathroom where my clothes are hanging. I shut the bathroom door to Lipa's drooping face.

The robe drapes open. Water pools on the tile around my feet. I'm reminded that tonight is the last night of Passover and the night so many years ago that the sea parted and my people crossed it. The Chassidim in my town throw buckets of water on the floor and symbolically walk through it. I catch my reflection in the mirror, so much darkness in my face. I pinch my cheeks for an effect. My clothes catch on my wet body as I dress.

I pull my black hair into a neat ball with an elastic band. I adjust my new flowered scarf around my head. My husband bought it for me. It's a nice custom for a husband to buy his wife a special something before the holidays.

At the door, Lipa wishes me a good Yom Tov and pats me in a sorry way. She lets me out and locks the door behind her. I can hear her labored breath as she attempts the stairs. She lives three floors above.

By now my father and husband have surely returned from the synagogue. They won't make Kiddush over the wine at my parents' home until I arrive. My single cousin Naomi is coming for the holiday meal and will make a wolf whistle when I walk in. This I am dreading.

It's turned cool. A breeze moves across the courtyard. My skirt drapes to the ground. I follow the red brick wall with my hand. Nachlaot is a ghost town. The men are all home. Even the holy Chassidim who extend their evening prayers saying Psalms have returned home. In the distance a family sings the prayer over wine. The gray building in front of me is so out of place. Small gray bricks line its façade. I hear a rustling, a rumble come up from behind, too quick.

Pain shoots throughout my neck. I stagger forward. Try to run. A boy leaps in front of me and puts his hand on my back and with the other plunges a blade into me. I yell but I hear nothing. A sound. The silver of the knife, the black rubber handle. My mouth hangs open. It comes again, then again. I put my hands under his neck and push up. The boy cups my back as if we're dancing. The knife is lifted out of my body to above the boy's head. He looks at me. The horror in his face scares me, maybe a reflection.

"Ya Allah," he exhales and stabs the knife down with finality. A blow. I hear a crack, hints of my voice. The boy chants other Arab words over me. I think he is blessing me. He runs. With no hand to prop me up, I drop to the ground. I try to scream. My voice is swallowed. Bile or blood or something awful chases up my throat. What has he done?

The oddest things come. *I forgot to tell Lipa about Fraha's fifty carbs*. From the ground I watch my hand shake. Crazy boy, looked like my cousin Yaakov, this boy, dark like myself. *What have you done?* But no words come, only a long slow hiss.

The sleepy eye of the window shade from the gray building moves. A cat approaches and licks from a small pool collecting in front of me. I'm on my side. It should have been Philadelphia, I think.

*Fraha's next to me on the bus, my high school class, all twenty-six girls ramble along on a trip to Masada. It's the rainy season, so our teachers watch the hills around us for falling rocks. Roads are suddenly closed.*

*The girls are singing—Esther, Malka and Zohra, our resident songbirds, give us a treat in harmony. "Kol HaOlam koo-lo. Gesher tsar maod."*

*Fraha calls to our teachers. "They aren't so great. Why just Esther, Malka and Zohra? Always Esther, Malka and Zohra. Why don't we all get to sing?" Fraha joins the singing with gusto. "Gesher tsar maod." She squeezes my knobby knee. "Sing, bird," she says to me. I try to hum along.*

*"Shut up, bird. Your voice stinks." Fraha holds her nose.*

*"I know. My middle name is Shira, but I can't sing," I tell her.*

*"And I'll never be thin. Big whoop."*

Fraha's just through the next courtyard. With my shaking hand I feel for my chest, but I can't lift it there. My chest is destroyed.

I try to move onto my side. I see a small child come out of a doorway and I pray he will see me. He's in a holiday outfit, black slacks and a vest like a cute little banker. He must be around two. *Help me, banker.* I hear a woman call him. The boy lingers. I see a hand come out of the door to tap his head in. The door shuts.

The cat comes to my nose and licks, the little Nazi. He is soft and I am glad of him all the same. My trembling hand finally reaches my wounds and my fingers sink easily into one of the cuts. It isn't far to the bone.

*The bald tires of my family's van make funny noises below us. We are on a holiday trip. I am not sure which year it is. I am young and in the front seat of our family's sixteen-passenger van. Our van is the color of a dark sea. I have the front seat because it is my special day. All of us get a chance in the front seat with Abba. Our mother doesn't mind the back; anyway, she needs to nurse a baby on the way. My father asks me questions about the parsha, the weekly Torah portion.*

*"Okay, Nehama Shira, you're up. Who was Avraham's wife?"*

*I look sideways at him.*

*"Too easy, okay," says my kindly father. I sit up straight in my seat, feeling my new orange barrette that all us girls got for the holiday.*

*"Why did Sarah laugh?" he asks, splitting his attention between me and the road.*

*"Because God told her she would have a baby, but she was too old," I say.*

*"Correct," booms my father, informing my siblings in the back that I got a win. "Was she too old? Did she have the baby?"*

*"Yes, Abba." I roll my eyes.*

*"What was the baby's name?"*

*"Yitzchok. Easy, Abba. Think better," I tell him.*

*"Who was Avraham and Hagar's son?"*

*I must have been young because this is basic information, yet I'm a bit stumped. It comes.*

*"Yishmael."*

*"Very good, Nehama Shira. Yishmael."*

I think on the Arab boy.

His forefather was Yishmael. Ours was Yishmael's father, Avraham. I want to tell this boy that Yishmael died a tzaddik, at peace with his father, at peace with his half-brother Isaac. I want to tell him we are related, even if our thinking would deny it. Our features do not. He was so dark, just like us. My body is a crime under me. My legs stack on top of each other like a doll. I am relieved by nothing now. Childless, wounded, left for dead. I have never known what it is to have extra money in my bank account. And I have purchased nothing in this life without too much thought. I'm unlucky. I know better than to die in savage thought. The vulture stays, the smart bird takes flight.

*We have parked our huge van by the Dead Sea. My father is rolling up his pants to just below his knees. We walk together. He holds my hand, talking to me about my prize-winning Torah knowledge. I tell him my name is Nehama Shira, but I can't sing. He tells me tut-tut with that now. Before we get to the path down to the sea, he turns.*

*It is for him to go to the men's side and me with my sisters and mother to the ladies' side. His parting words are about the Dead Sea. "They can't figure it, Nehama. Day after day, the yidden take the salt out of the sea. They mine it, extract the salt. Yet the salt keeps coming. It is a mystery, the salt of this sea." His face is like a child as he tells me this, his eyes eclipsed only by his large nose. His palms face the heavens bobbing up and down. "There is nothing alive in this sea. Not a piece of seaweed, not a fish. Nothing. It's dead. And the salt keeps coming. They can't figure it. It's a mystery." He walks away from me to the men's side, carefully negotiating the rocks under his bare feet.*

The pool in front of me has grown. Something is sticking out into the air. I try my hand at it. The knife is coming out of the space between my shoulder and my neck. I can't move it. I let myself be distracted by a flood lamp hanging from a balcony down the little banker's street.

*Ora, her name means light, draws me into her family's cave. Ora is my cousin on my mother's side. She is by far the most beautiful in our extended family. Instead of the clay-brown skin we all have, Ora's has the beauty of the brown, with a bloom of rose in the cheeks. Her lips are full and open as she tells me her brother, my cousin Benji, has a friend from the army who they all think is my other half. He has come twice to their Shabbos table. He is originally from the States. Chicago. His family made aliya fourteen years ago, when he was nine. He is a combat officer in the army and is good with numbers. He's on the back patio, she tells me. My shoulders fall. Ora pinches my checks and asks why I don't touch up with makeup more often. I ask her why she didn't tell me in advance that I'd be meeting a man. She tells me that would have made me nervous. I have to give her a nod, though I don't want to. With Sephardim, our cousins are our sisters. They tell us if our blouses are too tight, if our hair is not with the times, if our thinking has gone wrong.*

*The house is packed with people, mostly my family. All of them are winking and poking me with elbows as Ora leads me to the back patio. It seems everyone is in on the joke. It's late May and my aunt and uncle are having a barbeque for the holiday Log B'Omer, the day the Romans stopped killing Rabbi Akiva's students over a thousand years ago.*

*The patio is hot, a day's heat collected in the stone. My face falls when I see my husband for the first time. He looks like me if I were a man and good looking. The sun is setting hot pink and orange over the gray buildings behind us. Already I am sure he won't go for it. He could have someone voluptuous, I think. As I approach, he stands from the chair where he sits. The last rays of the day come in to frame him. I find myself wanting to tell him how the sun animates him, but we're strangers. Just then a tray of minted beef kabobs falls from the serving table and my beautiful cousin attends to it instead of making a proper introduction. My future husband has an embarrassed smile on his face, as if he is not disappointed with what he sees. He puts his hand on my cousin Benji's shoulder it seems almost as a support. He waves with his other hand and says, "Hi, I'm Ari."*

*I mutter my particular back to him. "Nechama Shira." Why I told him my full name I'll never know.*

*"Nehama Shira." he repeats. "And are you a comforting song?"*

*I find this to be a sign.*

*"A comfort maybe," I say, "but not a singer at all."*

*"Of the two, a comfort is always better." He smiles, leans in.*

*On our wedding night, how you made sense of this bird-like body, more a girl's than a woman's. I never understood how you wanted to touch what you did. As if you had a plan for the first time we would touch. A map of what you would do. And how complimented I would forever be by that plan for this bird of a bony body. How in the first few weeks we were married the rains came and the world stormed outside the windows we would look through for our years together. How we sat on the couch side by side watching the dark days. How you told me when the wind started to shake our windows at dusk that whatever would come for us, you were happy to be side by side. And in the stillness of those moments that passed between us, no words were said, no thoughts came to me. I have never felt more alive except for in that space between you and me. I have always thought of this.*

I am under now. Lights blare in my eyes. I hear sirens. Men are yelling and trying to move me. A dark-haired man with an American accent is yelling something like "hold on." But I am under. My body shakes uncontrollably. "She'll swallow her tongue," he screams. A familiar voice calls, "Nehama, Nehama!" I think Fraha has found me.

*I am on the bus again, moving. My friends are gone. I am alone. I can hardly see the inside of the bus. I am conscious only of the Judean hills sweeping all around. The gray hills that border on brown, the pale pink that lingers. I am almost sure there is red in the clay below. Rocks bed themselves into the hills as the silver brush ambles along. I am under the brush. I'm the song, the Shira, the breeze beneath the silver brush, softly I go. Hashem achad, God is One. The blessings I received and the ones I didn't, my identity, this life I held too tight, now lost to the moment, replaced by the next living moment, formless. Free.*

*Tonight is Shivii Shel Pesach, the last night of Passover and the night my people cross the parted sea. Every year we all cross the Sea. Not one of us, alive or dead, is missing from this yearly pilgrimage. Towering walls of water on either side of us, spraying a mist. Others are in front, and others behind, surrounded as we go. I am walking.*

*Wulf Losee*

# A BUTTERFLY MANIFESTO

1. Burrow deep deep into the image.

*Be the worm gnawing down to the seed of reality.*

2. Hold true to Great Uncle Ezra's dictums: "The Image is more than an idea. It is a vortex or cluster of fused ideas and is endowed with energy." Images, are the magical invokers of emotion. Focus on the image, and the words will emerge to describe it.

*The poetic process is the metamorphosis of gnawing worms into the butterflies of gnosis.*

3. Ezra also said: "...Use absolutely no word that does not contribute to the presentation." Excess adjectives and adverbs weaken the presentation of an image. Don't prune too much, though!

*A moth is just a pest to be swatted, until you mention the lime pale kite-wings of the Luna.*

4. Grandpa Stevens said: "Not all objects are equal."

*The butterfly feeder, even though it is as red as candy dye, is waiting for a visitor.*

5. Uncle Ezra interrupts, again: "As regarding rhythm: to compose in the sequence of the musical phrase, not in sequence of a metronome." The English language, as it's spoken, is irregular in its rhythms.

*A butterfly whirls and tumbles on the off-beat flutter of its wings. Follow its flight as it travels to unexpected flowers.*

6. Rhyme should remain invisible lest it detract from the image, for a rhyming word is usually less than perfect for the image; and rhymes can over-force the rhythm by making our breath pause for the rhyme.

> *A butterfly drenched with dew in the morning cannot fly. Thus it is with rhyme upon the image.*

7. Irony is a post-Modern sin. Brother Hoagland said: "Ironic distance is the latex condom of poetry."

> *The colors of a Luna Moth fade inside the killing jar of irony.*

8. Master Lu reminds us: "False feelings are a slap in the face of grace."

> *A butterfly wallpaper print is suitable for the sentimental person. True feeling requires that the butterfly be able to fly away when it's called elsewhere.*

9. Regarding the poetic voice, you are the second person in a poem unless I can make you the first.

> *Your attention is the butterfly. The image is the nectar in the flower. This poem is my net.*

*Sarah Van Arsdale*

# TAKEN

The video of the girls
abducted from their dormitory
                    a spare concrete square
                    in dusty, far-off Nigeria
will begin in seven seconds.

While I wait, a man on the screen
runs water from a hose
into a blue plastic pool.
It's the start of summer in America.
He makes a joke about his daughter—
how they can't communicate.
He's buying her a new cell phone.

In the video, the camera pans the girls
massed grey and black.
They are reciting words without apparent feeling.
There are so many of them, their shrouds so dark
that they blur into a single breathing animal.

My needs
are so easily satisfied
that sometimes I feel I'm disappearing.

I once was a girl, alone on a Greyhound bus
heading back to my boarding school
where no one was watching.
Classes were held in a reformed barn.
Smoking was allowed in the old milking room,
concrete-walled, stinking, freezing in winter.
We huddled there, child-refugees from the wrecks of our families,
and at night, found our way to one bed or another,
dragging our broken hearts.

I navigated the Port Authority
of the nineteen seventies, weaving
among tight-skirted, beaten-looking women
and men who sized me up.
I was careful to keep my face expressionless as a penny.
Then boarded another bus,
which sailed out into Jersey
where I paced the farmhouse kitchen,
the upstairs rooms echoing.
Everyone else had gone: my mother to her new apartment,
my father to his new, still-secret family.
Only the house remained,
the stained glass window my father made,
my mother's fragrance lingering in her bedroom,
the books still on the shelves,
the willow tree weeping its branches to the wet, wet, grass.
Like a nuclear disaster
where the buildings are intact
but all the people are gone.

I could so easily have been taken.

But I wasn't, and now, I'm far from any home,
in a wilderness of my own making,
and at last, someone is waiting for me,
wondering where I am and when I'll be home.

And the moon rose
a hammered silver disc
over the baobab tree.

*Joseph Colonna*

# THE FLOATING WORLD

THE AIRPORTS ARE STILL POISONOUS, the anchorwoman said. A fallout path filled the screen above northwestern Queens. LaGuardia was especially toxic: the cloud had strafed it hard. JFK, because of lucky winds, fell outside the threshold ring; still, the "tarmacs will stay closed."

I switched off the TV. She drew the monsoon shutters. Our futons lay, side by side, beside the dining bench, so I rolled them up with our comforter and our foot warmer and sheets.

"It'll be okay," I said.

"No, it won't," she said.

I heard the TV humming itself cool, then turned to find the moon was falling through the monsoon slats.

"I've got the water boiling for tea," I said. She had tears in her eyes.

Since the only American newscast—all others were Japanese—occurred at 3 AM, we'd built our lives around this hour for the past two months. We had laptops, of course, and the internet—but there was something about watching the news together, even a rebroadcast from the night before—about huddling in front of a television set and hanging on the evening anchor's words that must have felt like home to us because we kept doing it: waking at three, eating toast, pouring rice porridge into bowls; I'd smoked a morning cigarette and pretended the news we were about to watch wasn't fourteen hours old.

"Maybe you can fly back into Baltimore," I said.

"I'm not leaving without you."

"Or Pittsburgh. Someplace else, safe. Sylvie? Syl? Hey, look at me: it's gonna be okay."

"Central Park is gone."

She huddled round the dining bench, which had a brazier for heat. She muscled down a bean cake. I proposed we take a walk. She shook her head with red lips, still powdered from the cake.

At dawn, I jogged the river paths. I bought noodle cups from a Quickie Mart then warmed them back at home. Sylvie woke after noon. I served us soba lunches. As sun poured through the fingerbreadth that I'd left between the shutters, trees could be seen swaying in the yard with fat autumn plums. She milked a cigarette from my foil pack and lit it on the brazier grid. She pierced the gray skin of the standing bath with the cigarette then wriggled off her sweat clothes and her favorite Vermont socks. Naked, she leaned on the splash wall; her legs showed two months' growth. She squatted to the plastic pallet-floor where her razor lay in the drain, then clutched the rusty can of foam. She glanced at me then at the tub.

"Tomorrow is the day," I said, "you're flying home."

"The rubble—Times Square—is a hundred feet, more in many spots."

"We're running out of cash," I told her, "the amount we brought—our allowance is finite here."

I dialed the number for Nippon Air. I demanded to speak to higher-ups. After I snapped off the phone and turned to find Sylvie slouched on her study chair, I told her:

"Osaka to Heathrow is up for grabs then Heathrow to any airport outside the affected zone, north, maybe west, maybe Buffalo. Maybe Montreal."

She had wrapped herself in a bath towel; it looked like she hadn't showered. She was staring at a spot on the floor, and I followed her eyes to the spot: the mat we'd bought for her chair, a kind of occupational bast support for the shoulders and the back, had slipped down off the chair and onto the floor. The bast must have blended, in her eyes, with the tatami straw that covered the floor because she seemed fascinated by the coincidence of the texture, the color, something I tried, really tried, to validate, or at least comprehend. After a few moments of standing like this, I lifted the mat off the floor and slid it behind her back. I then smoothed her hair and kissed her cheek. I went out to clear my head.

Through the warm skim of the afternoon—through alleyways of medieval stone, I saw trees red with maple leaves, and the sun was in the leaves, and I came upon an old ramen-seller who bowed at my approach.

"Terror," he said then deepened his bow.

"Terror," I said.

"My friend Gail invited me to Japan!" Sylvie had said months before, a Wednesday, outside my work, "we can both go, together—you can quit the firm."

All I knew was that Gail was her friend from college. I clicked my briefcase shut.

"Maybe you can live off your savings a bit," she said. "You've paid off your law school debt."

At the time, I'd been working as an attorney for a Brooklyn firm that prosecuted ortho-crime. The firm consisted of two partners, five associates, six paralegals, and me. Counsel rabbis would shuttle defendants into our paneled office, and the client would defer to the rabbi, who would defer to the defendant's wife. Since the High Holy Season had just begun (it was early September), the office seemed empty each week for hours at a time. Left alone, I began to take my lunch along the promenade. As the wind kicked off the river, I imagined myself into Far-East scenes, bamboo groves, shrines.

"If I have to study two months for the LSAT exam," Sylvie said the next day as she packed her bags, "I may as well study in a foreign place—a free place, with you."

She stacked her study books and her vocab cards, and her "quick and dirty" practice test, then slid them in her favorite suitcase. She laid her favorite scrunchies and slippers beside the books and then a box of sharpened pencils, then slotted a box of energy bars in a mesh inner-pouch.

"That's the Kamo River in the background there," Sylvie said as she held out a photo of her friend's house, which she'd shown me twice already, "and that's an old-fashioned backstreet and a traditional *izakaya*."

In the photo, Gail was waving outside her tiny house. Ridge tiles glistened on her steep roof. The walls of the house looked wooden. She had short brown hair and blue eyes. She was wearing a winter kimono.

"She's in China for a while," Sylvie said as she nodded toward the picture, "visiting her two kids—she lost them in the divorce—so we'll have the whole house to ourselves. It has heated toilet seats."

Our cab sped toward the airport. To the west: Osaka Bay. Aware of Sylvie's eyes on me, I paid the driver with a breezy nod—"nice Yankees cap"—then lifted her luggage from the trunk. We wheeled it toward the entrance door, which whooshed back on its frame. Not counting the quirk of rolly carts, the murmurs of the main receiving hall seemed unpunctuated. A smooth rotunda came next, and loose departure queues, and I felt Sylvie's hand around my hand, as if trying to pull me back. I could sense, though, whenever I looked at her—whenever "New York" blipped on a wall screen—a brutal knowing efficiency that she tried to mask as fear.

"We want to go back," I told an agent.

"I'm not leaving alone," Sylvie said.

Unable to converse in English beyond the basic travel-speak, the agent resorted to a pantomime in which I'd increasingly felt at home: a bow, a wave toward another desk, a gray weight of suppression.

"Hello," a woman said behind the second desk. She wore a blue ink-washed uniform and a smile of coy regret. I explained ourselves in general terms then showed her the last traveler's checks we had to our name.

"It is all booked up into Washington and Pittsburgh," the woman said then gestured toward a hallway-full of standby Westerners, "all the safer upwind ports."

Sylvie swiped back the lick of sweaty hair that had fallen in her face then rolled her bags up the hall toward the taxi stand. I watched her pass a knot of youths cursing in American English then the woman behind the desk produced a numbered list. She added our names to the list then we hailed a cab back home.

The next day, I went for a walk to a shrine sale, this one at Toji Temple. What looked like hundreds of merchants in the open air sold crafts and food and antiques from long wooden tables. I wandered past a tip cart full of daikon radishes and examined an umbrella stand made of bluish porcelain. I wasn't there to buy, though; I was there to sell, or try to anyway. For the past week, I had made a daily habit of wandering the city for temple sales, to hawk our souvenirs. I'd even devised a system: instead of lugging each item to the temple grounds in the hope of an appraisal, I figured it was easier to bring a photo of it on my cellular; and so I'd set about snapping a picture of the Hello Kitty foot warmer we'd bought at duty-free and the dishware kit with the cherry blossoms stenciled on the edge; I'd even practiced the Japanese for "How much?" but just in case I'd brought a paper scrap on which I'd scribbled "¥ = ?" My first two trips had been failures (I barely managed a word), though on the third I got a bid: a fair exchange—100 yen—for a ceramic paperweight. On this day, though, I'd arrived at the market stalls hoping to sell the wooden wall clock we'd bought when we first arrived. It featured the numbers of the Japanese zodiac and a nice *washi* paper background, though what I hoped to get for it, pricewise, seemed beside the point. I knew it would be nothing, or next to nothing, certainly too little to make a dent toward airfare costs and food, but somehow I felt that, if I could keep in the world of bargaining, even if only once a day, that that might lead to something else, bigger, of commerce maybe, of feeling. I held the "¥ = ?" paper next to the photo of the clock then next to the one of some chopstick rests made of fake bamboo. The merchant wore a new-looking Yankees cap and a kind-looking expression, though he shook his head in a way that meant, politely, "no." I moved on to the next table and the next—and finally wheedled a fair appraisal bid on the clock, and a tepid one on the rests. Feeling satisfied for one day, I strolled the long way home to find Sylvie crossing toward her phone. She was showered, it seemed, and dressed.

"Gail!" she said as her phone rang, and she checked the incoming number. I heard a female voice—"I've left Shanghai"—echo from the receiver. Sylvie seemed to ask after friends in Sunset Park and Cobble Hill then fall into a hard-spun stretch where she didn't speak at all. She teared up and then Gail must have said something philosophical, something about social love and resiliency because Sylvie's face clouded over but without any tears. I never knew what to say.

"Gail caught a plane to South Japan," she said after she hung up.

"I don't understand."

"She joined a gathering—a kind of camp."

"Is she coming back to the house?"

"It's around the Hiroshima Dome."

That night, I slept through the 3 AM news. I slept through soba lunch. I woke to find Sylvie fully dressed. She held her iPhone and her purse.

"I want to come with you to the shrine sales," she said. "I want to sell my Cornell shirt."

I shook my head and told her, "You should keep your lucky shirt." She insisted, though, so I bathed and grabbed my phone, and together we set off. She brought a photo she'd taken of the straw mat, the one that covered her study chair, and I brought the "¥ =?" sheet. As she swiped her thumb, though, across her phone, past her photo of her mat and her lucky shirt, I noticed that she'd taken a photo, probably when I was in the bath, of her LSAT books. Gently, I slid the phone from her hand and deleted the photo. And though I wanted to calm her or scold her, or say whatever Gail had said that had clouded her face with peaceful disbelief, she seemed to nod in a way that said "Don't worry, I won't sell the books." I stared hard at her, for confirmation, and she stared back in the firmest way I had seen her stare since we'd first heard the news. We approached together, hand in hand, the first market stall. Since the mat had mashed sweat-frayed ends, I braced to be rebuffed, but the merchant, despite appearances—he had a sinister long fortuitous hair dangling from his chin—wrote her out a healthy bid. Sylvie smiled for what felt like the first time in over two months.

"We deserve a fancy meal," she said as we strolled from the temple. "Pickled mackerel. Sea bream."

"The profits should go toward an airline ticket—you need to take the test. Besides, you might need money when you get home. Unforeseen expense."

We left the temple for the alley lights of the Gion District. Apprentice geishas minced past. Sylvie stopped at a teahouse window.

"Here, dinner," she said, "with servants and the works."

Another geisha smiled at us with mollifying handsomeness. We made a right at Alley Twelve, past upscale sushi menus outside *machiya* shops. Sylvie read "deluxe" off of one menu, then "pike eel" off another, and I began to sense, more than the idea of dinner, she was enjoying the lawyerly effort it took to bring me round to it.

An agent at the departure desk led us off a snaking line. She sat us down in an anteroom. She poured out two dark teas in brown wooden bowls.

"Terror," a suited official said as he entered the room.

"Terror," I said.

He bowed shallowly.

"A seat has opened on the list," he said, syllabizing each word. "The flight—which is due to leave in less than three hours—would land you in Boston Logan, with stopover in Detroit."

I asked about Newark or JFK, and he shook his head and sighed with genteel despair.

"The hangars in Newark are mass morgues," Sylvie said. "You slept through that news, I guess."

The official drew blue expeditor forms from his metal drawer then slid both forms toward me. In irritation, Sylvie stood. She dragged her luggage cart out of the room, and I nodded in apology to the suited man then I followed Sylvie past the conversion desk for yen-to-currencies, past the agent saying "sōrī" to a family in Yankees hats.

"The test," I said when I finally caught up, "that's the reason we're even here."

"I'm not going," she said. "Not without you."

"The logical reasoning, the reading comp—"

"Who knows if they'll even have a test—their website: 'TBD.'"

"I'll catch a flight soon enough—once my Chase card starts to work, I promise I will—"

"Chase?" she said with disbelief. "Try Indian trading."

We spent the next hour next to a wall of orange coin lockers. She shook her head and crossed her arms. She dropped her study bag. The Stock Exchange, I reminded her, might regroup in safer hills, and when it did—I squeezed her thumb—"the retail banks might recoup," then she could wire me some cash. She shook her head and paced the wall. We went through this for a while. She looked drained in the way of a woman who'd been stunned by her relief.

"Maybe Gail's ex-husband can lend you money, wire it down from Shanghai?" she asked.

"Maybe I'll sell her heated toilet," I said ironically.

"Boston Logan."

"Through Detroit."

Two redcaps nodded as they passed with benevolent distrust. I slipped my hand in Sylvie's hand. She drew me close to hug.

"I'll review the parallel reasoning," she said.

"I know you'll do just fine."

"The MOMA is gone."

"I know."

"St. Patrick's, a fiery hole."

The moon glowed in the frail dome. Canvas tents ringed the base. I approached the camp through a small park, where the subway left me off. I held my charger and my mobile phone. Figures drifted in the dark between pale strings of naked bulbs, or milled beside parked cars. A Mercedes, a limo. A shiny chartered bus. A mother and father in golf pants lit incense silently, while their children studied textbooks in the headlight beams. Businessmen clapped in anger, it seemed, or maybe it was shame, though whatever the case, it was always up, always toward the dome. And since they seemed to be staring past me, I wound past quiet families deeper in the camp—past boys in crisp club ties texting on their phones, and girls, as if just come from school, in navy uniforms. No one wore Yankees caps.

As I wound toward the dome, the camp grew seedier. The tang of stale propane and sour rice wine crammed in my nostrils, and gas generators droned, and I passed the left-open flaps of clean vinyl tents. I followed dizzy curls of smoke deeper in the camp then found myself at the outer edge, at the far side of the dome. A group of teens sat on shattered rock. Tobacco ends of cigarettes red-bobbed in the night. One girl harangued in Japanese toward the naked dome;

then a boy, in the same direction, took up her tone. A man posed for a photograph with a mocking out-sprung hip then waited for a woman in tight black jeans to snap his photograph. She was wearing a green t-shirt and *geta* clogs made of mud-stained wood, and her hair was black and shiny and very long. Unsure where to go, I left the group. All I knew was what I felt: an orphan's wanton inwardness, a need to hear Sylvie's voice. I wandered back toward the denser camps. I hadn't heard from her in days.

"May I use your generator?" I asked an old man near a tent. He looked tired but clean, well-fed, but lost in bitter vigil. I held up my phone and charger like dumb hieroglyphs. The man turned his back without a word. I strolled back down the central path. In the dome-shine of the next tent, I found five ragtag boys with flat stares; I knew better than to ask. I wandered toward a low wall made of cast concrete, and I must have dozed off for a while with my phone in my lap because when I finally opened my eyes the dawn was in the dome. Sub-economies had wakened in the tents, of beer in exchange for cigarettes, for Pendleton blankets and socks. It was all done in muffled grunts, without urgency or fear. I watched, unsure what to do, as a man posed for a photograph. He *V*-ed two fingers in the air, but instead of peace it seemed in sign of a greater camp-wide grudge. I stood from the lamp, against which I'd slumped and slept the night, and since I only had a one-yen note left (I used the others toward the train), I began to search the nearby tents for handout-rice and beer. I gripped my phone in my pocket and, as I approached each tent, tried to give my eyes the spark of what I hoped was mutual aid.

At the curve of the next path, I found a crooked brown hoop tent made of rough mesh. I paused, and then peeked my head inside through the open flaps. I held my yen, out of habit, at my side in case I had to haggle. Dead coals occupied the rutted earth. Mold-tinted pots. A groundsheet contained a blanket and a meditation stool. I stepped out a moment to collect myself, though towards what I wasn't sure. I stared up at the broken ribs of the bombed-out dome. I lost its shape in the sun. I found it again then lost it again, then a large tree in the middle ground, between me and the dome, seemed to overshadow it.

After I returned to the tent and peeked inside I zippered the flaps behind me. I lay out on the plastic sheet and stared at the convex roof. I slept a while with my cell phone flat on my chest. When I woke the screen still read "0 messages." The light outside looked queasy with dusk and smoke from cooking, so I assumed that it had come time for supper, as such. I exited the tent. I found a man next door selling wrapped soaps from a shanty bench. He didn't ignore me nor, as no one had, did he welcome my presence either. He regarded me with—maybe there was a word for it in Japanese—whatever opposes charity.

Across the way, the black-jeaned woman from yesterday was sweeping out a tent. Her jeans were still snug and very black, but her shirt was ripped in parts. With her back turned to me, she swept the dooryard of her tent, next to which sat a generator block that hummed placidly. I approached with my arms at my side (I feared I'd begun to smell) and my phone in my hand, and I said, as she turned:

"Hello."

She smoothed down her hair.

In one hand, I held up my charger and phone; in the other I scratched my stubble. I nodded past her toward the generator.

"My phone just needs—" I began to say. "If you don't mind."

She managed a smile of wounded pride, as if I'd insulted, not her, but her property, her tent perhaps, her yard. She resumed sweeping the yard. A moment past, like this, in silence.

"Go back," she said.

I paused.

"To my tent?" I said.

She shook her head and gripped her broom. I drew back a step. She swept with slow deliberateness around a conceptual stack of welcome-rocks, and I began to imagine, as she did, she'd meant "to where you're from."

The next day I kept my phone off to conserve its battery. I stowed the phone on the low stool at the back of my tent, then stood outside my door. In exchange for my last temple-yen, the soap merchant next door ladled me some porridge. My head, with the lightness of relief, began to swim with the dusk, with the senile "u" of white lights strung in the dark. The next morning I traded two cigarettes for a pad of soap. Alone in my tent, I washed myself then powered-on the phone.

"Landed in Detroit," I heard Sylvie's voice on the voice message, "then took a bus to Pittsburgh. That's the closest I could get. Your parents are okay; they send their love. They were upstate when it happened."

She seemed to choke up a moment, or draw from the phone; her voice grew suddenly thin. She said Wall Street was trying to remake itself "in the Meadowlands" and that the Yankees were playing their "home games down in Baltimore." The message wavered on the edge of cutting-off, all static and distance-hum then she said something about "the test, next month," then something about "Western Union." I closed the phone and slid it on the meditation stool. I lay down on the blanket. I stared up at the roof. The moon, through the plastic ridgepole, threw loose arrows across my face of blue and gray and white. I waited for dreamless sleep. Camp-drunks clanged jerry cans in some distant tent, and I lay on my side and watched the moon lick the pegs of my tent. The ragged edge of a voice—someone, maybe two people, maybe a group was singing on the central path in some drunk but ancient tongue.

However long I finally slept, I didn't know. When I woke up, though, it seemed that the zipper on my tent-door was being drawn slowly down. The woman in the black jeans met my eyes through the *A*-shaped gap. Neither of us spoke. Her breath had a faint inner scrape of beer and cigarettes. Her face looked flippant and clean. She lowered to her knees, and we sat that way for what felt like hours, eyeing each other like that, then I leaned back on my blanket. I waited to feel, as I lay there, shrewd in pointlessness. Her shape, her brown scrounger coat, inched closer toward my groundsheet, through the moon falling in filtered pools, through the tent roof. The edge of her forward knee brushed against my thigh, and I felt her side press against my side, the warm gibberish of her hair, and her cheek paddied against my chest. Her breathing evened out. She smelled of petrol, rice, chewing gum. The starkness of autumn leaves. I stared at the fanning ridge supports that gave the tent-roof its shape. They met—there were four—at the vault of the roof, in a small flange-like bulb. And as I lay on my back and stared at the bulb, as the woman fell asleep—as my eyes traced the four ridge supports, their common lift and curve, I had to believe there was some game—something learnable in this, of logic or proportion. Something to do, I thought, with gravity or the tyranny of fourths—something that Sylvie was solving, maybe right now, something on the test. She was acing the logic, the reading comp—she was checking *B*, effortless, the analytic part—she was anxious but firm, within herself—she was somewhere in a gym—in the hills, western, safe, safe, in a testing bunker—she was midway through the writing part. I lay on the plastic sheeting. I stared up through the tent. I closed my eyes and tried to sleep.

*Bruce Graham*

# HOT PEPE

YOU MIGHT HAVE SEEN MY PICTURE. The photographer was Andy Lopez, and he was with United Press International. The photo was included in the book *Moments: The Pulitzer Prize-Winning Photographs*, by Tess Press in New York. He was sent to experience the first heady weeks of Fidel Castro's overthrow of Batista and his friends in January, 1959, and to witness *El Commandante*'s so-called justice. He kept the picture by a trick; when he was told he couldn't keep any photographs, he palmed the film and gave my *jefe* a roll of blank film.

The scene was soon after Fidel Castro and his *barbudos*, his bearded ones, had arrived in Havana and taken over the government of Cuba. In the swift aftermath the new government conducted a trial, of sorts, of Jose Roderiguez, who I heard was called Hot Pepe, an agent of the old government. He was immediately sentenced to death. The execution was to be carried out at once, and that was when Lopez took his picture.

Of course, I'm not Hot Pepe. In *El Commandante*'s regime, as I learned was common with similar setups, appeals and delays did not trouble, as they do in democratic countries. It was only when I looked in the book recently that I even saw Lopez's photograph, and there I was, forever twenty-four, forever staring through my sporty sunglasses, beret pushed back on my tousled hair, gripping my old Mauser rifle with both hands, legs spread, civilian pants dragging on the ground, cartridge belt at my slight hips.

The other members of the firing squad were gathered about, some of them also in the photograph, the bearded man in charge to my left, expression betraying an almost self-conscious desire to get on with it, the others behind us, two with blank looks, one smirking.

If you saw the picture you probably didn't pay much attention to me or the others who were assigned to deal out *El Commandante*'s justice, or vengeance, or political cleansing, or terror, or whatever you care to call it. At the time I gave no thought to what Lopez was going to record with his camera. I may have preferred that my family, in the Havana suburbs, not see me in my assigned role that day. I had no beard, and was not one of the *barbudos* who had come out of the mountains with Castro or rushed to join him when he was taking over the capital. I was simply among those who stepped forward when offered work with the scratch military units being quickly put together by the new government, to keep order in the streets, round up people from the Batista regime, guard against an uprising in favor of the old government. I was instructed in marching and handling a rifle and placed on guard duty around The Castle. I happened to be with a couple of dozen like myself on the day of Hot Pepe's trial and sentencing, and chosen by the grizzled man from the mountains to be in the firing squad for this execution. We were given single bullets for our rifles when Hot Pepe was brought into the courtyard.

I had no love for *El Commandante* or his followers, but no reason to dislike them either. They were giving me a job and pay and a certain status in the new Cuba. I had been out of work for almost a year and didn't have any liking or hatred for the old regime either, things had been bad for a couple of years and didn't look like they'd get any better. My father had worked at one of the capital-area gambling and party places, and my mother clerked at one of the shops near where the cruise ships came in. I was a regular churchgoer until I took work at the sugar factory, and attended the religious school until eighth grade. But I drifted away from the Church and went with the wind, the money from the sugar plant was good. When I was twenty-one I took up with Estella Vargas, who I later found out had been passed from man to man for a couple of years until she latched onto me. A year later we had a baby, who got sick and died because I couldn't afford medical care, it was becoming difficult to obtain during *El Commandante*'s insurrection. Estella left me, and I had trouble with the law trying to get her back. I spent a few months in jail, and lost my job at the sugar company. The only work I could find was with the city trash collection crew, and this paid a lot less than I was making before. After a year of that I was let go when I got to fighting with another worker. I was still out of work when I joined the militia, in the New Year euphoria after the old boss, Batista, and his closest cronies fled the country. All this time my mother tried to talk me into moving home and my father berated me for a deadbeat and a shirker.

I tell you this to help you to understand the effect that the Hot Pepe situation had on me.

We were getting together to do the job on Hot Pepe, just waiting on The Prosecutor to come from inside The Castle to give us the word. I wasn't feeling very good about what I was going to do, Hot Pepe was older than my father, frail and unkempt, face lined as if run over by a truck. He was in a simple shirt and trousers, and didn't appear to be a villain and criminal, the way the official government newspaper—that was all that we had to read, when we took the time—described anybody who had worked for the old regime. He shuffled across the courtyard, looking around with a frantic expression on his face, I took it to be fear, pushed by a pair of bearded men in fatigues and army caps, toward the wall assigned to those to be executed. My cartridge was in the rifle, ready to go on its way to the target.

Suddenly a figure moved from the doorway into The Castle toward Hot Pepe. The man was clean shaven, hair neatly in place, all in black, except for a streak of white on each side of his neck, onto his breast. He wore a long coat, familiar to me as I had seen its sort often. He moved rapidly, with firm step, and with authority, as if with a spirit of command.

For a moment I expected that the man would shout out orders. Instead, he went to where Hot Pepe stood, and spoke softly to him. Hot Pepe fell to his knees toward the man. The anxious look of a few minutes before left him. A trace of a smile appeared on his face.

The stranger was a priest, his gown was what they usually wore, but I couldn't think of its name. The gadget around his neck was what they wore when they heard confessions, I knew that from the time of my First Communion, but I couldn't recall its name either.

The priest joined his hands and held them out to Hot Pepe, who was saying something. He went on for a minute. The priest nodded and whispered in reply.

Our squad leader snorted and muttered an obscenity.

Hot Pepe didn't seem to notice. He nodded toward the priest and stopped speaking.

The priest lifted his right hand as he continued to speak, pressed his fingers to Hot Pepe's forehead, and made the sign of the cross, then rejoined his hands.

Hot Pepe reached out and touched the priest's hands.

A man behind me, the one smirking in the photograph, made a vulgar comment.

The priest held out a crucifix and Hot Pepe kissed it.

"Get on with it," came another voice from behind me.

It must have been about this time that Lopez took his photograph, because The Prosecutor appeared in the doorway and shouted, "No pictures."

The priest spoke louder, something about remembering Hot Pepe in his masses, and straightened up. He turned toward us.

I had the feeling that he peered at each of us in turn. And I felt that he stared steadily at me for a few seconds. He then spun on his heels and went toward the doorway, with a firm stride. The Prosecutor stepped aside, then moved to Lopez.

Lopez was standing with his camera in front of him.

"No pictures," said The Prosecutor. "I could take your camera."

"I'll give you the film," said Lopez.

The Prosecutor held out his open hand toward Lopez.

Hot Pepe struggled to his feet and licked his lips.

Lopez fumbled with the camera and placed a roll of film in the Prosecutor's open hand. I know now it was a blank roll, in place of the one he took from the camera.

The Prosecutor closed his hand on the film. "Now, out. You men," said The Prosecutor, pointing toward us. "Go away. I need higher authority's word to execute this man. You, Cold Pepe, will go to a cell."

Lopez sauntered into The Castle. Two regular *barbudos* moved to Hot Pepe. They seized him by the arms and disappeared with him into The Castle. I couldn't help noticing that his face no longer was fearful, but seemed almost peaceful.

We milled about, and within a few moments I had stacked my rifle with the others inside the doorway and was headed toward the barracks.

The memory of what I had seen, however, remained with me. The next day we were called to the courtyard, where Hot Pepe was brought by two guards from The Castle. His clothes, his disheveled look, were the same. The frantic expression of the day before was gone. He was pushed against the wall. At our leader's command we raised our reloaded rifles, took aim and fired.

From the way the old man dropped and our group leader's nod of satisfaction I knew that enough slugs had struck the prisoner to send him into the next world. But not every bullet fired hit home. My aim was off. I know, because I couldn't bring myself to aim at the withered frame of the old man staring at us. My shot struck the padding on the wall a few inches above his right shoulder.

My thoughts were confused when we marched from the courtyard, while a crew dragged away the lifeless frame of Hot Pepe, who The Prosecutor had referred to as Cold Pepe. The man had been a corporal in the Batista army, but he seemed much too old for active service. And I could not bring myself to understand what he could have done to deserve this fate.

One day, many years earlier, the man had probably been as I, new to a unit, trained, armed, and drawn into serving what was then a new regime, that had taken over a few years before I had been born. Perhaps, as I, he had few ideals, few ambitions beyond survival, few roots to direct him to avoid Batista and his henchmen. Had he at first gone along and remained silent, then fallen into the ways of his superiors, then adjusted to the comfort, the privileges, the money that came his way from association with the government? Had he extorted from the vulnerable, mistreated the weak, lorded it over the powerless, forced his manhood against the will of women and girls, even murdered?

In short, was Hot Pepe so different, at the beginning, from me, and would my later years be so different from his?

Even more to the point, would my years in general be so different from his; was my present way of life so different from his?

Would I one day be facing a firing squad of young men not yet born, but fated to work their will on the society, that would no longer have a place for me?

Would I be allowed the last chance that the mysterious priest provided Hot Pepe?

How many others would be afforded the final rites at the end?

For a few days these thoughts swirled about me, until I was granted leave and returned to my home. My family knew of my service in what was spoken of as the "people's militia," but I said nothing of my assignment to an execution. My father was tolerant of my position, but expressed discontent over what he called the "lawless actions of the new bosses." He challenged me to say how *El Commandante* was any different from the exiled Batista. One of his points was particularly telling: "His men will meet the same end as the ones abandoned by Batista."

His comment caused me to think. Hot Pepe had made a career of working for his *jefe*, who served his superior, who followed the orders of his boss, and so on up the line. In the end, the few who could escape did so, leaving everybody down the line to face the music alone. They had no more safety from above.

My mother urged me to attend mass on Sunday, which I did without argument, to her surprise. I felt out of place, however. She was understanding when I avoided receiving communion. I remembered the admonition of the nuns and priests that to take the Body of Christ while not in a state of grace was a great sin, a sacrilege. I was aware of my poor relationship with the Church, but could not explain to myself why I should avoid what the clergy called a sin, when I ignored Church doctrine in so many other ways.

One part of the mass hit home with me. During his sermon—what is now called the homily—the priest stated, "Put not your faith in princes," supposedly from the Bible. Many around me may have thought that this was a reference to the effect of the old regime's perfidy in absconding so suddenly. I, indeed, remembered the pathetic figure of Hot Pepe, old and facing death when the masters he had served so well deserted him. I, however, also took it as a reminder of my vulnerability when one day another uprising came along.

My service in the militia soon came to an end with the organization of a new military force. My group leader's earlier compliments on my attitude turned to a thinly disguised warning that my future was dim outside of the regime. A few weeks at home, and odd jobs, with my father goading me to "do something," and my mother's obvious joy at my regular attendance at mass were accompanied by serious thought of what lied ahead. To the amazement of both of my parents, and my brother and sisters, I expressed resentment at the new regime's negative attitude toward the Church.

To make a long story short, if possible, I entered the seminary, to my father's puzzlement, and my mother's amazement. The way was not easy, but with disdain, rather than hostility, the communist regime allowed ecclesiastical institutions to survive, under sometimes strict, usually simply nettlesome, scrutiny, so that the Church struggled along with respectable visibility. Now, almost fifty years later, I look back on my career with gratification, having done everything that I was able, reaching believers, and, most important, the imprisoned, the ill—those who, like Hot Pepe, were under a sentence of death, for one cause or another. More than one of those were erstwhile adherents to *El Commandante*'s regime, even a couple that I knew during my brief tenure at The Castle. In my fancies I wonder if, in what appear to be his last days of mortal life, when he has released his grasp of power, and is isolated, debilitated, and not able to dominate even the Cuban public arena, watching history march on without him, the old worshipper at the shrine of Lenin thinks back to his days as a student in Catholic schools and under the Jesuits, and the precepts of the Church about which he heard so much. Does he think of asking for what once was known as the Last Rites, now the Anointing of the Sick, as a way to at least have some chance to enter the gates of Heaven? Has he pondered the saying, posted in my humble parish church, *Tempus Fugit, Memento Mori*? Would he have the courage, or the opportunity, to seek what Hot Pepe sought and received two generations ago?

I will not have my photograph in a picture book, as a priest, only as a sort of revolutionary, a role I am not proud of, and have not followed since. I do not know whether to be thankful or regret being where my photograph showed me as one of *El Commandante*'s assassins. If I had not been where I could see the wretched man, and the determined priest, I would never have been taught the lesson that brought me into the arms of the Church.

Thank you, Andy Lopez. You do not know the gift you have given. Or perhaps you do know, your gift to me.

*Grace Bondy*

# CRIMP

IT'S LATE JUNE OF 1966, and in the small town of Poplar Grove, Arkansas, the devil is beating his wife.

At least, that's what Wes Davis would call it. The remaining 1,672 residents of Poplar Grove would just call it a sun storm. But Wes is a stranger; an alien. He was born and raised on a farm in middle Georgia, and in the six months that have passed since he moved to town, he hasn't been able to shake that Deep South vernacular, that scarlet drawl.

No one knows why he moved to Poplar Grove, let alone how he was able to find it on a map. Aside from a handful of the town's oldest residents, no one can remember another outsider ever living among them.

He isn't very well-liked: There is only one person in all of Poplar Grove he considers a friend. He expects they'll be married by the end of the year. Or, rather, he *expected.* Now, he fears that if he doesn't marry her within the next few days, he'll never be able to. He thinks she would make a good wife. She isn't the most beautiful girl he has ever met, and she is sometimes a little too quick to trust her heart when her mind would suit her better. But she is kind, generous, and he has come to love her more than he ever thought possible. And she lets him call her Mags even though she insists everyone else call her Maggie.

On the western outskirts of the town, Wes stands on the front porch of his rundown home. He knows it's on the wrong side of the train tracks, but it was the only rental available. And he likes the openness of the landscape. The vast expanse of rolling hills. He has always had a fear of confined spaces.

He lights a Marlboro Red. It's his third cigarette in the last fifteen minutes, but he doesn't care. He needs the distraction, the buzz. Anything that will keep his mind off of the draft.

Mags will be there soon. She works at the Five and Dime, but no one comes in on draft days. Still, the manager always plays the readings on the loud speaker. He says it's in case a customer comes in, but really, it's because he can't get out of work and has a boy drafting age. Wes reckons that's why he gave her the rest of the afternoon off. Because he was relieved it was Wes, and not his boy, and he felt guilty for being relieved.

When Mags finally turns the corner and Wes can see her coming up the street, his entire world is encased in gold. He is reminded of beautiful visions from his childhood: Shafts of dusty sunlight slanting through the attic windows; fields of grain glowing yellow in the late afternoon; sunlight the color of ripe honeysuckles, and days just as sweet. All of these memories lend themselves kindly to Mags. Her hair is wet and stringy, her shorts stick to her thighs, her heavy green work shirt clings to her stomach and she's got tears in her eyes. But in that light, there's something about her that's ethereal and flawless: She's glowing and vibrant and bright, and Wes doesn't think she's ever been so beautiful.

By the time she climbs the stairs and is safely under the porch overhang, she's soaked through. She doesn't seem to notice.

She takes one of his cigarettes, lights it, and exhales in a thin, low stream.

"They called my birthday," he says, even though he knows she already knows.

"It was below a hundred," she says quietly, sitting down. "What are we gonna do?"

He can tell she's trying to stop crying. Her hands are shaking and she won't look at him. She's trying to be strong.

It's not working.

He can't stop thinking about how beautiful she looks, dripping wet and sobbing, in that golden light. He knows now isn't the time, but he wonders if he's ever loved her more than he does in that instant. If he'll ever be able to love her more. But she's looking at him, waiting for an answer.

He sits down next to her, but doesn't touch her. "I was number forty-seven, Mags. There's nothing we can do. I'm twenty-two years old. I'm healthy. There's no way for me to get out of it."

She nods, her eyes fixed on something in the distance that Wes can't see. He wants to marry her. He really does. But he's a soldier now, and as hard as he tries, he doesn't mind.

"I can volunteer," he says, hoping to cheer her up. "It'll be quicker. And who knows? Maybe I'll get a better assignment."

He glances at her cigarette. She's already smoked it damn near down to the filter.

"The pay is good," he continues. "I'll finally have enough money to get you that ring we keep talking about."

With a single clap of thunder, the storm breaks. The rain slows; the sunlight fades. Gradually, the sky darkens, leaving a dull, listless flatness in its wake. Little by little, Mags is robbed of that vivid, remarkable glow. This moment has a distinctly bitter edge to it. He knows he will never be able to reclaim it: He will never be able to reclaim the way he feels about Mags while she is cast in that watery, deep-June sun.

"I don't care about the ring," her voice is soft. She stands up, taking one last drag of her cigarette before stubbing it out. "I'm gonna go dry off."

She walks inside, letting the door slam behind her. She isn't a good liar.

Wes finishes his cigarette, deciding to go into town tomorrow. He'll go to the recruiting station and sign up for the service. He'll go to the pawn shop—the good one—and pick out a ring. He'll splurge. Buy her something really nice. If he can scrape together the money, he'll even buy her something gold.

He flicks his cigarette into a puddle. It hisses as it goes out.

Tomorrow, he wonders, where will he go first?

They are married on the Fourth of July. Not for sentimental value, but because it was the only day they were both off from work.

Mags borrows a white sundress from her sister, Wes irons his only button-down shirt, and they take the train to Signal. Signal is the only town on the train line with a courthouse. Wes doesn't mind. Mags doesn't want to get married in Poplar Grove, so neither does he.

It's 2:30 on a Monday afternoon, and they have the entire cabin—the entire *car*—to themselves. They stretch out, make themselves comfortable. Wes opens the windows, and Mags leaves to find a glass of water. She returns with a bottle of champagne.

"Look," she exclaims, laughing as she struggles to open the bottle. "I told the girl at the bar that it was my wedding day, and she gave it to me. Just gave it to me. Can you believe it?"

She finally manages to get the bottle open, pours a glass, and pushes it towards Wes. He shakes his head in refusal, but he smiles a crooked, playful smile.

"No thank you, ma'am. Mama always said ladies first, and if I were to drink that before you had some, I reckon she'd find her way back from Heaven just to set me straight."

She takes his free hand with both of her own, her smile bigger than the whole county. No, bigger than the damn state of Arkansas.

"Your mama raised you right. I bet you're one hell of a husband."

He leans in. Kisses her briefly. "In an hour or two, you can ask my wife what she thinks."

For the rest of the trip, they drink their champagne in silence. Mags' hands are shaking, but he doesn't let go.

The marriage office is in the basement of the courthouse. The air conditioning is broken, the justice of the peace keeps calling Mags *Megan*, and Wes is so nervous he can't quite get the ring on her finger. But all of that goes away when Mags smiles and whispers, "I don't care what my first name is as long as my last name is Davis."

Instead of a reception, they find a table in the courtyard garden of a French restaurant and drink champagne they can't afford. The air is sweet with the smell of flowers, papier-mâché lanterns twinkle above them, and water babbles gently from stone fountains. A calm night falls, and they are lost in a blissful, private intimacy.

They don't need to talk.

In that garden, with the soft glow of the lanterns and the gently gurgling water, it's easy to forget. With the scent of honeysuckles heavy in the air, it is almost too easy to pretend their days aren't numbered.

Wes reaches Vietnam before August can break.

He's stationed in a small farming town southeast of the capital. In some ways, it reminds him of home. But he tries not to think about home.

There's a lot of downtime. A lot of standing around, rifle in hand, *protecting the people,* with only his thoughts to keep him company.

He spends a lot of time thinking about colors.

Red is the color of Poplar Grove. Red like rust. Like the cars, the homes, the land. Old and tarnished.

Vietnam is red, too. But red like blood. Blood spilling, splattering, drying. A fine, red mist. And then there's green and brown and black. They all mix together, bleeding into each other. There's nothing simple or singular about Vietnam. It's not one color. It isn't easily categorized or compartmentalized.

What Wes finds more unnerving than anything—more than the relentless heat, or the endless hours spent wading through rice paddies and thick, bloody bogs, and even the violent, shadowy death that is always present—is the way it never really gets dark at night. The night sky is the reason why he thinks Vietnam is more red than anything else. Enemy fire lights the horizon like fireworks on the Fourth of July. Always like the Fourth of July, which makes him smell honeysuckles and taste champagne.

Needless to say, he doesn't sleep very well.

With seven months left in his tour, Operation Crimp begins.

Wes' company must relocate to CủChi, but none of the trucks can pass the water to get to them, and dispatch can't spare enough helicopters to move them. The Lieutenant spends the better part of a week glued to the CB radio, arguing with mission control. He only makes matters worse. They end up walking.

It takes eleven days for them to make the 200-mile trip. As they draw closer, the jungle begins to thin out and the distinct smell of burning wood and napalm fills the air. There are whispers of B-52s. Of tunnels.

He knows something is wrong before they reach the clearing.

The tree line comes to an abrupt, jagged edge, and the ground is still smoking. The land is barren, save for smoldering splinters of wood. It is a pockmarked, barren moonscape.

He had heard stories of the tunnels when he first arrived, but he figured they were nothing more than ghost tales. Something the vets told. To try and scare the new guys. They weren't supposed to be real. There wasn't supposed to be a trapdoor hidden on the floor of the jungle that dropped off into the pits of hell. Against all hope, as the days go by, he wishes that the higher-ups are mistaken. That there aren't dozens of Viet Cong, concealed below them.

But then, one morning, there's an excited shout and the camouflaged trap door is suddenly open.

The next few days pass in a blur. There are strategy meetings, new assignments. They send wave after wave of poison gas down the trap door in hopes of flushing out the Viet Cong soldiers, but nothing happens. And then, one afternoon, Wes is summoned into the Colonel's tent. The Colonel sits at his desk, smoking a cigarette. He is much older, with the unmistakable harshness of a man who has spent the majority of his life in battle. He smokes like a chimney and always shouts when he speaks.

"Davis?" He asks. He doesn't even look up.

"Yes, sir."

"You're being reassigned. How strong are your knees?"

Immediately, he knows what this means. He's being sent into the tunnels. He's being sent to his death. And he's powerless to stop it. He stammers, "Very strong, sir."

The Colonel nods. "I don't give a rat's ass about what you do tonight, as long as you're ready to go at 0600 hours tomorrow morning. Now, send in Danielson."

"Yes, sir."

He finds Danielson, relays the message, and returns to his bunk. He writes to Mags. Tells her how much he loves her. How much he misses her. He doesn't mention that he will never see her again.

For the first time since stepping off the plane and into the jungle, Wes is truly scared.

Wes wakes with a start. He sits up, looks around. No one else is awake. The sun has not yet risen and the bunk is eerily quiet. He thinks about going back to sleep, but then he hears the familiar *click* of a lighter from beyond the confines of the tent and figures it's a good enough reason to get up.

He pulls his boots on, grabs his cigarettes, and makes his way outside.

Danielson and a man Wes doesn't recognize sit by the trap door, smoking silently. They both flick their ash into the tunnel. Danielson catches sight of Wes and beckons him over.

"This is Shellman," he says, nodding at the man beside him. "He's going down with us."

"Davis," Wes says. He begins to extend his hand, but he is struck with the absurdity of the gesture. Formality and tradition have no place on the battlefield. "Wes Davis."

"You're a Southern boy, ain't ya?"

"Georgia, born and bred."

"No shit. I'm from Augusta."

"Small world. Perry."

It's comforting, in some small way. Wes hasn't heard a Southern accent in a long time, and he can tell that Shellman's got that no-nonsense, tough-as-nails attitude that can only be developed by doing back-breaking labor during the Georgia summers. It's familiar. He grew up with guys like Shellman. He's still terrified of what they're about to do, but now, he feels a little bit better.

At exactly five 'til, the Colonel joins their ranks. He explains the mission, and maybe Wes is imagining it, but his voice is softer than usual. Compassionate, almost. But he's *probably* imagining it.

The mission itself is relatively straightforward: Survey and map the tunnels, identify any hostiles, extract any fellows, avoid confrontation. There's to be no combat. Just exploration. Information.

The Colonel gives them each three flares, a week's worth of rations, a battery-powered lantern with an extra battery pack, several heavy spools of twine, and mapping equipment. He has one AN/PRC-6 walkie-talkie, which he gives to Danielson. The range is supposed to be about a mile, but he warns them it'll be much less underground.

Without a single word of encouragement, they descend the rickety rope ladder, holding on so tightly their palms are rubbed raw.

They set up camp at the foot of the ladder, where the ground is flat, smooth, and easily fortified. From there, tunnels extend in six different directions. Two have already collapsed, and are impassable. For each remaining tunnel, Danielson ties the end of one spool to the ladder.

The work is slow and methodical. Danielson leads, lantern in hand; Wes behind him, mapping their progress; and Shellman in the back, unraveling the twine to mark their progress.

In the tunnels, everything echoes. Every cough, every footstep, every single goddamn breath reverberates endlessly, back and forth, again and again. No one speaks because their words are never laid to rest. It's unnatural. Unsettling. All-consuming.

Other than the artificial glow of the lanterns, they are cloaked in darkness. Eternal, impenetrable darkness. There's no daytime, no nighttime. No way to measure the minutes passed, the hours elapsed. As it seems, time does not exist. Not in the tunnels.

The air is damp and stale. The ceilings are low, the walls narrow. Wes has always needed space. Big, open spaces. One bad childhood experience of getting trapped in the crawl space below his house ruined him for life. He has tried to deny it, to conquer it, his whole life, but to no avail. Claustrophobia, he once heard it called. Now, it follows him everywhere he goes. The fear is constant—unwavering. He can feel it with every move he makes; sees it lurking in the shadows, just beyond the weak band of light. He doesn't eat, doesn't sleep: It doesn't want him to. Won't let him. But he's a soldier, and he must soldier on.

But then, on the third day, shit hits the fan.

They're making their way back to camp, about a quarter mile deep, when Danielson steps on the mine. Within an instant, he's gone from the face of the earth. Erased completely. Before either Wes or Shellman can realize what has happened, the ceiling caves in and they are trapped in total darkness, the explosion still ringing in their ears.

"Wes?" The voice is vague, distant. But if he focuses really hard, he can hear it. "Wes, man, c'mon. You alright?"

"Yeah," he stutters, waiting for his eyes to adjust to the darkness. They don't. He reaches forward, brushing his hand against the fresh barricade. It's less than a foot away, but he can't see it. "Yeah, I'm alright. Are you?"

"Goddamn peachy."

"I don't have a lantern."

"Shit. Shit. *Shit.* Rations?"

"No."

Shellman pushes past him. Tries to survey the damage. Wes can hear him pulling at rocks, attempting to clear a path, but he doesn't help. It's useless. He knew from the beginning that he was going to die in the tunnels. Why fight it? There's nothing they can do now. They have no food, no light. Less than a gallon of water. Shellman can't get the walkie-talkie to work. Mission control has no idea that they're trapped. There will be no help. No rescue. No one to swoop in and save them. And eventually, Shellman realizes that. Little by little, he stops trying to clear the rocks.

"Four more days 'til we're supposed to be up top," Shellman says suddenly, sickeningly hopeful. "I reckon if we don't make it, they'll send someone. Sooner or later."

Wes doesn't respond. He has resigned himself to death. To stagnancy. Just like everything around him. Time passes and nothing changes. The pitch black darkness, the moist cold, is constant. Unforgiving. He can't see the walls but he can feel them pressing in on him. Closing in.

Once, he hears Shellman speak in his sleep. *Hearts and minds*, he says.

Wes had heard LBJ talk about hearts and minds in a few of his speeches. Win the hearts of the Viet Cong, and their minds will follow next. That was the basic idea.

He laughs at the absurdity of it. It's more like grab them by the necks, and hope their hearts and minds follow.

After a while, he wonders what will happen to his body once he's dead. Will the Viet Cong find it? Or will the tunnels claim him? Use him as an example. Turn him to stone and say *Look what happens to those who try and tame us.* He can't decide, but he knows it won't be pretty—whatever it is.

And then there's Mags. Poor, sweet Mags. What will become of her? In his mind, he finds himself replaying the draft day like a roll of film. All through a sepia lens. Over and over again, he sees her coming up the street, blindingly beautiful in that watery sunlight. In his last moments, he recalls how fiercely—how vividly—he loved her while she was consumed by that deep-June sun. He manages to smile.

Halfway through January, Wes wakes up in an army hospital in Laos.

The doctors tell him he will never regain his vision. That the damage done by six days in total darkness is irreversible. But he is alive and so is Shellman and they're both being honorably discharged and awarded Purple Hearts. He even hears that Danielson is being posthumously nominated for the Medal of Honor. He knows not to trust rumors, but he can hope.

At first, he finds his blindness devastating. Choking. It is far too similar to the darkness of the tunnels, and as hard as he tries, he can't stop himself from thinking about their shadowy depths.

And then, the day before he is to be flown home, a nurse removes the bandages from his eyes, helps him into a wheelchair, and takes him outside.

"It's the first sunny day this month," she says. "Doesn't it feel nice?"

But it's beyond just *nice.* It transcends meaning, or feeling or definition. He tries to explain it to her but he can't find words beautiful or poetic enough to do it justice.

He can still see the sunlight, filtering through his eyelids.

And it looks just like Mags' deep-June sunlight.

*Zoë Meager*

# How to Select for Animal Testing

FIRST, FIND A LOCATION. Find a shabby farm that keeps its neighbours at arm's length. Find a house with a rusted roof, with guttering that dribbles down the sunburnt boards. A place with a back door that is always open and a front door that is always shut. Where inside, the rooms that were once the happiest have been given over to dust. Find not much of a garden, just a go-between passing muddy messages from house to field.

Discover the surrounding fields; they bloom in the wet and perish in the heat. Squat animals internalise the grasses' wisdom; observe them closely. See their football-shaped heads, watch their bums jiggle when pressed to a jog, detect the texture of their greasy fleece. Listen to the sounds they make too. Use your instruments to interpret the bleats and analyse their herd behaviour. See if you can pick one out from the others. Name them. Make it a game.

Next, pay close attention to the tiny animals in the hedgerow, the ones who are nervous to stay inside it, and cautious when leaving. These are the ones who fly, just like you. Gather some of their feathers that have fallen in the grass; record your thoughts on their method of flight. Note how they care for their young, who arrive in orbs humming with life and sit on stormy branches while they harden, ready for life.

Make sure you locate the old animal who remembers long hot days with sand beneath its hooves. Who recalls the weight of little ones clinging to its back. The one who stands on the same four legs, in the same spot, day after day. Not near to the house and not far away. No longer useful. Not wanted, yet not unwanted, yet. Send for samples of the smell of its thick neck, and have a hair plucked from its mane, and twist it round your finger the way the children used to.

Now, find the animal closest to the house. Train your lens on the one who was neither the runt nor the pick of the litter. Who is caught between pleasing, and sinking its teeth ecstatic into the animals of the field. Notice its sleeping quarters, like the farm house in miniature, but dirty and cold and with only a front door, always open. See it look up at the moon. Zoom in on its worried eyebrows. Focus on the shadows behind its eyes, filling the space where memories of its mother should be.

Last, look to the dingy farm house and find two animals inside who don't see each other anymore. Find an animal who turns up the stereo and sings along to Bonnie Tyler's *I Need a Hero* instead of finishing the vacuuming. The one who writes sad, disappearing poems in the condensation of the shower door. The same animal who will run outside through the night's lonely darkness, who will stand under the perfect circle you beam blue onto the grass, arms upstretched in a thin white nightie, begging to be taken with you.

Find the other one too—the one who spends all day among the animals of the field, knows them better than his own beating heart. Who believes deeply that one animal once died to save all of some, but none of the others. Who likes nothing more than to eat other animals, skinned and cut and hot. Find this animal who loads the fleecy ones onto a truck while whistling loudly to blanket their moronic cries. See what you think.

Find all this, then visit once again, at night. Hover over the house and field and take your pick. Choose an animal you want to take back and commence your animal testing.

*Terrance Manning, Jr.*

# Pig's Heart

YOUGHIOGHENY RIVER, PITTSBURGH. River sand red by the creek, early March. It was unusually hot for spring, one of those days everything melted together across the Allegheny skyline, flies buzzing over river water, bristling in the bushes, mud on boots, dried sweat, and a tee shirt wrinkled and browned. Even the sky had started to melt away, dripping over the hills all pink and orange. It had been two years since Levi Douglas's father died in his sleep, left him with the pig they'd hunted, that they'd intended to kill, but didn't—named her Hank.

Now Levi climbed into Hank's pen to repost the trough she'd knocked over and chewed up like an ear of corn. He propped it to the plank nearest the willow tree draped over the hog's pen. It had rained a week and everything was mud: him trudging through it; Hank rolling, mouth opened. Before he could reach the trough, she charged him, excited, and by then three hundred pounds and costing more to feed every week. Levi's boot stuck in the mud. She took him sideways in the air and he came down so hard he thought he'd broken his wrist.

"Get back, girl." He kicked her in the shoulder, and she stopped grunting, shied away long enough for him to stand, yank his foot from the mud, and climb over the fence. He looked back in at her, feeling bad for hitting her, wrist aching, nose burning from the chill lingering in the wet air. He knelt down beside the lower plank.

"Come here, girl," he said, breathless, but in a gentler voice. "Come over here."

She waddled over and settled. He ran his good hand down her spine. A splay of white hair at her back twisted around her chest, making her look like a wolf-pig—little tusks growing from her lower jaw. He opened and closed his sore hand to make sure he hadn't broken it.

"Levi, you alright?" he heard a voice yell from behind.

Turning, he saw Shawn Rybar, who he'd been working for laying brick nearly a year, fast-walking toward him.

Levi waved.

"Watched it from the driveway," Shawn said. "Thought she killed you."

Levi smiled and leaned back on the fence, Hank behind him, snorting, rolling in the mud again, sniffing everything she came near. Shawn was a tall, stooped man with dark eyes, pools beneath them like he never slept. He'd gone to school with Levi and usually had the right work at the right time, mainly bricklaying. He had a clean-shaved head and found a way, no matter what, to talk about work.

"Everything alright?" Levi asked.

"Figured I'd drop by to see if I could get you Saturday–Sunday. I'm short Gary and Luke. Need a good hustle man to climb scaffold." He shook Levi's sore hand.

"You know I spend 'em with my girl here." Levi thumbed behind him.

Shawn leaned over the fence, reached his hand in to touch Hank. She sniffed her way over to the willow tree, splashing down in a puddle of mud. Shawn smiled, leaned his back on the fence, mirroring Levi.

Levi looked back across the yard to the house, where a woman stood with a little boy wrapped around her legs. She seemed small, frightened, or curious, standing with her jacket flapping open. Levi squinted, straining for a clearer view. Aside from a few nights over the years, after drinking or spending time with people he didn't spend time with anymore, it wasn't often there was a woman around the house.

Shawn said, "Takin' my cousin Linda and her boy into the city. Boy's sick. Damn weather. I have to meet a guy anyway. You remember Linda, right? Married Bobby Crawson."

Levi knew Crawson from high school, a year or so older. Kind of guy to spend money he didn't have, always a different girl in his arm.

"She still with him?" Levi asked.

"Not since November. Ran up to Oklahoma. Ain't been back."

"That *his* boy?"

"No one else's." Shawn waved for her to walk up.

Levi leaned his foot back on the lower plank. He could hear Hank behind him, sloshing through mud. He watched Linda approach and figured Bobby Crawson either died in Oklahoma, or he was plain stupid to leave this woman.

"Linda, you remember Levi Douglas?" Shawn said as she came closer, her nose and cheeks glowing red from the wind.

"I knew your Daddy," she said. "Used to come in the store and pick watermelon near an hour." She smiled and Levi thought she looked pretty with her hair pulled back, strands of it falling down in her face. "He was a good man," she said, like she'd never thought of him the way most people in the town had: a drunk, a dreamer, whatever else. She was a little older than Levi and had wide brown eyes that smiled even when she wasn't. He remembered her.

"She works down Grove Convenience. Good job," Shawn said.

She pulled her son closer.

"Momma loved watermelon." Levi gave her his hand. "Good to meet you."

"Was sorry to hear he died," she said, her forehead flushing.

Levi nodded, *Thank you,* with a smile, thinking suddenly of his father, the week he died, when he'd gotten a call from Joe at the local bar, asking to pick him up. At the bar, his father was leaned close to some man's cheek slurring, "Rode the whole way down, son of a bitch; no one's telling me I didn't."

"It's late, old man," Levi had nudged him, wishing his father would leave, that he'd finish his beer and walk. Wished he hadn't come himself, having to apologize on the way out, *Sorry fellas; you know how he gets*, embarrassed later to show up around the docks until the guys forgot, and he'd wait for his father to forget, too.

Still, his father cried, "My boy watched the whole damn rodeo. She jumped around screaming like a dyin' horse. She fought, too. Ask my boy. Two of us were like hogs wrestling in the mud."

"Damn drunk," the man said, and Dale had grabbed him by the collar and took him off the stool. Everyone shuffled, piling into each other, pulling, pushing, screaming, *Damn fool.* A bottle broke, and Levi felt a punch in the head. A stool ground across hardwood. Another punch in the head, someone yelling, *No feral pig,* and Levi heard his father screaming, *No one's telling me I didn't.* Levi stood up, real fast, his father breathing deep in Levi's arm and facing off with a yelling crowd, *Douglas boys are nothing but trouble*, as Levi dragged him through the bar fumbling, *Fellas, I'm sorry* before he ran out the front.

"This here's Jonny," Linda said, as if she'd noticed Levi's distraction.

"Good to meet you, Jonny." Levi reached his hand out. Jonny kept his arms wrapped around his mother.

"He's five. A little shy, but he's a handful of smoke when you get his engine running." She smiled again, small teeth, and one turned a little sideways, making her smile even prettier to Levi.

Levi leaned back into the fence. Everyone stood for a moment in the sound of the wind kicking around, then Hank started grumbling. Jonny, standing level with the lower slit, saw her and pushed his face into Linda's leg, a little smile bending up on his cheek.

"That's Hank," Levi said. "My girl."

Everyone came near the fence, looked into the pen.

"Good company," Linda said.

"Only one I got." Levi smiled.

They were quiet for a while, watching Hank run the gamut in the pen, splashing mud, Jonny laughing here and there, Shawn reaching, unsuccessfully, to pet her. Linda asked, "How long you had her?"

"Little over two years," Levi said. "My daddy and I caught her. She's a good girl."

"She wild?"

"Not no more."

Linda smiled, and Levi gave the lower plank a kick thinking of those summer days he and his daddy built the pen, arguing over what shape it should be and how big, how muddy to keep the pen, how big Hank would get, what she would and wouldn't eat, whether or not she really sounded like Hank Williams when she sang—*Just like Hank,* his daddy'd insisted.

"She got a good heart," Levi said.

Linda laughed suddenly, like a hiccup, as she leaned over the fence. Levi watched her, eyes smiling, her hair falling some from a bunch she had pulled back, holding Jonny's hand. "Where's a pig's heart?"

"Same place as yours." Levi looked at Hank running around, thinking about extending the pen, giving her room to move.

Shawn smacked Levi in the back. "Saturday–Sunday good?"

"I need the work," Levi said.

By the time spring crawled into town, Levi had run into Linda a number of times, different places, like the post office or in line at her store, where he went to buy vegetables and beans for Hank. He asked Shawn about her, offered to take her into town, drive her to work, to dinner maybe. Eventually Jonny started talking. Levi had them come by the house often, where they'd walk up and watch Hank snort and grunt for a while, if it wasn't raining, or they'd walk down around the perimeter of the property, by the creek. Linda talked a lot about Jonny, how he loved trucks, and she thought maybe he'd grow up to work on trucks, or if nothing else, own a truck. Levi talked about the land, getting work, extending the pen and the house, he hoped, or how he and his father used to want to build something by the creek, but they never had the time. She'd tell him a little, mostly in pieces, what happened with her husband Bobby, how he'd been going back and forth to Oklahoma near a year, for work, longer every trip, before he stopped calling. Levi wanted to reach for her, to ask if she still loved Bobby, if she'd have him back, but he nodded instead, thinking it might not be right to walk with another man's woman like that. Linda was quiet some days, for a long time, looking off or watching the clouds roll by in the sky. Other days, she'd laugh, tell Levi how she used to dream of being a teacher, any kind of teacher—she just loved the kids. And most of the time they'd walk along quietly—watch Jonny, Levi chewing on a stick, Linda pulling her hair back as it fell.

Jonny always laughed when Hank rolled in the mud, so they'd stand sometimes beneath the willow tree, guarded from the rain, just to watch her.

"We were hunting," Levi said. "The day we got her. Looked the whole damn day for a good one. A good shot. Something with meat on the bones."

Linda pulled Jonny to her. Jonny reached his hand into the pen and touched Hank.

"We hiked all the way through Yellow Thicket Run, into the valley," Jonny said. "They say it's the most pig-populated place in Louisiana. That's where you find them. Rummaging. Vigilant. Can hear a fly buzzin' if they want to. Pigs got good ears. And they're smart too. Ain't dumb like you'd think." He knocked his knuckles on the plank so Hank would come lie down in front of Jonny.

Linda smiled and watched Jonny run his hand along her hair as she lay. "Be careful," she said.

"He's alright," Levi said.

Linda watched.

"We hit the valley mid-day, July," Levi said. "I remember that. Hot like hell and we were sweatin' through but we kept pushin'. All empty and quiet. Everything. I mean, real quiet down in that valley and I thought, well no wonder they hear you comin', there ain't no wind down here."

Linda laughed.

Jonny scratched Hank's back. "She's dirty," he said, wiping his hands.

"Keeps her cool," Levi said. "And warm when she needs it."

Hank breathed rhythmically.

"I figured, we take the hills back, we'd find them rummaging in the heavy thickets that run that whole stretch above Yellow Run. Daddy said no. We wait in the valley, post in trees, and they'd show up, he knew it. And he was right. We sat in them trees the better half of the day, and I was damn near sleepin' when she showed up, alone, white strip there running from neck to belly. They don't do that normally, come alone, but she did. She's brave, Hank. She wasn't much more than two hundred pounds, but she was a fighter. She sniffed everything, gruntin' and whippin' her head side to side. Walked right under Daddy's tree or I'd had my gun lined on her."

"You was gonna shoot her?" Jonny asked, looking up, his hand stopped on her side, lifting and falling as she breathed.

"Course not," Linda said.

"Needed a better look," Levi said, "Through the sights."

Everyone was quiet.

"Come here," Levi said to Jonny and jumped over the fence and in the pen with Hank. He reached over and grabbed Jonny up under the arms and pulled him over the top plank.

"No, no," Linda said, reaching her arms.

"He'll be alright," Levi said. "I'll hold him."

Hank stood up and Levi dropped Jonny down on her back, laughing. "Grab hold of her." Hank started running through the mud. Levi moved beside her, holding Jonny as he jumped up and over and laughed and mud splashed over everything, Hank grunting and honking the same short, breathless, guttural grunts she'd been breathing for years. Levi thought maybe she was laughing, too, or smiling, happy for the company, happy to breathe the same air rolling in the pen, the same smells of old trough and pig fur, happy for most things, but not all things. Happy to forget, for once, how lonely the pen could feel with no voices rising up into the willow leaves, how quiet the night could be with just the sound of crickets crying or insects buzzing.

By January, the next year, Linda couldn't keep the heat on, let alone make the rent at her place, so she and Jonny came and stayed with Levi, who emptied out the back bedroom, where he normally slept, for the two of them, thinking that could change, sometime, if Jonny wanted his own little space. He took his father's old room, the same blankets still folded on the dresser, the same half-drunk can of beer still dusty and stinking on the window sill that Levi hadn't quite gotten around to cleaning up or throwing out.

In April, a few days before Jonny's seventh birthday, Levi had him standing on the front bumper of the old truck, teaching him to check the antifreeze, letting him dump fresh oil in when Linda walked up with a guy with a clean shave and a button-down with no undershirt.

"Met this guy down the store," she said. "Got to talkin' 'bout Hank."

"Heard the hog's near six hundred pounds," the man said. "Had to see it to believe it."

"That's right," Levi wiped oil from his hands with a rag and walked around the front of the truck.

"I said so," Linda laughed and smiled at the man.

Levi still cleaned oil from his hands.

"We standing here all day or can I see him myself?" the man asked.

"She," Levi said.

"Who?"

"I said she, dumb prick. Hank's a she." Levi stood stone still, staring at the man's clean-shaven face.

"Levi."

"Calm down there, buddy," the man said. "I'm here to offer a good deal. If he's—if *she's* clean, well-kept, and six-hundred pounds, the way little Linda here's told me, I'm willing to offer one hundred CWT, and that's *per* hundred. It ain't cheap paying for a pig that big to eat."

"You said yourself, Levi," Linda said. "If you ever had the chance, you might sell—"

"Not for sale." Levi felt something stirring like a mix between pissed and embarrassed, wondering how many people she'd told that things around the house had grown a little tight with work coming in small bursts—all at once or not at all.

"It's a good deal, Levi," the man said.

"I know you?" Levi imagined Linda smiling her pretty smile at this man. Imagined her liking the way his face looked young, a little bright in the sunlight, pretty, like he'd kept it safe from the cold in the winter, guarded from wind and dirt. Made Levi sick, jealous, angry.

"Levi," Linda said.

"Not that I know of," the man said. "I just know little Linda from the store."

"Levi, we could use the mon—"

"Listen, now, dumb bitch, she's not somethin' for sellin'." Levi stared the man in the face, watching his eyes waver a little. As he stepped back, he saw Linda's face change.

"Hey, buddy, you got the wrong idea," the man said.

"Take your money," Levi pointed into the man's face. "And go back to where you came from. Old Hank's not somethin' for sellin'. We're gone past that point. I'll be damned some pretty prick like you come on my property talkin' 'bout good deals."

The man reached out to swat Levi's hand away and Levi stepped sharp, jutted forward, and flat-palmed the man in the chest, knocking him hard into the side of the truck, the bang sounding louder than the actual impact.

Everyone stood real still, kind of held, stuck by the unpredictability of a moment like that, where one move might set something crooked. Linda moved slowly over to Jonny and ran into the house. The man backed away from Levi, reached his car, and flew backward out of the driveway, dust flying up and floating evenly in the air after he left.

Later that night, Levi got drunk up by the pen with Hank. He hadn't gotten so drunk since the year his father died. He spent most of his time then working, fixing things, feeding or cleaning or watering Hank's pen to keep her healthy. He never understood why his father jumped out of the tree that day, or decided to catch her by hand, or why he wanted to build the pen and *fatten her up*, but he knew something in the old man wanted to keep her, name her, and Levi wouldn't sell her. For no price, he knew that. But she was getting heavy fast, and he figured he might cut her diet, if he could, because the rate she was eating cost more than he could afford. Most of the time, though, she went hungry, sleeping more often, lying in the mud beneath the tree. Or she wouldn't listen when Levi called—not the way she used to. He'd knock his knuckles on the plank like his father and she'd open her eyes and they'd stare for a while, contemplating, waiting for one or the other to give. Levi understood she was getting old and hogs, he'd heard, could be real short-tempered or cross with age, but he knew better. Hank had a good heart. She was only hungry, and he figured he might have to extend the pen.

Levi headed back down to the house after a while, knocking an empty can on the top plank and whipping it at Hank, for no reason, mostly pissed. He whispered, drunkenly, *I'm sorry, girl, I didn't mean it*, and she grunted. He headed back across the moonlit yard.

"Linda," he yelled into a quiet house.

Shawn had less and less work over the winter, and Levi knew he needed a steady job, at least a job he could depend on having after summer's heat. He could feed Hank that way, and Linda and Jonny. He could keep the truck running, the yard straight. Things had seemed a little easier when his father was around. Even drunk he'd at least been another hand. Levi missed the old man, or at least the man his father wanted to be.

"Linda," Levi said again, feeling his way along the walls in the dark toward the bedroom. He felt like apologizing, making her laugh, anything to see her smiling.

"Linda," he yelled, knocking over something in the dark, something cutting across the silence, and the bedroom door opened. Linda slipped out, pulling it shut behind her and leaning on the wall, moonlight spilling in through the window.

"I'm not doing it, Levi."

"You bring some prick, gonna sell my pig?"

"Keep quiet, Jonny's sleeping."

"The hell with that," Levi said and turned, Linda moving quickly to get in front of him.

"Don't you walk away," she said.

"If it's the money—"

"Not the money, Levi."

"I'm no button-shirt guy," he said. "Don't expect it either."

"I don't want no button shirt."

Levi pictured Jonny awake in the bedroom, under the blanket, listening, frightened. Levi was sure the boy was angry. Too frightened to move, but burning up with it anyway. "This point, she's not for sellin', Linda. I don't need no one tellin' me different."

"Not about selling her. Not about shirts. You'd rather be up in the pen drinking with that feral pig than anything else."

"She ain't feral," he said and thought Jonny must have hated hearing Levi yelling at his mother, must have wanted to tear up out of the covers and crash into the hallway screaming and shouting he wouldn't have no one calling his mother a bitch, or a dummy, or *damn whore, you can't keep your mouth shut, the least,* the way his father used to say to his own mother before she left.

"You're just a jealous woman," Levi said.

"What'll Jonny think?" She moved as he moved. "He sees right in you. Can't hear you talking like that."

"I can't be no one's Daddy," he said.

"Damn you," she said and pushed him.

"Damn you too," he said, wanting to leave, thinking Jonny must have been awake in the bedroom by then. He heard it, Levi was sure, despite insulation and closed doors and whispers. He could hear in the night.

"Go on, feral pig," she said and pushed him again.

Levi shoved her back into the wall, shouting, "She's no feral pig."

"You don't got your Daddy in you," she screamed, crying, her hair sticking to her face. Levi wanted to whisper, *Sorry, baby, I didn't mean it,* but he yelled, "She's no feral pig," and he punched the wall just to make the noise. He knew Jonny wasn't sleeping, he was never sleeping, and he wondered why Hank had gained so much weight, or how three years had disappeared in the wind since they caught her, and he knew he couldn't let her go, despite the pain, he couldn't leave the pig. He left Linda crying against the wall, left the house and fell asleep in the dirt beside his truck, just kneeling for a moment to take a break, a breath, and before he knew it, he was nearly sleeping, thinking he should teach Jonny how to change a tire on the truck, how to change the starter, how to smile when he's angry, look angry when he's sad, how to dream out in the night, unafraid of the dark, or objects covered in moonlight.

Levi wasn't good at saying sorry so he never did. It took a while to make up with Linda. Took hours, then a day, then just past a week before she smiled again as he unloaded hay off the back of the truck. He dropped a bale down into the dirt and looked up at her through the dust watching him. He winked—the first thing he thought to do. She smiled, and it felt right, like saying sorry, saying, *You know I didn't mean it. You know I love you. I can treat him good. I'll treat Jonny good.* He hoped she understood.

Then in May, Levi sent Jonny back to water the pen, something he'd done a number of times. He'd have to hook three hoses and run them all the way across the yard, up to the fence, and get the water pouring in at a steady rate, nothing that might startle Hank. Linda was at work, and Levi was stacking Versa-Loc in the driveway when he heard Jonny scream up on the hillside, behind the house.

Levi dropped the block and walked toward the yard to look for him.

Rounding the corner, he could see Jonny's legs sticking out through the bottom slit of the pen, pointed hard and straight toward the sky, and the black top of Hank's back above the fence. Jonny screamed. Levi took off running—pushed hard across the yard. He hadn't had much use for running over the years and his legs felt heavier than they'd ever felt in his life. Like he wished he could up and fly—be inside the pen. He could see Jonny's pointed legs, hear the terrified scream, muffled, unmuffled. Everything burned in him. He could hear his own voice screaming *Hank, no*, his breath choking out the words, and Jonny squealing under Hank, swinging his arms to free himself, but helplessly.

Levi flipped over the top of the fence, into the pen. He crashed into Hank. He reached around her neck and twisted her sideways to pull her from Jonny, but she wouldn't budge. She jumped. She snorted. She knocked her trotters across the kid's face. So Levi punched her in the stomach, only once, but still, she kicked. So he punched again, and again, every brutal pound of her like punching stiffened mortar. He only wanted to frighten her, but Jonny kept squealing—horrified and shrill—Hank's trotters knocking his head back and forth until the last hit shoved his face violently into the ground and the muffled sound of his voice, like a grunt or pause, startled Levi so suddenly that he yanked his knife off his jeans and drove the blade into Hank's throat. Just happened, and she screamed, a loud, piercing sound, and Levi wrestled her back, easier now, and stunned. Then thick, hot blood poured down his wrist and over the mud, over Jonny and his face and chest, so much that it surprised Levi—the warmth of it, the sound or feel of the knife in his hand, or Hank's relenting, or that he didn't feel sad or sorry, but angry and scared—and Levi scooped the bloody boy into his arms. He dove between the pen planks in one sudden, uncalculated movement—his knife left butt-end poking from Hank's throat.

Jonny cried as Levi ran down the yard with him in his arms. Levi laid him on the porch. "Let me see," he said.

Jonny cupped his hands over his face, crying hard, and Levi said again, "Let me see it," unsuccessfully before peeling Jonny's bloody fingers from his face, sickened with apprehension, with all the possibilities or horrors that might lie beneath, nearly dizzy when he saw just a scrape and swelling cheek, realizing that the blood was all Hank's.

"You'll be alright. Be tough, boy."

Jonny cried a little less, and as he blinked his eyes open, they were sheer white and alien on his tiny, blood-covered face.

"Just a scratch," Levi said, trying to laugh. "Got you good, didn't she?" He smiled, nearly wanting to cry with fear and anger and everything else he couldn't name or understand, that "she" reminding him now that he'd run his knife through Hank, and he hoped Jonny couldn't see it in him. "Just a scratch," he said again. He took Jonny into the house, into the back room beside the garage, and lifted him into the utility sink. "You'll be alright," he said. "You sit. You're okay, now." He turned the faucet on, checked the temperature, pulled a drywall sponge from the shelf.

The blood was already drying on Jonny's skin, cracking some around his eyes when he winced in pain, or cried, "It hurts," and Levi said, "Well it's gonna," as he pulled the kid's bloody shirt over his head, revealing a pale chest. He wished Linda was there, wished she could tell Jonny that he was safe, that she loved him, and Levi could run back to the pen to where Hank lay bleeding out in the mud. But he wet the sponge instead, wiping pig's blood from Jonny's neck, rinsing it out, and wiping again.

"Tilt your head," Levi said, sponging.

Jonny peered at him, his body quivering beneath Levi's hands, most likely from the pain setting in as the excitement wore away, and Levi didn't know how to tell him gently that he'd feel that pain for a time, that he'd hurt longer from the memory, so he moved the sponge over Jonny's cheeks, holding it lighter where the scratch was, and he thought again of Hank, of the day his father fell from that tree. Or his father's version: that he jumped. Though Levi had seen fear, or revelation. He'd never said that to his father, but he saw it magnified, illuminated down the sights of the gun: his father moving to slide and dropping his rifle. And for a moment, he missed the sound of his father's voice, the way he used to say, *Bastard put up a fight*, because to him, it was always about the fight. And Levi couldn't remember if he or his father had intended to keep Hank, but he knew it didn't matter. He'd kept her. For as long as he could keep her, he'd kept her—the last thing he knew his father had touched, and loved.

Jonny winced, from pain maybe, but this time, he closed his eyes, as if to ignore, as if not to show Levi he was hurting him. "I know," Levi said, cleaning off and revealing that beaten, scratched half of Jonny's face.

Mud from Levi's hands wiped away with blood, dirtying the sponge, but his arms stayed filthy with it, mud-caked and drying. And a smell rose from the utility sink, from the warm-water steam—a smell like Hank, when he'd washed her, a smell he'd grown to stand, or love. Like life, or the extension of it, and as he washed Jonny's face, careful not to hurt him or smudge mud onto his tender skin, he couldn't help feeling sick thinking about the pig, unsure whether from a certain grief or a certain regret, a certain resentment for keeping her in the first place. And Later, after Levi would bury Hank by the creek, insects buzzing in the bushes, after Jonny's face turned black and blue, swelled, and healed, leaving only a scab, Levi would take Jonny some days to work, sitting next to him in the truck pretending to drive, or helping unload hay or brick or light lumber from the bed and when he'd sit in the dirt, leaving Levi to finish alone, saying, *I'm tired from workin'*, Levi would smile and tell him, *You'll be alright—you're tough*, and Levi would believe that somehow he could care for the kid, could raise him, protect him. And now, as Levi finished cleaning Hank's blood from Jonny's face and neck, from behind his ears, there was a pale stain of her blood left on his chest, the bit that had soaked his shirt and dried, so Levi wiped that away, too, his arms still muddy and cracking. Water poured from the sponge, running down Jonny's stomach and into the sink, then swirling a moment by the drain before it disappeared.

*Matthew Stephen Sirois*

# Follow the Doe

IT HAD BEEN A LONG TIME since the old man quit hunting, but he'd kept the rifle, still. An ancient, single-shot model from Sears and Roebuck that had sat high away on a shelf for the past twenty-five some-odd years, evading spring cleanings and tag sales. Whenever Tom had caught a glimpse of its wooden stock, a chestnut gleam behind suitcases and ski masks and gloves with no match, he'd looked—wondering about the heft of the thing, the chill touch of its barrel—but always he let it be. Strong taboo and mannish grist, for a boy. He imagined the gun to be one of his father's totemic items, though Dad himself didn't seem to remember it was there.

The story of how Tom's father had given up hunting was a family parable, the particulars sometimes changing, but the moral intact. It gave the man, to his son, both myth and humanity. A person with a past full of trials. Tom retained the story, heard it hum within the white noise of his conscience; let it shape him in small but accumulative ways.

One morning in winter, maybe a year after Tom's birth, his father had driven his pickup to the general store on North Pond and purchased a box of Springfield shells, his annual doe license, a thermos of black coffee, and a ham-and-egg muffin that slowly spun in a glass case by the door. He spent the ten-minute drive home eating the muffin and then perfunctorily smoking half a Winston, his big orange coat and his cigarette fire the only colors brightening the county road at dawn. He pulled the truck slowly past the "big house," where his parents slept, past the mobile home, where his young wife slept and his son had likely just begun mewling in the dark, past all the standing, man-made things and onto a logging trail for another mile before he killed the engine and simply sat. A few breath's worth of time in the quiet.

The family property in central Maine was wide and wooded, the preferred hunting ground for Tom's dad and his brothers. And it was customarily with these brothers, those by blood and those by marriage, that Tom's father had gone hunting deer. The season which brought them together from disparate lives, away from work and wives and all the other silhouettes that waited for them on brotherhood's shrinking horizon. But on this morning, for whatever reason, on this last morning, Tom's father was alone. He would start and end the day alone. This, Tom knew, was an important part of the story.

Tom's father left the pickup unlocked and his keys on the bench seat, checked that his thermos and knife and compass and watch were all where and as they should be. He slid back the bolt of the rifle, well-oiled and obeying his cold, red hand. He slipped a cartridge in the chamber as he walked, his boots sucking at the mudsickles of the logging trail, an even, unhurried pace out from under the quickly blueing sky and into the dark, close trees.

He walked for hours. He noted tree bark and tree limbs. Hollows in the ground and anything still bearing fruit. He detected pathways where most anyone would see only brush, and then, in a moment, he doubted himself as most anyone might. When the silence grew so complete that his pulse was audible and the woods could not possibly be less alive, he leaned the rifle on a stump and pulled out a Winston and held his thermos between his palms and spat. The early snow had told him nothing in these hours of tracking. Nothing, as he swallowed the last drops of coffee. Nothing, as the noontime sun carved half-dollar cavities into the snow beneath his feet.

And then, a doe. Tom's father had already relented, turned to track his own footprints back toward hot, running water and meals wrapped in plastic and the Patriots at Chicago. The doe skittered into his life, completely unaware, out of that panoply of vertical lines and slouching boughs. He stopped still and watched the tiny animal mirror him, suddenly frozen and achingly conscious, the both of them bristling with the shock of having overlapped worlds. His thoughts were on the one shell in the chamber of his rifle. He weighed the situation, quickly, too many factors to dwell on any one. The doe seemed to occupy some in-between space of fortuity in that moment. She was small, and she was distant, and she knew that he was there. But the hunter was un-moneyed and recently wed. An infant son at home. A meager wage to earn tomorrow, and the next day, and the next. He took the shot.

BANG, the gun shouted, a brick through glassy silence. The doe, a hundred yards away, felt a strange fire bite into her flank before hearing it, as bullets travel faster than their bang. Without thought or hesitation, as Tom's father squinted down the hot barrel, she bound. Over the leafless blackberry tangles, over the fallen trunks of last year's thicket. Into the dark parts, the sanctum, the place where coyotes are bamboozled and men only poke around outside of, wondering. She jumped and kicked and danced through these obstacles, fleeing the fire, fleeing the bang. Ignorant of death, and bred for movement.

He knew he had to follow the doe. Having winged her, blundered the shot, he was bound to follow. The hunter's mistakes do not go unnoticed. He felt the world's breath on his neck as he watched his quarry spring, leaving a red sentence behind her in drips and splashes. Tom's father cursed softly, shucking out the empty shell, digging with stiff fingers for another, and running.

Spoor traces in the snow pack, frantic hoof marks, snapped branches and fading light. For hours this was his life, dizzy with minute concentration, as the doe used her last, great reserves to flee. No discernible goal, only away, away. Deeper and deeper into the twilight he found himself drawn, until he could no longer be certain that this was still the family plot, until landmarks and the sun's declination stopped informing his search and he, like the doe, followed a path of pure and hectic struggle. He was exhausted and hungry. He'd thought many times to curtail this insanity. But the tiny stains of her blood before him, showing black and oily in the gloam, insisted that she was close. The doe had run as far as her blood would carry her, every explosive leap a rejection of the cold earth below, costing her another ounce. Unable to run any longer, she reluctantly hid.

There were coarse, brown hairs caught in the evergreen needles, and hasty scratch marks in the snow. If sunset were any nearer, he might not have seen these. The doe may have spent her last hours alone, with only her defeat and a black chill crawling toward her heart. Tom's father approached the tree slowly, a sort of holy torpor weighing on his limbs. He reached out to a low-hanging bough and pulled it aside, ice crystals in his palm going liquid, shedding wan light on the cavity where she was curled and panting.

Dark, wet eyes. Big, pretty eyes, in his own words. A phrase which cropped up in every retelling, with a shake of Dad's graying head, with a penetrating look at his son. Tom felt at times that this was the point of the whole story. Those beautiful eyes which would haunt his father forever, containing every lesson he'd learned the hard way in their depth and blackness. The doe did not move from the spot, did not move in any way, and returned Tom's father's gaze, unblinking.

For several minutes they considered one another, themselves, their shared—if uneven—circumstances in this forest, far from either of their kin. Tom's father may have sworn, or prayed, or wondered what his own father might make of all this.

It was this moment that Tom had no real knowledge about, a moment that he knew had occurred, but could only imagine. A void, here, of time and distance and identity. And so, in order to understand this one moment in his father's story, Tom had to become him. To lock eyes with the doe. It was the only way. His only keyhole through which to peer at the man who was his father.

He fired the second shot. The second of the day, the last of his life, he'd decided. Or perhaps she had decided. He'd think about that question, from time to time, as holidays brought Tom's uncles together to swap hunting anecdotes. When someone said, Why don't you come out for once, Hank? That doe still got yer goat? The life he'd shed, which came cloying back at him through the lips of his brothers over brandy and beers as Tom sat there, wondering what his father might say. Hoping he'd rebut those middle-aged boys for poking a long-dead fire, extinguished by larger factors than just the doe. Tom wanted to see them shamed, but his father would only smile. He wasn't bothered.

He placed the muzzle over her neck, probably because of those eyes. Or, because he believed in the abstract that we call *sin*. Or, because he knew that the memory of this shot would come to him whenever he spoke to his children, or sat down to dinner, or watched his wife sleeping, or drove along a winter road. The doe, for her part, never flinched. Frightened beyond fright. Dumbfounded as Moses.

He shut his eyes and turned his head against the sound. He squeezed until he felt the recoil, until the explosion shook him and shook the snow from the pine branches down to the ground.

And then he was alone.

*William E. Burleson*

# Men with Nets

WE STOOD IN THE SPRING-SWOLLEN RIVER, sun falling behind the birch and poplar trees lining the tops of steep, rocky hills on each side. The north shore of Lake Superior, the final destination of the rapid, freezing-cold water, was a hundred yards away or so, and between us and it were six other men, all standing knee-deep just like us, dressed just like us, all looking for the same prey. Hip-waders. Wool and Gore-Tex. Hats with earflaps. Beer bottles and flasks. Men standing at the ready, nets, aluminum with nylon filament, poised in front of bodies and resting on shoulders, buckets near on shore, handy for when the onslaught came. Some in pairs and some alone, we all looked downstream, waiting, while the din from the stream battering rocks drowned out any conversations, unless the man stood right next to you.

"I am so fucking cold," I said. It was maybe forty-five degrees and dropping, but clear and windless.

"And you wonder why I never took you?" The weather-beaten, stubby man—my father—propped his net in the rocks to clear his hands, reached in his plaid coat, pulled out a fifth of Old Grand-Dad, and took a drink.

"Because it's cold?"

He put the bottle away. “Because you are a whiner, Johnny. You’ve always been a whiner. You’ve been complaining since we set out this morning. No one wants to listen to that.”

“Is that why, Dad? Really? Is that why? Because I want to know,” I said, my voice rising in pitch as well as volume.

“Look,” Dad said, “I never thought you wanted to go.”

“You could have asked.” Other dads took their sons smelting. All my friends went. Three or four days in the north woods with your pop under the pretext of bringing home a bounty of little fish.

“Would it have been different? Would you have come?”

I didn’t answer.

A week’s vacation with my wife and my twelve-year-old son—both back in Cold Spring with my mother and sister, warm, waiting for our return the next day—was my first time home in many years. My wife’s idea. A boy should know his grandparents, to which I said, good luck with that. That it was smelting season was a coincidence. Dad wanted to go even though we were visiting, and to that I said, go.

Out of nowhere, Mom asked if I would take him. She said his driving scared most sane people, and she worried for all the innocent drivers. At first I thought, no way. Not after all this time. But as hours passed, the idea grew. I thought it might give us a chance—maybe a last chance—to get to know each other, man to man.

Now there we were, finally, after a lifetime, in the frigid stream, me now a middle-aged man, and my father, seventy-two but looking eighty-two from a lifetime of Pall Malls.

Water pushed on the back of our legs as we held our nets in front of us, one hand on the black plastic handles, the other choked up the poles, the end of mine floating in the water, pointing to the lake. Each spring in rivers pouring into Lake Superior, smelt swim upstream in great masses like miniature salmon from the ocean. We were in the Split Rock River, but it could have just as easily been the Knife, Beaver, Baptism, or several other streams coming out of the hills into the lake. I’m told smelt fishing is all about timing—they only run a couple days but you never know exactly when. My old man had stood in God-knows-how-many rivers over his lifetime, scooping smelt and dumping them in a bucket. Will I be standing in the river thirty years hence, in my seventies? Not a chance.

It used to be that men from across Minnesota went up north and brought back buckets of the little fish, more than any one family could, or would ever want to, eat. Every Minnesota town had at least one smelt fry annually in the spring, usually a fundraiser at the VFW, fire department, town bar, or, in the case of our home town of Cold Spring, the church. Mom and Dad would load my sister and me in the Vista Cruiser and drive to Saint Andrew's Lutheran, where for five dollars everyone but me would get a basket of a dozen and stand around folding tables on the church lawn socializing, rediscovering each other after another brutal winter—"...Lost a few perennials..." "...Ya, soybeans..." "Twins will break my heart again, darned sure..."—while I looked for certain young women in the crowd no longer wearing their heavy winter bulk, giving me a glimpse of their promise of summer. As for those batter-dipped little monsters, I'd never eaten one, myself. Never a one. "At least try it," my mother would say. But I refused.

The frogs and crickets sang their songs as if in harmony with the river and rocks, the incense of campfires completing the scene. The full moon rose as the sun set, light dissolving fast. I knew that if the smelt were to run it would be now. Looking downstream, I expected the men closest to the lake to kick into action alerting us to the run, but they all just stood there.

"Johnny, you got to understand. It was one of the few times I could spend time with my friends. You can understand that, can't you?" He shifted his weight on the slippery rocks.

I never thought of him having friends. Hard to wrap my mind around, really. Not that I didn't understand; I knew it was difficult for men of his generation to have friends. They were expected to work hard and provide and, if they had time, to devote it to their families—friends were for youth or the army, and, if cut of that cloth, the bar.

"Did you go with friends or did you know people who came back every year?" I felt a crack in the wall between us and wanted to gain some leverage.

Dad ignored my question. "Every day I went to work and every day I brought home the bacon. Didn't I?"

"Yes, but..."

"But nothing. What more can a man do? Once or twice a year I went fishing. So what? A man has needs. Go to work, go home, go to work, go home, all to a half-shit job. He has to live a little. He needs something of his own. If that's being greedy, so be it." He reached for his fifth again.

"A boy has needs, too." All my life he came home from work, took a shower, read the paper, drank beer, and went to sleep. Little interaction was likely, or at least of the positive variety. The only time he recognized my sharing the same space on earth was when he meted out some punishment for a chore not done or a bicycle not put away.

"Yeah, well, you turned out okay."

An unprecedented moment of praise. Another crack in the wall? Perhaps.

My father worked at the co-op his whole life. Being the youngest of four boys meant he would not be working the family farm, the mantle unquestioningly passed to the oldest. He had no options. Me, I had choices. I hung out with and eventually became one of the kids who would have been good at sports if only they would have applied themselves, who would have gotten good grades if only they'd have paid attention. I had choices. I chose to hang out down at the river, first on bikes and then in cars, getting stoned, making promises to willing town girls. When I turned eighteen, I chose to leave and go as far away as I could, which meant the army. Eventually I got as far away as the desert of Saudi Arabia in Iraq One, filling the honored role of one more useless grunt with an addiction to opiates.

All water downstream, so to speak.

We stood in silence, listening to the rocks. It became dark, the only light the full moon and fires at campsites, no flashlights allowed in the river. In the moonlight we could see someone up ahead put his net in the water, but it turned out he was just bored, swishing around for a moment for lack of anything else to do. No fish. It occurred to me maybe we were hunting snipe rather than fishing smelt. Maybe it was all a big practical joke—the fish at the VFW brought in secretly from a fish wholesaler in the cities. I wondered how long we would stay. We had two rooms waiting for us at the Viking Motel in Two Harbors and that meant a long drive back.

"You know, this isn't at all what it used to be," he said.

"Yeah?"

"This river used to be packed. In the seventies, you could barely move around for all the men standing out here, and forget about getting a campsite! Oh, boy. Now look at it. I can't remember the last time I got a good catch from any of these rivers. They haven't run heavy in twenty-five years."

"Good memories?" I asked.

"Yeah. A long time ago, now."

"If the smelt don't run, why keep coming?"

"So many memories," he said, leaving me unclear if that was an answer to my question or if he was talking to himself.

Smelt don't belong in Lake Superior or its rivers. They were imported and took hold all too well when trout, who loved smelt, were being wiped out by another foreign species of fish, the sea lamprey. Seems as if nothing really belongs.

Now trout are recovering and back to eating their fill, and the smelt population is way down. And yet, a handful of men still go. Why? Is it enough to catch the few slimy stragglers who don't know their days are over? Hope that one day they'll come back? A habit so ingrained it's in these men's DNA? To think about it, I couldn't recall him bringing smelt home. Did he give his catch to Saint Andrew's? Didn't sound like him; he was more the sort to take more than his share, rather than share his.

"Tell me some of them. I would love to hear," I said perhaps too fast, with perhaps a bit too much enthusiasm.

He didn't look at me. It was too dark to see his face, to judge what he was thinking.

"Where did you stay?" I asked.

"Huh?"

"Where'd you stay when you couldn't camp? You said it was often hard to get a campsite."

"Duluth." He got out his Old Grand-Dad and took a pull.

That was news. Maybe I *was* getting to know him, if only one disconnected fact at a time.

"Why not Two Harbors?"

He didn't answer. I thought he couldn't hear me.

"Why not Two Harbors? Wouldn't that be much closer than Duluth?"

He snapped back, "What is this, an interrogation? What's it to you where I stayed? Can't a man take a fucking breath once or twice a year without everyone looking up his ass?"

Blood rushed to my head. Enough. Enough of the water and rocks, enough of the water in my boots, enough of the cold, enough of waiting, hoping. I was wasting my time. There were no little fish. I couldn't believe how stupid I was. As if, through sheer force of will, I could make something happen, make something from the nothing. There would be no fish to net that night, and no amount of hoping and pretending would change that. "Let's get out of here," I said.

"What?"

"Let's get out of here. The smelt aren't running. We're freezing to death. We have a long drive."

He laughed. "Quitter."

We put our nets and empty buckets in the back of his old F-150 and got in, me behind the wheel. I started it up and cranked the heat. I turned on the lights, illuminating the trees along the shore and the men in the river, who looked back, expressionless, ghost-like. I started down the gravel path toward the highway. He popped in the cigarette lighter, and pulled out his pack of smokes, tapped one out, and lit it.

"I wish you wouldn't do that."

"My truck, my rules."

His rules. His rules meant I could never live my life in Cold Spring. After the army helped me sober up, I moved to Kansas City, having a connection to a good construction job. I worked hard. I moved cement blocks with a forklift during the day, and went to school at night. After I graduated I got a job in the office wearing a tie, I met a wonderful girl, got married, and now our son. I'm not perfect, don't pretend to be, but my son and I go fishing often, just the two of us, and we talk, and he knows his dad. A man does indeed have needs.

Have needs.

We bumped slowly over the washboard road, curving up steeply. "Where are your friends now? The ones you used to fish with?"

"Oh, who knows. You get old, people die, you end up alone. That's how it is."

"Did you have fun in Duluth? Did you know people there?"

He didn't answer.

The smelt don't run anymore. There are no more smelt fries on Main Street, now a lost culture, long forgotten. Hard to believe that there were once buckets of little fish coming out of Lake Superior; hard to believe that for one weekend a year men would leave their families to become men with nets.

We got to pavement and Minnesota 61 and stopped. "One last question." I turned in my seat to face him. "Why didn't you ever bring home smelt?"

"What?"

"You never brought home any smelt."

"Oh, don't be silly. I did many times. It's just the nature of things that sometimes you catch your limit and sometimes you are skunked. Stop breaking my balls."

"Where did you stay in Duluth?" My voice again found that little boy pitch with adult volume.

"I thought you said that was your last question."

I slapped the steering wheel, hard. "Why didn't you bring home any smelt? Where did you stay? What did you do? Who did you see?" All those years wondering, assuming my flaws as a boy, as a man, were irreconcilable, while in fact another agenda played out, having no connection to me at all.

"Like I said, a man's got needs. Grow up."

No, smelt didn't belong in Lake Superior, or the Split Rock River, or anywhere else in Minnesota. Those lonely little fish were bit players in a greater drama of communities and churches, families and duty, a father and his secrets.

*Hannah Silverstein*

# LAND RECORD

The neighbors call this "the Carpenter place"
twenty-five years since Carpenter built it,
though records show four different families all
have inhabited these solid stories
since his hammer struck nail to beam and strut,
stick frame and pine rafters rising over
foundation, dug in cliff-shadowed hillside.
Before Carpenter, Ward kept this parcel,
eleven ledge acres sold one bad year,
against taxes on his well farmed hundred,
here where his Abenaki forebears stood,
above the rock lip, seeing thin valley,
to the *caw* of these ravens' ancestors,
who dove and soared in these same thermal drafts.

A paper in the town clerk's office claims
we own this spot. That hemlock, this beech stand,
those yellow birch. Fox den, deer bed, bear nest:
deed and title, signed, countersigned, witnessed.
Four walls, roof, skylight to let in the stars.
We painted the kitchen, replaced the wood
stove, added porch and deck, fought blackberries
out from the garden, cut a new back door,
paid bills, made love, buried cat and dog, slept.
Five years in October, we've made our home
here. How many more years, before what trace
we leave sinks any root? Until one day,
thinking of us, the neighbors, nodding, say,
*Remember them, up to Carpenter's place?*

*Abby E. Murray*

# Ode to Norteño

There is a kind of embarrassment you remember
without feeling sick: that time we lived across the street
from a Mexican family that sold produce from a U-Haul
by day and blasted norteño in the yard all night.

It was a Tuesday, because all that is good and right
is obscured on Tuesday. We were drowning in the Nightly News:
more of your friends dead overseas, a helicopter
driven into the desert floor like a tent peg,
women begged for food with toddlers asleep in their arms,
and our money flashed on the screen in a series of red arrows
pointing down when the accordions rumbled over the street,
platoon of violins that shook the standing water of our sorrow.

We decided to cross the street together and ask
for a lower volume, that was all, though we intended to slouch
into our hips to show them how exhausted we were,
how much we deserved to hear our television
over their songs, that we had earned the sound
of the broadcaster's tongue against the teeth of his words.

When we opened the backyard fence everyone turned
to see who had arrived. A teenager, the one who drove the U-Haul,
wheeled a volume knob counterclockwise with his thumb.
The air over their yard seemed cooler than the air over ours,
the grass beneath their pecan trees like the ocean at night
while the yellow lawn below our dogwoods
lay brittle and smashed by the heat.
Pear-shaped lightbulbs dangled between the patio awning
and the pecan branches, gold light shining on the laps and foreheads
and paper plates of the family as if Christ had been dining there
only seconds before. The screen door slapped
and a woman yelled inside the house, *Felix! Two plates!*
The call of our back-peddling. We saw ourselves unmoored

in the gilded glow of summer, our lives like burning boats.

We said we'd come to buy vegetables.
They gave us two peppers, five limes, a head of lettuce
the size of a bowling ball and when we offered to pay
they held their hands up, palms toward us, because they knew
it wasn't our wanting to a quiet music we would regret
but what we might do afterward: carry the vegetables home
in our hands, consider eating them whole
while they were cool and full of juice,
then chop them into a salad instead.

*Anna Goodkind*

# SEVILLA

AVA WAS GLAD WHEN HER FRIENDS suggested walking down to the river. She'd been drinking slowly, and so she jumped at the excuse to say, "You guys go check it out, I'm going to sit here for a bit and finish my drink." She listened to the girls' voices slowly fading into the dark as they made their way to the lit bridge, and watched them stopping to catch their balance and doubling over in laughter when their thin heels stuck between the ancient cobblestones. Soon the small bar and its outdoor tables were quiet, free of the girls' chatter and giggles, and Ava could feel the man's dark eyes on her face as she sipped her drink.

She had seen him watching her all night, over her friends' heads. Diana and Jacqueline hadn't noticed him at all. They'd been too engaged in their own conversation about their trip to the *discoteca* the night before to notice the staring man behind them. Normally Ava would have discussed him with her friends; she would have lowered her head and whispered to her friends, *don't both turn around at once*, and then *tell me if you think he's cute*. The girls had analyzed many young men this way, both in Spain and in New York. In Spain the men were more forward. Any of them who knew any English at all considered themselves fit to approach the girls as soon as they heard them talking with each other. Carlos had been the most fun; he'd introduced himself, kissing each of the girls on the cheek and declaring, "I am in love with you" to each. All the Spanish men they had met seemed to like Jacqueline best, though they couldn't pronounce her name and most often ended up calling her *Yac*; with her long blond hair and miniskirts, she was the typical American beauty. Ava was smaller and darker and not nearly as exotically American as her two friends.

Before they'd left New York the girls had discussed ways to hide their American identities.

It had been Perry, their suitemate who was staying in New York, who'd suggested, "Why don't you buy some Canadian flag patches and put them on your bags?"

And Jacqueline who'd added, "Yeah, and say *eh* a lot."

But the girls hadn't done that, and it probably would have been pointless. It seemed that everywhere they went people knew instantly that they were Americans, and most were excited and intrigued. At every bar the girls went to, men of all ages dropped Hollywood names—*Hey Madonna, hola Julia Roberts!*—as they struck up conversation with the "beautiful American girls." And when the girls told people they went to school in New York, someone would enthusiastically shout "Empire State!" or "Sex and the City!" and buy everyone a drink.

But this time was different. The man at the next table hadn't approached them. And Ava hadn't asked her friends if he was good-looking. She knew he was. He was darker than the others they had met that week. His hair fell in shiny black curls over his broad forehead; his eyebrows were thick and slightly furrowed as he stared at her above his caramel-colored drink. It reminded Ava of one of those subway situations; riding the subway in New York she would often find herself staring at the various people sitting across from her—the woman peering over shopping bags on her lap and by her feet, the man checking his phone, the girl reading and chewing a purple fingernail. And as her eyes shifted from face to face, she noticed that many of the other eyes in the car were doing the same. Once in a while, two pair would meet, and most often one or both would look away immediately. However, there were those rare days when Ava's eyes met a pair that stared back, stared long and hard, taunting her, refusing to look away. And as much as Ava wanted to herself, she couldn't right away. The stare would bore into her sockets and spread through her nerves down her arms, until she shivered and shifted her gaze to her hands in her lap, or the transit map on the wall, or the child swinging on the pole at the other end of the car. The dark-eyed man with the caramel drink had that same persistent stare.

Ava tugged at her cotton skirt. But no matter how much she pulled at it, the bottom halves of her thighs remained uncovered and stuck uncomfortably to the mesh of the metal chair that had etched itself into her skin. The first thing Ava had noticed on the taxi ride from the airport to the hotel was that all the Spanish women wore pants or long skirts. Not a single mini-skirt walked by as she pressed her nose to the window, then rolled it down so she could hear the Spanish that accompanied the waving hands of people on the sidewalks—strange sounds that rose loud then faded as they drove—and breathe in the occasional spicy smell of bitter citrus, oranges that were still bright among the vibrant green leaves, and just beginning to litter the sidewalk below. Ava had worn her jeans the first day sightseeing, but the weather was unseasonably warm that week and her legs had cooked in the denim under the midday sun. The girls went shopping, and Ava bought a long skirt with layers of white gauzy material that wrapped around her legs when the wind blew. When the fabric softly hit her calves she felt pretty and European. But now it was their last night in Seville and she'd wanted to wear the brand-new black miniskirt that she'd bought especially for the trip. She'd felt the eyes on the backs of her legs as she'd walked down the narrow streets that day. And now at the outdoor bar by the river, her thighs pressed to her chair, she wished she were wearing the layers of white fabric that had covered her legs most of the week.

When she looked up, the man was coming towards her and she smiled slightly as her eyes met his. "*Hola*," she said.

Without acknowledging the fact that she had spoken, he sat in the chair opposite her and said, "Where are you from?" His English was nearly perfect. But Ava wasn't giving in that easily.

"*Los Estados Unidos*," she said.

He smirked. "Yes, of course I know that you are American. I heard you order drinks earlier. Your accent is, eh, not so good." His smile, with big teeth shining white against smooth brown lips, almost made Ava forget that he had just insulted her. But she was hurt by the smirk, and even more so by the words that came with it.

Ava had always been told that her Spanish accent was excellent. The Mexican bag boy at the grocery store in New York was impressed, as was everyone she had spoken with that week in Seville. She was the only one of the girls who really knew Spanish; Jacqueline could only say *hola, adiós*, and *¿Donde está el baño?* so that Ava had to inform disappointed men who approached her friend in tapas bars and dance clubs *Ella no habla español.* Yes, Ava was the one who really cared about the language, and the culture; she was the one who'd studied the maps of the narrow, curvy cobblestone streets of the old Jewish quarter. She'd pointed out the delicate terra-cotta and brick patterns at the top of La Giralda, and proudly informed Diana and Jacqueline that the cathedral had once been a mosque when the Muslims had ruled this part of Spain, and that then there'd been no cross, but rather a minaret with four copper spheres, the Muslim symbol for unity, at the top of the tower.

Later, looking at paintings in the Museo de Bellas Artes, Ava had noticed a blue-robed Virgin Mary who stood on a crescent moon, another Muslim symbol, but she hadn't bothered telling Diana and Jacqueline. She'd stood by herself in front of the painting, looking at Mary's smiling white face, round and rosy-cheeked, her deep blue robes flowing in delicately painted folds down to the strange shiny white crescent moon, holding the virgin hovering in space, the grey and blue heavens spreading beyond.

And now this man with the dark eyes and thick eyebrows was making fun of her accent, she who had expertly guided her friends through Southern Spain, where people said the Spanish was unintelligible to foreigners, for almost an entire week. Offended, Ava looked down into her glass, and picked at a small piece of orange peel soaked in wine, between the melting ice cubes.

"Let me get you another drink," he said, and before she had time to object, he had called the waiter over, "*Oye, hombre,*" and ordered, "*un tinto de verano, porfa.*"

"Tinto de verano, what's that? I was drinking sangria."

"Don't worry, this is better." He winked at her. "What we drink. The same, but better."

She felt that somehow she had been insulted again, but she wasn't sure why, and so she accepted the drink. "*Gracias*, thank you," she said, and smiled at the waiter who put the perspiring glass in front of her. It did taste a lot like the sangria she had been drinking all week, but more bubbly and less fruity sweet; she did indeed like it better, but she wasn't sure she wanted to say so to this man, not yet at least, and so she simply smiled and took a second sip.

"Your name is?"

"Ava," she said.

"And where are you from in Los Estados Unidos, Ava?" He pronounced her name with an *e* sound—*Eva* it sounded like.

"New York City." It sounded strange to her, in English. She had been telling people where she was from in Spanish for days.

"Ah, of course." He took a large sip of his drink. His fingers were long and smooth as they curled around the glass, and his nails were perfectly trimmed, his cuticles neat and round, almost womanly. "Twin Towers," he said, nodding knowingly. Then, "I am Abrán. I work at the bank."

But after he'd told her his name and his job, she didn't know what to ask him next, so she smiled and took another sip of the drink, which had begun to taste less alcoholic and more juice-like. A horse's hooves clopped along the cobblestones on the next street, and Ava thought of the carriage ride the girls had taken their first night in Seville. The horse had been silky white and speckled grey on its bottom, which bounced up and down as it walked ahead of them. The driver had stopped in front of the university, which was lit up at night, the marble glowing, and he'd stepped down with Diana's camera to photograph the girls in the carriage. They'd offered him a tip, even though their guidebook had said it wasn't expected. "No, no," he'd said, shaking his head; he'd seemed insulted.

"You like Sevilla?" Abrán asked.

"What? Oh yes! I love it, it is the most beautiful city!" Ava leaned towards him resting her chin on her hands, her elbows on the table.

He asked her how long they would be in the city.

She told him they were leaving the next day.

"That really is a shame," he said, leaning towards her across the table, sticking out his lower lip and furrowing his eyebrows in a sincere pout.

She laughed.

"I am only getting to know you now!" He smiled at her, his white teeth flashing, and she felt her stomach flop excitedly.

She quickly looked away from his playful, glittering eyes. She began to describe all the exciting things they had done since they'd arrived almost a week ago.

She told him about the flamenco dancers they had seen, in the beautiful theater attached to the hotel, the vines climbing the wall behind the stage, the flowers and candles lining the edge of the stage separating the audience from the dancers, the edges of the women's black dresses moving the flickering flames as they gathered their skirts in one hand and stomped their feet in perfect rhythm with the music.

She felt her cheeks flush as she described the curvy, graceful dancers—or maybe it was the wine that made her face hot. She told him about the Ferris wheel ride they'd taken, and how beautiful the city had looked from above at night, buildings sparkling along either side of the river, the cathedral tower hovering over winding streets. Twirling a dark curl around and around her finger and smiling at him, she told him about the *discotecas* they had visited, dancing together to loud Spanish music late into the night.

He laughed and said, "You Americans really need to learn how to slow down, appreciate the Spanish lifestyle." She liked the way his *R*s rolled off his tongue, dripping like ice cream and vibrating in her ears. He leaned back in his chair, stretching out his long legs, and finished his drink, tilting the glass far back and shaking out the last drop.

But now she couldn't stop talking. She told him how they had planned to go to a bullfight, but then, when she'd seen part of a fight on TV in the hotel one night, it had made her so sick she'd decided she couldn't go. She'd felt so sorry for the bull, she said. She said it was cruel, and asked him if people really still enjoyed that.

"But it is tradition, you see," he explained. "Part of our culture. People do not want to give up their traditions, even when the times are changing."

"But the poor bull!" she cried, hearing her voice suddenly high, slightly whiney.

He frowned. "Maybe you do not understand..." He repeated that it was tradition, mostly a tradition the older Spaniards liked and the younger generation wasn't usually too interested in. "But sometimes," he raised one thick eyebrow, "the bull wins. And then it becomes exciting."

Ava sipped her drink and looked past the small round tables on the outdoor patio to the dark river, at the Torre de Oro, the tower with the gold dome that used to hold treasure, half-lit and glowing eerily in the streetlights across the river. Diana and Jacqueline were small black figures walking beneath the lit bridge, and she could hear their faint high-pitched laughs. A car sped by on the bridge, too quickly for her eyes to capture, disappearing and leaving a blurry phantom behind that faded quickly among the spots of scattered light. She blinked. The sweet liquid in her glass and the two glasses that she'd had before were filling her head, weighing her eyelids, seeping through her ears so that the sounds of nearby voices, cars, and some far away music seemed to come slowly towards her through water. "Abrán," she asked, "do people ever swim in the river?"

He said no, not really; he thought maybe they used to, but it was considered too dirty now. "Do you know that we are in a drought?" he asked, looking out over the river.

She shook her head.

"We are always in a drought here. They say in a few years we will be out of water."

"Oh, no, that's awful!" she said.

"Yes, and so you will think about that the next time you American take your thirty-minute shower."

"Ava," she said. She thought maybe he had forgotten her name; many of the Spaniards they had met called them *American girls* because they could not remember or pronounce their names.

"My father came here on a boat from Morocco."

"Really, why?" she asked.

He looked at her. "Because people in his country were starving."

"Oh." She saw that the thick muscles in his neck were taut.

"He worked on a farm in a *pueblo* outside of the city, making just enough money for room and board. He met my mother when her family came for vacation. They ran away together."

Abrán's English was almost perfect, but his accent still stood out on certain letters, *R*s mostly—and *S*es. He held his *S*es longer than any native speaker did, letting them hiss and fade like air from a balloon. The sensual sounds filled her head, along with the rhythmic clopping of the horse's hooves on the next street, and she thought that she might fall asleep here by the river with this strange man's tongue *hissing* soothingly into her ear. "That's so romantic," she murmured.

"Yes. And then her family rejected her," he said, looking back towards the river and the shadowed buildings and flickering lights beyond. Then he turned back to her. "You know, I have been to New York before."

"Really?" She wondered why he had not mentioned that earlier, when she'd told him where she was from.

"Yes. Two years ago. I went to visit my cousin. She lives in Harlem. Do you know it?"

"I've been there before." She yawned. "Got on the wrong train once."

He made a noise that sounded like a half-laugh, half-grunt, shook his head slightly and looked away, toward the river.

*Shit*, she thought, *what did I say?* And then he spoke again before she could remember.

"Funny thing," he said.

She smiled to herself, thinking that he had probably heard an American say that phrase before.

"Funny thing," he repeated. "On the way into the country, I was stopped by security policemen. A 'random search'...they said."

She nodded. "Airport security's been very tight lately."

"Yes, of course." He paused. "But then, on the way back, when I was leaving New York, was another 'random search.' Of me. Again. Funny, no?"

"Yes, that is kind of funny, I guess."

"And so then I am wondering to myself, what is random? Perhaps, I wonder, these Americans are not so good with the numbers. Perhaps, they can only count skin?"

"I, I'm not sure what you mean..." She tried to focus on his face, but it was blurry, outlined in dark curls, and her eyelids felt heavy.

Suddenly he sat up straight and leaned over her, so close she could feel his warm breath on her face. "You Americans," he breathed. "Think you rule the world."

"What?" And then she understood. She smiled. "Oh, no," she explained. "I'm a Democrat."

"You are an American." He was breathing heavier, and faster, in warm bursts that made her blink. His breath smelled like whiskey, mixed with an almond scent that she thought came from his hair. She inhaled, and felt dizzy.

"You are a princess," he whispered, hissing quietly and leaning closer.

She was surprised when she felt his sticky palm on her thigh. A light shiver ran up her leg and her cheeks felt hot again.

"Perfect white princess. Best money can buy."

She watched his mouth, watched his tongue roll with each *R*. His large brown lips looked soft and warm and she wondered if he would kiss her.

"Grown from hamburgers and Coca-Cola."

The weight of his hand on her thigh became heavier.

"In the land of freedom. Freedom and democracy. That is what you call it, no? That is what you fight for. What you kill and die for."

Suddenly she felt a sharp pain in her thigh, which grew more intense as his fingernails dug deeper into her skin. She looked up at him. Her eyes widened as she stared into his, dark pools, shining like the river.

"Freedom for big fat white oil men. Suits and shiny black shoes."

She opened her mouth but did not speak. Her face was frozen and stiff, her eyes wide. She could not look away from his face, his eyes, could not look at her thigh that burned now.

"You are not real." Small flecks of his spit fell lightly on her hot cheeks. But she did not move to wipe them away. "You are not clean. You are money and Coca-Cola and hamburgers. You do not want to see the bull die, but you stuff yourself with hamburgers and watch the world starve."

Then he looked down, and she did too, at his clenched hand gripping her thigh, the skin stretched taut and white across the knuckles tense with strength. He shook his head slightly and blinked, as if he did not recognize his own hand. He quickly released his hold. His hand, once again soft and smooth as milk chocolate, rested limp and lifeless on her thigh. He looked at her, then back at his hand. He lifted it quickly from her leg and reached into his pocket. He dropped two coins on the table in front of her, and stood. His chair scraped loudly against the cobblestones.

Ava watched the coins spin, a gold and silver blur, clinking gently against each other, until they fell flat on the table. She studied the engravings outlined on the gold center, overlapping the silver border and framed with stars. She suddenly gasped and realized that she had not been breathing. She looked up and Abrán was gone.

She could hear Diana and Jacqueline coming back up the street from the river. They were singing *Feliz Navidad*, blending strange sounds for the Spanish words they didn't know and clapping loudly off rhythm. Soon they came into sight. Laughing, they leaned on each other and started the chorus again.

Ava looked down. Five white crescents shone against her skin tanned slightly pink by the Spanish sun. She grazed her hand lightly over her thigh, then tugged at her mini-skirt to cover it.

*Kevin Fortuna*

# WEDDINGS AND BURIALS

THE IRISH HAD COME OVER IN FULL FORCE for the latest Fahey wedding. When I got to the reception, Dee Dougherty and her sister-in-law Anne Fahey were huddled in front of one of the floor-to-ceiling windows overlooking the cemetery, sipping from clear plastic cups of white wine and whispering to each other about my husband. They stood with their backs toward me. I'd just fetched my own chardonnay from the nearby bar, and was heading toward them to say hello when I overheard them.

"That's it? That's where he did it?" Anne said.

"Yes—over there, in the fourth row. The Linden grave. It has cameras on it now, and you can see the little security sign."

"Imagine such a thing. Jesus. Jesus in holy heaven."

When Dee Dougherty said "Jesus" with her Cork accent, it sounded like "Jay-zuhss." Like some kind of drunken banshee. She always was a loud one, and she liked her wine. I circled around them and saw them before they noticed me. Anne had a warm, kind smile on her face—which was still quite beautiful despite her more than sixty years. Her straight gray hair pulled back in a tight bun, those Audrey Hepburn cheekbones, that itsy pinky of a nose, those teeth lined up perfectly like a row of tiny white bricks—it all still did the trick for her. She'd always been a great beauty. I couldn't blame Eddie for picking Anne back in Cobh, when we were all just kids. As he put it, Anne got the face and I got the personality, and he was a face man. True enough. I could make the boys laugh like I was one of them. Brian used to tell me to stop being so funny, that it wasn't right that I was so much funnier than him. Women shouldn't be so funny, he'd say. Oh, Brian. What a fool thing to say.

So there I was, frozen in place, thinking about the harsh truth of Eddie's choice, trying to decide if I should veer off or go talk to the Fahey sisters as I'd planned. Fuck it, I thought. Coming here, I knew there'd be jokes and sly looks and clucking tongues, and I promised myself I wouldn't let any of it get to me. I took a swig from my glass, put my head down, and walked toward Dee and Anne, bracing myself for the jolt of embarrassment they'd feel when they saw me.

Dee saw me first and hugged me like she meant it, a little too fast and rough. "Oh, look who it is! Our little Rosie!"

Anne pulled me to her and air-kissed me, but her smile seemed genuine and never left her face when she saw me. "Rosie, you never get older," she said. "You don't look a day older than forty."

"She *is* like a bottle of fine wine that gets better with age," Dee spat, before tossing back what was left in her cup. A splash of wine missed her mouth and streaked across her cheek, glistening with reflected light from the chandelier above us. She couldn't feel it through her thick makeup, but it was all I could see while she blathered on. "What is your secret, Rosie? Wheat germ? Fish oil? Or is it one of those exotic fruits everyone is raving about now? Do you know the ones? Pomegranate. Kiwi. Cactus, maybe? Some Yank on the plane over talked Eddie's ear off about something called a Nonni. From Tahiti or someplace like that. Swore it cures cancer, stops the flu, destroys fat, and builds muscle. On and on. Talked about it like it's the bloody fountain of youth. He was a salesman for it, and tried to tell Eddie he should be one, too—*ha! imagine! Eddie!* Anyway, we got stuck on the tarmac at Shannon for an hour with some kind of mechanical problem and Eddie had his fill of the Yank and his Nonni, so at one point he says to your man, 'Look. Why don't you bring yourself and some of that magic Nonni potion up to the pilot, so he can pour it in the tank of this bloody plane and get us on our way?'"

We all had a laugh about Eddie taking the piss out of the Yank. I could just see him saying it, with the whiskey in his hand, the crafty smile on his face. I considered telling Dee about the droplet of wine on her face but decided against it.

"Now where's your Brian?" Dee asked. Her eyebrows scrunched with charmless curiosity.

"Oh, he's around here somewhere."

"Well, I need to say howdy. Haven't seen his handsome face yet. How's his work?"

"Good, good," I said. Brian hadn't had any kind of real job since being fired from this place, and Dee knew it full well. "I need a refill. What about you girls?"

Anne and Dee nodded, and I took their empty cups and headed toward the bar. As I walked away from them, the air on my face felt like freedom, and I started to unclench. Wouldn't it have been nice if someone slipped a little something in Dee's cup of wine? Nothing too crazy or dangerous. Maybe one of those party pills the kids had been talking about—a roofie or whatever they call it. Just something to put her over the edge, make her wobbly enough to lose her legs a time or two before the end of the night. I'd do it if I had one in my purse. I had some Paxil, but that would probably just make her more alert and happy. That wouldn't do. Maybe if I crushed up six or seven pills and put them in her drink it would get her. But no. The thought of it made me smile. But that was more the chardonnay talking than anything else. Chardonnay was my best friend right now, and I couldn't wait to have another. I got in line at the bar behind a bunch of strange young faces. Friends of the bride and groom, in a hurry to get drunk. My own children couldn't be here, or so they said. I knew better.

Now, I'm no great defender of my husband, but I do think if another man had done it—if, say, Eddie Fahey had done it—somehow it would have been turned into a funny stunt, or even a bit of delayed justice. A feather in his cap. But not so with Brian. Brian got crucified for it, and they still hadn't let him come down off his cross. Everyone asked why he did it, but it has always been pretty plain to me. He felt trapped and figured it would do no harm if nobody found him out. Figured he could get away with it. He'd been getting away with things all his life. The lifelong teamster pension that followed the Irish-football injury just before his twenty-sixth birthday, the girls he had before—and probably after—meeting me. Part of it was chance. Part of it was his good looks. (When we were vacationing in Los Angeles one time, he won a James Dean look-alike contest and we drank for free the whole night.) God knows it wasn't his personality, which had kept him unemployed and isolated for years. He couldn't get along with his own children, even now that they were grown. Brian got the face all right, but Eddie got the balls and heart and sense of humor.

The gambling debts had gotten out of hand, Brian said after he got caught. And he had gotten into debt with some brutal men who had threatened to harm me and the children. I can still remember the day he called me from this place in a panic. The cops were on to him, he kept saying. He was heaving and whimpering like a child. When I finally got him to calm down enough to make sense, he told me what he'd done as if confessing it in church. Later came his rationalization. Linden was a Nazi and the watch was contraband from the war. The family came to eat at the Natchez after the funeral, and that's how he found out about it. They'd tried for years to find the watch's rightful owners, who they suspected were prisoners at Auschwitz. The old man wanted to do the right thing in the end, and so did the family. Apparently the watch was a rare Rolex, one of the first ever made, and was worth more than $30,000. What got Brian in the end were his fingerprints on the axe that he used to finish the job on the grave's padlock.

Disgusted by the memory, and the shame and ruin that followed it, I decided to take a break before rejoining Anne and Dee. I got one wine refill instead of the three and headed to the far side of the banquet room, toward a hidden patio I knew about from the old days.

It took me back, being there. Back then, the Natchez Club felt like the world we'd never be part of, the world of the old people whose houses I cleaned. And this enormous banquet room seemed like a Cinderella dream. With its twenty-foot ceilings, dark wood floors, massive chandeliers, white tablecloths, and views of the cemetery and Garden District mansions. I remembered when Brian first got the job more than a decade ago. One of the Fahey cousins from our county owned a big interest in the Natchez, and he knew Brian had been a cook and barman back in Ireland. He gave him a chance, even though he resented him from their time playing football together. Probably on Eddie's say-so, born of some misguided feelings of guilt or regret about me, he made Brian the assistant general manager.

I had such hope for the future then, for a brief time. I never deluded myself to think that Brian would suddenly become the dream husband—after all, we'd been living pretty separate lives for years. But I did think he might've found a job he could keep for a while, and that maybe I wouldn't have to keep cleaning rich people's houses and offices at night to put the kids through college. A better life seemed possible. I imagined first communions and confirmations and graduations and the girls getting married here in this banquet room. Thinking about it now was pure silliness, though. It was too good to be true, and the unreality of it made me wonder from the start when Brian would find a way to fuck it all up. But I'd let myself hope against reason that it could last. And I guess I didn't expect him to blow up in such spectacular fashion.

I walked out a side door of the ballroom. I needed to be alone for a few minutes more. I needed to finish this cup of wine and clear my head before going back to the reception. I went past the ladies' room, took a right, and found the small patio off the kitchen. Good. None of the smokers had found it yet. The sun had set. The patio was unlit and stood some distance from the ballroom, but I could see the wedding party through the ballroom's big windows. I could see the wedding people but they couldn't see me. The newlyweds had been summoned for their first dance and they were moving around, to and fro, eyes locked on each other, self-conscious smiles on their faces. They looked positively miserable. Poor things. If they thought this was bad, wait 'til they saw what they'd let themselves in for. I thought of the other couples I'd seen dance on that same floor over the years, at the wedding receptions held at the Natchez when Brian still worked here, and at the other family weddings of the Fahey kids and two of the Moran family kids. Brian stopped coming to family events after he lost his job here, but I kept coming, maybe out of spite. Right here on this very patio, at Lucy Moran's wedding, only a little more than a year after his brother fired Brian, Eddie Fahey invited me out here for a smoke and professed his love, drunk as a priest. I could still remember his red eyes and his unsteady voice. The sadness of it. The exhilaration of being wanted like that again. The way he grabbed me and pressed up against me, like he was doing his best imitation of a movie star. The whiskey on his breath. The touch of his coarse, stubby carpenter's fingers, like big nail files scraping across my face and neck when he kissed me.

"Hello, Ms. Casey," a man said behind me.

Startled, I turned around and saw old Rodney Meeks, the club's handyman, sitting in a dark corner of the patio, smoking one of his trademark menthol cigarettes.

"My God. Rodney? Rodney Meeks? Is that you?"

"Yes, ma'am. In the flesh."

"Well, you're a sight for sore eyes," I said, still shaking from the fright he gave me.

"Nice to see you, too, Ms. Casey."

Funny how Rodney always addressed me as "Ms." instead of "Mrs." I used to wonder if it was a subtle dig against Brian. All these years later and Rodney still worked here. Amazing. I always loved Rodney Meeks. He had a kind of stoic wisdom. He always seemed glad to see me.

Brian and he didn't get along too well, from what I remembered. It had something to do with the fact that Rodney once upstaged him in front of the kitchen staff by lighting the gas pilot on a stove that Brian had struggled for hours to fix before proclaiming it broken and dead.

"Nice day for a party," he said.

"It is, indeed."

"So it's the old man Fahey's granddaughter getting married?"

"Yes."

"She sure is pretty."

"Yes. She got the Fahey looks."

Suddenly I wondered what Rodney knew. I wondered if he knew the whole story about Brian. I wondered, irrationally, if he knew about me and Eddie, if he could see the memory of our kiss that had just left my head.

"How have you been, Rodney?"

"I can't complain. An' nobody would care if I did. My health is okay. Doctor said I should quit the cigarettes, but I can't see how it makes much difference now. I only got so much time left anyhow. Only so many more weddings and burials before my own time comes. Figure I might as well enjoy what's left."

"How's your family, Rodney? How's your wife?"

"Betsy's been gone now about five years, Ms. Casey. But my boys are good. Both in college now."

"Oh, Rodney. I'm sorry. I'm so sorry about Betsy."

He nodded and looked down and we were both quiet for a few seconds. Then he raised something to his lips—a silver flask. He took a long sip from it. He saw me following it with my eyes, which locked with his for a moment, and then he lowered the flask from his lips and passed it to me in one smooth motion. I drank from it and the cheap whiskey filled my sinuses and warmed the back of my neck. I passed it back to Rodney and thanked him and we watched the people dance on the other side of the glass as if they wouldn't see tomorrow.

"Let me ask you something, Rodney. Now that all this time has gone by. What happened with Brian and that Rogers girl? Why did she tell the Faheys what happened, and how did she know about it in the first place?"

"Been a long time. Let me see what I remember. Armando and Brian planned the thing with the grave. I suppose you know all about that. What you might not know is that I was his lookout boy…" He smiled and shook his head. He took a drag from his smoke and leaned back in his seat. I got the sense that he felt he might've said too much.

"Rodney, you don't need to worry," I said. "This is ancient history. All is forgiven. In fact, Brian's here tonight."

Rodney's eyes widened. "He is? Well, I'll be. Guess time heals, like they say. Anyhow, yeah. So I was moonlighting back then as a neighborhood security guard, so I made sure nobody bothered us while we did the deed. Brian paid me five hundred bucks to do it, which was a lot of money for me then. Yep, sure was. I'm not sorry. I needed the cash. But I didn't bargain for the job we had in front of us. Had I known, I wouldn't've done it for five *thousand* dollars. The night we did it he waited and waited until the streets emptied out. Then he called us and we met at the club, must've been four in the morning. Brian had already done the job with bolt cutters and the axe, but he wanted us to watch the edges of the cemetery for him while he got the watch off the dead man. And everything was fine for a few weeks until the Rogers girl did what she did. Armando told her what happened, because he wanted to get in her pants. Hell, Ms. Casey, *I* wanted to get in her pants, too." I laughed at that, which encouraged Rodney. The whiskey had gone to my head. "Every damn man in this club did. She was *that* pretty. Not nice, you understand, but real good-looking and saucy. Anyhow, the Rogers girl told on Brian because she tried to blackmail him and it didn't work. She wanted half the money to stay quiet, and he refused. So then she threatened to sue and started running her mouth. She claimed Brian was harassing her..." Rodney paused to see how I'd react. I didn't say anything, and he kept going: "...or some nonsense like that. I never liked her, to tell the truth. Never trusted her. But I can't really say what happened for real and what was made up, Ms. Casey. Sure caused a lot of trouble around here 'til old man Fahey paid her off. She tipped them off about the axe, and once they found it in the crypt, it was over. Damn shame, really, since police in this town couldn't be bothered to look at it too deep. Had to have their work done for them. Linden was a bad man, after all. Some kind of Nazi. She should have just left it alone. But that's life. That's just life."

"Yes, that's just life," I said. Then I took the last sip of my wine. "Why leave the axe, Rodney? Why not burn it or throw it in the river?"

"Have always asked myself the same question. Guess we just left it there in a panic."

We both had a laugh about the axe.

"Thanks, Rodney. It was really good seeing you. Take care of yourself."

"Ms. Casey, there's one more thing. Do me a favor. Tell Brian thank you for me, would you?"

"For what?"

"Well, the way I see it, I owe him a lot. I'm still here at the Natchez because of him. He took the blame for the whole thing. Covered for Armando and me both, and I've never gotten the chance to properly thank him. He told old man Fahey that he made us help him by threatening to fire us. He really did right by us."

"Oh," I said. My cheeks burned, and for a moment I couldn't think or speak. "Well, Rodney, Brian is right out there in the dining room. No reason you can't tell him thank you yourself. I know it would mean a lot to him."

Rodney lowered his eyes and shook his head.

"Okay, Rodney. I'll tell him."

When I went back in, people were fanning out to find their assigned tables. To my surprise, Brian and I were seated at table five, the same table as Eddie and

Anne Fahey. Who assigned the seating? Oh, Lord. I made my way over slowly, scanning the crowd for Brian.

"There she is!" said Eddie, standing up to greet me when I reached our table. "How have you been, Mrs. Casey?" He gave me a tight, lingering hug. He held me too long and I let him do it. My head rested on his shoulder for a second and my eyes found Brian walking toward our table, watching us embrace. I wondered what he was thinking—and what Anne was thinking. Brian stopped where he was, about twenty feet away. He stared at me intensely, looking angry, defeated, and somehow satisfied all at once. I felt Eddie wrapped around me still. He was on his way to being drunk. I could smell the whiskey on his breath, and I could hear the raspy sound of him breathing. I remembered the sweet poison taste of his mouth when we kissed, the whiskey and tobacco. I let go, pulled away from Eddie, and sat down. I only turned my head for a second, just long enough to find my seat beneath me. But when I looked back, Brian was gone. I scanned the room but didn't see him. I wondered if he'd left.

For a few minutes, it was just me and the Faheys at the table. To keep things light, I asked Eddie about the Nonni juice and he told us the whole story of getting buttonholed by the American salesman on the plane from Shannon. The story was much funnier coming from Eddie. He had Anne and me laughing.

A few minutes later, the table had filled up. A few minutes after that, Brian finally came and sat down with us. Everyone was polite, but I could tell Brian wanted to disappear.

Eddie didn't make eye contact with him until the dessert came. Then he raised his knife and clinked it against his wineglass to silence the table. "I'd like to raise a glass to the lovely bride and groom, my niece and new nephew-in-law. May they live long lives together and make lots of babies. Hear, hear!"

Everyone raised their glasses and toasted the bride and groom. Then they started talking among themselves again, thinking Eddie had finished his toast. But he hadn't. He tapped his wineglass again, and the table fell silent a second time. "I'd also like to make a toast to someone who is making a homecoming of sorts. Mr. Brian Casey, who used to work for this fine establishment. He stayed away for a while, but he's finally come back to bury the hatchet."

Someone laughed. I don't know who. The hair on the back of my neck stood up. My face flushed. I looked at Brian, who was looking down at his untouched dessert plate. He looked stricken and suddenly old, and my heart went out to him in that moment. I reached out and took his hand in mine. Without thinking, I stood up and led him onto the dance floor.

For a while, we were the only ones dancing. We danced slowly and did not speak. By the second song, the dance floor had filled up around us. We danced and danced for what seemed like hours. I can remember Eddie and Anne dancing right next to us, and I can remember Anne looking at me with an apology in her eyes. All beauty and grace. I can remember slow dancing with Brian to *Unchained Melody*. I can remember trying to imagine what went through Brian's head the night he robbed the dead man. I could picture him skulking about that creepy cemetery, struggling with the wire cutters, drenching his clothes with sweat and constantly wiping it away from his eyes. I could see him cursing and groping through the darkness of the vault and having words with the men who helped him, talking down to them, and them hating him for keeping them there. It must've taken them at least an hour to do it all. What drove him? Were the gambling debts real? Did he do it to just get one over on Eddie? Or did he do it for me? The possibility that he had some kind of a noble purpose, however twisted, had never occurred to me until this moment. Maybe he needed to assert himself. Everyone had gone out and made their way in the world, but, for reasons he would never understand, Brian got left behind, stunted, working for the brother of a man who had scorned his wife back in Ireland.

Funny how Brian's mind filed the event. Long after it happened, he told me that nobody understood. People said he dug up a corpse, but that wasn't true. New Orleans is a swamp, so bodies are buried aboveground, in vaults and crypts, to prevent the coffins from floating away. Cities of the Dead, they call the cemeteries. He did no digging—just busted a lock to take a stolen watch off a once-evil man. And he planned to give some of the money to charity, some kind of Holocaust museum or something. Nobody understood poor Brian's true intentions.

At one point, they started playing the old songs, and the women started step dancing. A few songs into it, they played an old rebel ballad called *Kitty*, about a man who runs away and abandons his lover to escape prison. Before the first verse was sung, Eddie came over and poked Brian on his shoulder, hard. It was more of a shove than a poke, and I could feel the weight of it. "I'll have this next dance with your beautiful bride," he said. It wasn't a request.

I could feel Brian's heartbeat quicken with rage, and it scared me. He let go of me and tried to move away. But I held on to him and leaned forward and put my mouth up to his ear and whispered, "Wait. Please stay." Then I turned to Eddie, met his eyes, and said, "No, Eddie. I don't think so. Not now."

Brian and I finished that dance together. Then, before the next song started, we walked off the dance floor. With our backs turned to the Faheys, we kept walking arm-in-arm and left for home without saying goodbye to anyone.

*Joshua Bennett*

# PALIMPSESTINA

I spend most days studying the eloquent beast
juxtaposed against a given black
body living into its singular joy i.e. forsythia
& lemonade in the middle of July, steel
pan playing loud enough to feel it. Hands
aloft in praise mistaken for surrender, left

then right, slowly. Nothing left
to an officer's imagination lest he manumit the beasts
which call his corners quarters, think his hands
a tempest sent to scar the endless black
expanse. George Jackson bends steel
with every letter, & I can think only of the forsythia

growing in his lover's eyes, how *forsythia*
sounds like the name of a girl I knew before I left
town for hallways bereft of steel
-faced boys who named sorrow the beast
they slew daily, how they sustained a kind of black
humor about this business of being bound to one's hands

as conflict's only punctuation. Survival: how I lend my hands
to lyric's labor, as if forsythia
or chrysanthemum could bloom from black
ideas dancing across a screen. What is there left
to say about the dead space betwixt soul & beast,
the law as an eternal mouth, anxious for blood & steel?

Before I learned to steel
nerves in the face of a stranger's hands
swinging swift as a beast's
heart in chase or heat, my arms were forsythia
freshly grown, thinnest green, bad for business. Which left
only a world of fugitive black

letters to serve as my loophole of retreat, a black
wholeness to ease the wounds, flesh of gem & steel
to reflect the light of those that left
only faintest trace behind. May these hands
forever tend the soil of those songs, the forsythia
lives straining for air against the beast

-ly fear which seeks to quell the beast
who sleeps within, the voice left praying *forsythia,*
*forsythia, make a world of these hands.*

*Matt W. Miller*

## ABOUT THE DECK AN IDIOT

but bivouacked in this sea, set upon an egg, its single fin set up just right
for carving these shoulder high lefts, he wades the is of was and will be.

Summer slips the moon its light. August's old lobster boats putter across
an eastern scrim of night that is blue stone dissolving in old bone Atlantic.

To eyes bent west, the sun sets fat in the dunes, cottages, and marshes, tossing
its billion embers into the foam. He bobs hip deep between this fire, that gloam.

Waves like wine glasses mouth wishes and, burnished in the sunset, score a pink
so sore distinct from the night behind. Waiting for a set he stares

into eternity's roll inside those fragile hollows. And then a billow peaks.
He turns, paddles languidly from the scree of whitewater's roiling

gravity until board and he gut the earth, both yanked into a pull of birth. Everything
is easy, as if falling down a dream. He pops up, clumsy feet

gripping the wax. The sandbar bores its curl into the brine. He tucks into a
flicker of time, a mere dry tick in the barrel. And then the eye upon his babble

winks, the green room closes the door, the ceiling sinks. He cannot crouch out.
Arms fail and back bends. He flails, stumbles again. Any world watching

watches him thrown into spit of rose and milk. For all his able, for all his struggle
to stand against the fall or fall again to stand, for all the universe there

he scans, he goes about the deck an idiot. But bivouacked in this sea, paddling
back into the deep's horizon, he wades the is of was and will be.

*Don Schofield*

# DRILLING

*for Melitta*

Someone across the valley
is opening a well, or maybe a road
from your small house, its trembling walls and tables
filled with photographs of you smiling
beside your daughter, son or second husband.

"Mark reads to me in bed," you said
when I saw you last, your oxygen machine
softly pumping beside you, "holds me upright
so I can shower, feeds me and carries me
into the bathroom." Sitting on the porch,
breathing in that rich air, you insisted
he deserved some "hot young babe," not you
like this, admitted you had one last wish,
to live alone again. Turning to leave,

I saw the trees on Mt. Taygetos
covered in kudzu, as if dressed for mourning,
heard the cows lowing below your house,
in mourning too, imagined you laid out
on a steel table, alone at last. Now
it's all those photographs I see, your smile
growing larger and larger as it fades,
a coin dropped into a well, a gleaming.

*Anne Witty*

# FORBIDDEN RICE

I could brew a pot
of cinnamon
steam Forbidden Rice
and simply feast

the dark and purpling
flavors bring
to my tongue the spice
of kissing you

on a hot street canopied
by languid leaves
at the end
of summer

*Mariana Lin*

# MAMA

Puts on lipstick
No kissing, no kissing

Drinks too many saketinis
Is gone missing

Snake streets meet jagged
eyes, too much, too much—

So happy music empties, goes forward
like a crutch

It's how Mama can shimmy into
silk-bottomed panties

It's how Mama hums lullabies
and envies gay love, and kills kills

hope with cold-ironed words
smooth, no rounded edges

pane clean and mirror-slippery
to cradle baby, baba.

It's why Mama
eats elephants alone, no television.
No noise.

*Margot Douaihy*

# My Money

My money's on the guy in last place, the runt of the litter, the bloody knee.

My money's on the missing sock, the single Lego, the lock with no key.

My money's on the run-on sentence, the misplaced comma, the Fail.

My money's on the deer in headlights, the lost, the One White Whale.

My money's on the introvert, the B-/C+, the barely audible.

My money's on the The—ubiquitous, unanimous, invisible.

My money's on the iffy, the jinx, the artist screaming in the park.

My money's on the blinking cursor, the negative space, the space bar.

My money's on the secret wing, the Gelfling, the girl eating alone in her car.

My money's on the sun shower, Spring snow, the healers, the confused.

My money's on the Podling, the flat tire, the spinning wheel, the bruised.

My money's on the tattooed, kind-hearted outlaw, the dented and darned.

My money's on Sisyphus. Sure, the hill is high and rock is heavy,
but look at those arms.

*JL Schneider*

# YOUR WIFE IS A BIRD

On the way to work
ice sheets from a Buick roof
flap-jack like white guillotine blades
gutting the bland wind of commutation.
There's undecided temperature, a poem on the radio
about passengers and silence and something—always
with these fucking poets—something
about writing it down.

I take off work early
come home and drink the rest of the day.
I don't understand the rules. I thought the poet said
make a splash in the Dry Dept. Who knows how
long you're going to last. I thought he said be lightning
not the bug. Your cat is a stringed instrument—you don't know
how to play a cat. Your wife is a bird—you don't know
where she goes in winter—you don't know
who wrote this.

*George Drew*

## Just One Lousy Apple

*To Dawn Potter*

How many poems about that damned garden
do we have to endure? How many read?
Millions, it seems. And now another one,
by a really fine poet. It's a fine poem, too,
told from Eve's feminist point of view,
about how she couldn't say no to such
succulent temptation. One lousy apple,
and it was all over—for her and for Adam,
poor hapless tool, for you, for me. Eve
of course makes all sorts of excuses,
even blaming it on her having thought,
half asleep as she says she was, that it was
Adam's voice calling her from a dream's
sweet insouciance; that it was sexual,
the apple with her hungry mouth around it;
that in the end, she was whorish in her desire.
And so it goes, on and on, the tree taller
than any, the apple juicier, the myth mythier.
But jesus, we know what it was really all
about, what really drove her—boredom.
Boredom with perfection, boredom with Adam,
boredom with her status as First Spouse,
boredom with The Father and his rules.
All she wanted was a hot time in the cool
little garden, and by god, she got it,
for a little while anyway. We were about to say,
let's say it was just one lousy apple,
that's all; and let's leave Eve there drooling
in her fecund plot over the McIntosh,
or whatever the hell kind of apple she's
about to bite into. But oops—too late!

## Just One Lousy Apple

Now we've gone and done it, another poem
about what it opposes; another poem
about that garden. Though it's lovely to have
the mother of all whores to blame for the mother
of all mistakes, let's bury the apple once
and for all; let's take an eternal time out.
Oh, please, let's have a moratorium on myth.

*Melissa J. Varnavas*

## THE SOUND OF A PLASTIC FORK SCRAPING AGAINST THE BARK OF A TREE

Let me tell you about this
man this morning who

wore a baseball hat, pants, short sleeve
tee shirt. He was holding

something, I couldn't see what, in his
left hand. His right hand held a plastic fork.

He was on the other side

of the street, rotating
his body at the waist, swinging

his arms back
and forth. Back.

And. Forth.
Like a metronome.

He held the plastic fork horizontally
so the tines scraped against the bark to make

a noise.

Not musical, but not un-
musical, the repetition of it all.

I looked up from my walk, thinking:
*Bird*? Thinking: *What is that sound?*

The problem of identifying.

*What* is *that sound?*

Searching out its source like I
do the name of the unknown.

Cardinal? *No.* Dog? *No.* Weed whacker? *Must be.*
Distant train? Flag in the wind? Baby crying? But

no. None of that. Just this man swinging
his fork back and forth, back and forth. And all

I can think is: Off his meds. I hope he doesn't see

me. I hope he doesn't follow me. I am just
out for my morning walk. I walk faster. And I

forget about him.

When I come back this way again he is gone.
So I don't learn why he swung that fork,

Don't know if it was the motion of the swing,
the pressure of his hand against the plastic

handle, the vibration of it pulsing up
his arm as it scraped the bark, the space

between him and the tree filling up

with energy and the possibility of the coming
action, his feet planted in the ground.

The muscles of his back as he twisted, swung.

Or maybe it wasn't
the movement but the sound

that caught him,
a cicada-esque

memory repeating down
the cilia of his ear.

*Clark Knowles*

# THE TROJAN EXPERIENCE

MY BROTHER JUSTIN PLAYS IN A BAND called The Trojan Experience and they've been touring behind their latest CD for fifteen months and he's coming home tomorrow. He doesn't want to come home. He has to. My father called up Tad Burgo, the band's manager, and left about a thousand messages and held off on the service and waited and waited and the messages must have finally got through because Justin called his old friend Banks and told him to come over and tell my father don't worry he's coming home and Banks came over and did just that and my father said he wasn't worried anyway and then him and Banks stood and looked at each other through the screen door for a long time and then Banks turned around and got on his moped and drove down Best Street toward downtown, probably going to work at the Tar Pit, where he's worked ever since before Justin got famous. In The Trojan Experience, Justin calls himself Flame. The first time TE was on the cover of *Rolling Stone,* Justin was there with Mox and Q-face sticking out their tongues and holding beer bottles and the headline said *Straight Outta Troy*, which was technically true—the whole band was born and raised in Troy, NY—but also stupid. A strip of Trojan Magnum rubbers dangled out of Justin's shirt pocket like a string of sausages, some photographer's idea of a joke. After their second album on SubPop, TE signed to a major label and released *Flat Broke* and were anointed the saviors of rock 'n' roll. Justin sent Dad checks every month. They sat on the sideboard in my mother's blue crystal bowl. Once I asked my father if he was ever going to cash them and he picked them up and waved them in the air and then set them down. Later, they were gone. After *Flat Broke*, they toured for two years. They sold songs to Nike and Taco Bell and Budweiser and their concerts were always sold out and you couldn't walk down the street without seeing a Trojan Experience t-shirt or walk through the CD section at Wal-Mart without seeing a huge poster of the band or turn on the radio without hearing any of the five number-one songs: *Back Breaker, Boob Man, Total Fail, Sundried,* and *Greetings from the Gutter*. Of course, the three-year wait for the follow-up to *Flat Broke* combined with all the rumors of band infighting and producer trouble seemed like the beginning of the end. The band scrapped two whole CD's worth of songs and went to Istanbul to record new music. The resulting *Ne Var Ne Yok?*—which is Turkish for *What's Happening?*—surprised everyone, maybe me the most. By then, we hadn't seen Justin in over two years. He'd always been kind of a goof. Not stupid, but careless. My mother missed him, though. I was too serious. He was easier with his smile and better at parties and charming to her friends and acquaintances from her assorted knitting clubs and service committees, even when he had a safety pin through his nose, a short-lived experiment done mostly to freak out my father. *Ne Var Ne Yok* isn't careless or stupid. Justin has always been a furious guitar player, but now it's obvious that he's sophisticated, too, although he'd tell me to fuck off if he heard me say that. I could listen to *Ne Var Ne Yok?* again and again and still not figure out how it all holds together. It's not like the music some bands make when they get near their thirties. It's not soft or bogus or about how life is passing them by or how they're starting to understand and appreciate domestic life or the love of a good woman. It's loud and fierce and if you aren't chilled by Justin's ripping syncopation or Q-face's demonic bass lines or Mox's polyrhythmic percussion, you simply don't have a soul. Sasha Frere-Jones compared it to the leap that the Beatles took when they matured and made *Sgt. Peppers*, but before *Sgt. Peppers*, they made *Rubber Soul* and *Revolver* so you knew something big was on the way. When The Trojan Experience went to Istanbul, it should have been a last gasp, a flailing attempt to be relevant, but that isn't what happened. Even the names the band chose to call themselves suddenly sounded out of place—would a guy who calls himself Flame write such a howling, bone-crushing song like *Steal the Bread* in which a family urges their youngest child, a girl named Bella, to steal bread so that they can eat? Someone named Flame shouldn't write a song called *Great Dismal Swamp*, which is about Wal-Mart paving the world. And someone named Flame shouldn't write a song called *It's My Heart and It's Cold*, which is about, I think, brothers, and how much the singer loves his own. And the most crazy thing about the music is that despite all the strange Turkish influences—the opening sounds very similar to the Adhan, the Muslim call to prayer—and the added instruments and the two songs with orchestration and the closing song featuring a bass clarinet—is just how *hard* it all *rocks*. If you haven't heard it yet, I know it sounds crazy to say that something like this could rock at all. I'm not explaining it well. My mother loved this CD, too. When she first listened to it, she put her hands over her heart and tears welled up in her eyes and she reached over from her place in her bed and put her hand in my hand and we both listened. My father stood back in the hallway, outside her room because the smells in there made him crazy and for years I was the only one who could stand it, but we knew he was listening and we knew he was moved too, though if you asked him, he'd say that the last real musician was Chet Atkins and if I'd come out of the room, he would've moved down the hall pretending he was doing something or just coming from somewhere or adjusting the painting of the deer near the lake, which was always crooked. All of it was hard for him, of course, and no one blames him for being who he is. I only wish Justin could have come home sooner. The day before we heard he was coming home, I was sitting at the Tar Pit and Banks was mixing drinks for a bunch of sorority sisters from Russell Sage College and one of TE's songs came on the jukebox, an old one called *V-8*, back from when they were stupid and wild, the kind of punks who would have made fun of anyone making an album called *Ne Var Ne Yok?*, and someone told the sorority girls that I was Flame's brother and they gathered around me asking what he was like. They couldn't have known that my mother's room was suddenly empty or that my father was sitting in the recliner in the living room with a cup of cold coffee next to him on the table, or that I didn't know what to do with myself now that the one thing I was good at doing was no longer needed, so they were happy and bouncy and a few of them were wiggling their butts as the song beat out its primitive rhythm. *V-8* was about this car that my father had when we were young—some flat-roofed, big-wheeled monster that he held together with baling wire and duct tape. How would you describe your brother's music, one of the girls—I think it was Brianna—asked, and I said, You ever see one of those big old junky cars from the seventies? Brianna nodded, but she wasn't following me. You don't see them much anymore, I said, because everyone has a nice car these days, but I'm talking about a rust bucket with the seats all threadbare and if you lift up the floor mats you can see the street and one of the headlights only works when it wants to and the steering wheel is huge, easily twice the size of a new car's steering wheel and there's a suicide knob on the wheel and the radio only gets one station because someone ripped off the antenna and the back is jacked up but the shocks are worn down and the hood doesn't shut right and the doors stick and you have to use a pair of vise-grips to roll down the window because the crank has been gone forever and the side-view mirror is cracked and barely stuck to the car and the fabric is coming off the ceiling and hanging down and the seatbelts have been stuck back in the seats for so long that if you tried to pull one out, it'd be covered in old jelly beans and cigarette butts and crumbs from a sandwich that you swear you never ate, but you can tell that the car used to be something, a beast, something to write home about. Now, not so much. You get in the car and the person behind the wheel is sort of crazy, but you knew that before you got in and it doesn't bother you. You get in and he gets the car going pretty good. He tells you that the thing probably shouldn't go over fifty or so because of the shimmy, but he doesn't seem to be listening to himself. He pushes it up past fifty and close to sixty and you sense the car straining, adjusting to the added ten miles per hour. The hood starts to rattle, but it's all okay because the guy knows his own car, right? He knows what it can do and what it can't do. So when he pulls up on the highway, it's okay. You watch the speedometer going up and up and you notice the whole thing is shaking now, the whole car rumbling and roaring up through your legs and into your ass and up your spine and into your head because it's going seventy-five and that's way too fast. Even the speedometer is rocking, the little arm jiggling on its coiled wire between seventy-five and eighty and then eighty-five and ninety. But the driver is comfortable, one arm resting on the window ledge, the wind blowing every which way, so you get comfortable too. You put one foot up on the dash and the other out the window. Through the dash, you can feel the motor—God that thing has power! It's loose and straining and something is whining like crazy on the other side of the firewall, but the pistons are jamming and the wind is blowing against the sole of your right foot and the trees are a blur and the sunlight coming in the window is so bright that you have to close your eyes, not all the way, just 'til they're sort of half open and half closed and everything is caught up in a haze and you think for a second that you might be crying but you realize that there's nothing to cry about and what you're really doing is learning how to sing, that the car around you is really just a massive and complicated song and all the instruments are humming along, even when you aren't listening, and when that side mirror flies off the door and bounces behind you down the highway, that's part of the song too, a cymbal crash that slowly fades away, and the song is so good that you don't want it to end though you know it will. Please, don't stop, you want to tell the driver, but you don't speak. It's all in your head and your eyes are still half-mast. He guns it one last time to push you over a hundred miles per hour and everything exists in that final moment before the car breaks apart into a million pieces. That's what Trojan Experience sounds like to me, I said. Later in the evening, after everyone had cleared out of the bar, Banks said to me that I'd probably get laid more if I just said: Trojan Experience is balls-out rock and roll. Probably, I said, but sometimes you just have to listen to your heart.

*Mark Brownlow*

# Breaking into a Broken Home

After splitting a bottle of Beefeater and smoking the pot hidden in Dan's brother's pillowcase, Dan and I decided that to truly better my life, to allow me to overcome certain emotional obstacles and map out the path toward a stable adulthood, we had to break into my father's house. And it had to be now.

"Motherfucker," Dan said.

He shifted to the edge of the chair. We were in his living room. The chair had a floral print, creeping vines. Cigarette burns blackened the center of some leaves, as if a caterpillar had been lunching. A *Yellow Pages* replaced one leg. Dan stroked his chin like a psychiatric patient who believes he's the shrink.

"Look at the shit he's put you through. We need to pee on his rugs. We need to do *something*. Or else you'll be fucked up your whole life. You'll feel helpless, like you never did anything back. Like you're worthless. Don't let him get away with that."

"Let's do this," I said.

We stumbled together through the front door. Outside I looked up and I'd never seen that sky. Dan's house was on Great Plain Ave., with a gas station across the street. I practically lived at Dan's house, played basketball beneath the flood light in the back in my AC/DC t-shirt on cold autumn nights, had probably stood in this exact spot five feet from his front steps at least a hundred times, but the sky had just given birth to these stars. Snowflakes drifted as if searching the night for a home. They were blind and lost and it did something to me inside. Where had this all come from? Why had I never seen it before? The starlight between clouds was so fragile, trembling. Were worlds hidden in each moment?

I'd left my coat on Dan's couch, but a coat, any kind of self-protection, was crushed beneath that sky. It would have been impossible now to return to the house with its stern black shutters and blue paint peeling like shedding skin. I'd stepped into a stranger's dream. The pupil-less eyes of streetlamps stared unblinking, and yet somehow it all felt holy.

"A turning point," I heard Dan say. "You know where he lives, right?"

"The other side of town," I said. "Follow me."

"We're on a mission," Dan said.

My sneakers sank into the snow. My feet were someone else's. My head floated on my shoulders. And yet I saw everything clearly. I heard the crunch where snow had melted during the day and frozen again in the night. I smelled what I thought was chicken soup and tasted blood, as if I'd bitten my tongue.

I snapped a piece of ice from a snow bank and gripped it between my pink fingers. Light shimmered inside! How had it gotten in? How did light survive the darkness?

Dan and I didn't speak. For a moment I fell asleep standing and maybe dreamed and woke with no idea where we were going. This was the town I'd grown up in. My feet had worn grooves in this road. I'd trick-or-treated in the neighborhood. Stacy lived on this street. It hurt to think of her. I wondered if we'd really broken up, and yet she wasn't with me now. I tried to remember what had happened. Had we argued?

We crossed the empty road. The trees of a bird sanctuary huddled on the other side. I'd once dropped a cube of hashish in there, searched for it on my knees in tears, and then later discovered it miraculously, as if God had meant for me to pluck that hashish from among the leaves. And now I heard an animal groaning, suffering between the same bare maples.

I approached the dying thing warily. I wanted to help it, rescue it from death, from pain. The trees had rolled up their dark sleeves, revealing bony arms. Only a few more steps. I wanted to whisper in its furry ear that the next life *will* be better, whether it were true or not. I wanted at least to offer the hope; it was a gift I could give. I stretched out my hands.

Dan stepped from behind a tree, wiping green spittle from his chin. "Temporary set-back," he said. "Let's continue."

I counted the houses. We'd passed only six.

"Shit," I said. "This'll take all fucking night."

I'd been in my father's house once three years earlier when I was twelve. It wasn't his house. It belonged to my parents' friends, and their family, and my father was living there. The husband had stayed for a while. Where had they all slept?

But the husband was gone now, and my dad lived with the wife and her two children. Our families had met in church.

My younger brother and I were invited to their home. Here's what I remember: everyone acted as if things were okay. It was easier for my brother and I—we could believe it because we weren't old enough to know any better. For all I understood, this was how divorces worked. My younger brother, who was eight, asked my dad's new wife, although I don't know if they were married yet, "Are you and my mom switching places?"

I remember a leather recliner in the living room, where I sat when the son, the first kid I'd known with a "hyperactive disorder," called my dad "Dad."

I remember sitting on a bed with the daughter, a teenager dressed in black and listening to The Cure. I wanted to ask her why she was frightened—she seemed that way to me—but I was only twelve and I didn't have the question. She showed me her secret writings about teens in trouble, about boys and girls making out, about breasts being touched. She read to me with the door locked, the notebook flat in her palms like a holy book, in awe of the power of her own words, of her feelings, and maybe then I realized writing could be a way out.

Later we all played Monopoly in the living room.

Months after the visit my little brother would call, maybe the first time he'd dialed a phone by himself, wondering when we could come again, and he'd hear my father's voice in the background saying, "Tell him I'm not here."

Would you believe my father read to me every night when I was a child?

Dan and I stood outside the Friendly's at the edge of Needham Center. The windows framed the town, threw back its thin reflection. The town but not the town. The cars, the people, all life incinerated, the empty streets powdered with its ash.

We placed cold hands on the glass, peeked into the empty restaurant, the light sucked from it by the night, the deserted booths where families in spring devoured greasy hot dogs and burgers and cherry-topped sundaes while discussing little league games and teachers and birthday parties. I pressed my nose flat against the pane. I wanted to hurl a rock. I wanted to take off my shoes and cut my feet with the shards.

"Have you ever had a Jim Dandy?" Dan asked. "Five fucking scoops of ice cream. I could shit my pants just thinking about it."

We wandered past Scorby's, the camera store, and the Music Center, where I'd rushed to buy John Lennon's *Double Fantasy* the day after he was shot. The lip of the awning was swollen with ice.

We took a break and sat on a bench in the town common, the bench at which the biggest, fattest kid in our high school, who always wore a denim jacket with the sleeves cut off and who was world-renowned for selling great pot, had hung out among autumn leaves that lined the street like orphans. He had rings of curly hair and was nicknamed the Woofenmonster. He'd sat behind me in my freshman English class. While Mr. McDonough, who was deaf in one ear, lectured about Scout in *To Kill a Mockingbird*, the Woofenmonster recited from memory page after page of *A Clockwork Orange* in a crazy whisper.

It was that kind of town.

"Do you think there are roads out of here?" I asked Dan.

"Not tonight," he said.

"My ass is wet," I said.

"I feel absolutely nothing," Dan said.

"Have you ever broken into a house?" I asked.

"Not that I remember."

"I mean, how does it work? Do we smash a window and turn a latch or something?"

"I think we just figure out our options once we get there."

"Sounds like a lack of a plan."

We stood across the street from the house, the snow burying our legs to the knee. We were the only ones on Earth now. We'd inherited the abandoned night, but the stars had been replaced with glittery glass jewelry, the entire scene staged in cardboard and paper snow, and I wanted to give it all back.

The house was a Colonial, built at least 150 years before, like many of the houses in my Massachusetts town. People had lived and probably died in there. People had fought and made love and raised families, people my dad and his new family didn't know and never would know and probably never thought about. Between the same walls. And Dan and I stood outside of it all, studying the windows for vulnerability, any weakness, and I wondered if kids from a hundred years ago had ever stood in the snow where I now stood, filled with as much hatred and confusion and emptiness as I felt, or whether I were the first.

I knew no one would be home because my mother had told me that my father had taken his new family to Florida, to where my own mother, who'd never touched a palm tree, had always dreamed of escaping.

We walked behind the house in the silence that comes before something gets broken.

The patio and lawn had vanished in the snow, but a narrow walkway had been carefully shoveled to the edge of the patio, probably by my dad, and then neglected and layered with snow again. Piled snow softened the shapes of patio furniture. Briefly I felt afraid. Hidden ice made our feet slip. We followed the walkway to the back door, which was locked, and then found a window that looked into the living room, where I could see the same recliner I remembered, only now everything—the television, the couch, the lamp—was drawn like a charcoal sketch.

"Do you wanna do the honors? Or should I?" Dan asked.

Honors? Where had that word come from?

"It's all you," I told him.

"No, really," he said, "it's all *you.* But I'll take care of this part."

Dan used his elbow, protected by the denim sleeve, to smash a hole near the window latch. The glass rang as it shattered inside, while the few shards that broke toward us made dark shapes where they'd fallen.

"Easy as pie," he said.

"You're like MacGyver."

Then Dan reached his hand through the small hole and unlatched the window.

When he brought back his hand I noticed drops of blood, and the blood and the places where the shards had fallen together created strange patterns on the white paper snow.

"A MacGyver in training," I said.

"You don't have a band-aid in your pocket, do you?"

"I'll take over from here," I said.

I lifted the window from the outside as more shards released from the pane and dropped into the snow and into the house.

"Beauty before youth," I said.

"No, no, I insist," Dan said, gesturing with his bleeding hand toward the opening.

I checked the frame for broken glass then wiggled through. It was a reverse birth. I was squeezing myself into a murky womb. It was like opening your eyes under water.

As I dropped to the floor I felt the painful pricking of glass through my shirt like tiny animal bites, but none of the bites were deep enough to matter.

Dan followed, dripping blood onto the carpet.

I pulled him in, guiding his shoulders to keep him from falling.

"Maybe you ought to wrap that in something," I told him.

"Shouldn't this be *your* blood?" he asked.

I took a cushion from the couch and slipped off the sleeve and helped Dan wrap his hand. "If you pass out, let me know," I told him.

"Don't worry," he said. "I have plenty of blood."

As our eyes adjusted, the darkness became home and the light outside was strange and unfamiliar.

"I'm hungry," Dan said.

"My dad always had beer in the fridge," I said.

Dan walked into the kitchen and I stood in the living room alone, my soul blurring with the edges of solid things—chairs, a television, a table, the couch—their corners erased. I found the square of carpet where we'd set up the Monopoly board. I sat in the recliner. It made me want to cry or vomit, so I got up. Where was the anger? I'd imagined destroying this house, but in the end I only wanted to destroy myself. What exactly, I wondered, had I done wrong?

Dan returned.

"There's nothing in the fridge except spring water and mustard. Want some?" He handed me a plastic bottle of water.

"So what now?" Dan asked.

"I don't know. What do you suggest?"

"Let's pee on his rugs like I said. Give him something to remember you by." He reached down to unzip.

"I don't know," I said. I felt as if I were on a lightless stage after the audience has gone home, and who pees on a stage? "Let's look around first."

"Okay." Dan zipped up. "Let's steal something," he said.

"Like what?"

"I'm not talking about money, or jewelry, although I'm not entirely against the idea. I mean something that's important to you. Something he took from you that you want back."

"He didn't take anything from me."

"That's where you're wrong," he said.

Downstairs my dad had set up a study. Books filled a shelf, the titles partially visible, fractured by shadow into single words: "*...Falling...Misremembered...Years...Ghost...Fried...*" none of which made sense alone.

I recognized the green swivel chair I'd played beneath while he corrected college exams. He'd never shooed me away when I came to disturb him.

Dan saw me looking at the chair. "You want it?" he asked. "I'll carry it for you."

I reached out to touch it but then stopped myself. I was afraid. Would the frame burn my hand?

"Let's go back up," I said.

We followed the stairs to the main floor, and then the next set of stairs to the top floor where everyone slept. Our boots trailed snow and road salt along the plush carpet. "That's the daughter's room," I said, pointing at the door. "I remember. She read me something about a boy taking off a girl's bra. She must be eighteen or nineteen now."

"Is she hot?"

"You wouldn't kick her out of bed for eating crackers," I said.

"Let's check it out," he said.

The bedroom smelled of young woman, of perfume or apple-scented soaps and lotions, soft and inviting, promising.

"I wonder where her bras are," Dan said.

"Come on," I said.

I pulled him out and we opened the door to the bedroom we thought was the son's, but it turned out to be my dad's. I could see the bed sheets flat and tight, without wrinkles, the outlines of pillows even mounds beneath the headboard. I recognized his leather slippers by the bed, and I crossed to the window to look outside at the night. I was a bird, drifting on currents of wind above the snow-covered street. The beauty suddenly shocked me—the ice along the light poles, the snow rewriting the night in powder and dust, the trees paused as if about to speak the final answer—the eternal secret— but waiting. For me. How could I have imagined not being a part of this?

"Found something," Dan said.

He had been rifling through drawers with one hand, pulling apart clothes in the closet, on a mission.

But instead of a diamond ring or 24-carat necklace, he was holding what appeared to be an open book.

"Ah, look at you," he said, bringing the book closer to the light through the window.

It was a simple, cloth-bound photo album.

There were pictures of my brother and me as toddlers playing Wiffle Ball with my dad, towheaded kids, our skin lightly browned by summer sun, my dad in a Red Sox cap grinning and seemingly proud.

"Close that fucking thing," I said.

"I told you he had something of yours."

"Find me a match," I said.

Dan returned it to a drawer.

"Oh, fuck it," he said. "I'm not having as much fun as I expected, and obviously neither are you. Let's quit this place. There's nothing but bones here anyway."

I followed him down the stairs. We could simply unlock the back door and escape, an easy out, but I stopped. Dan stood on the frozen welcome mat beyond the door looking in at me. In the darkness, could he have really seen me?

"You don't want to do this," he said.

"You go home," I said. "I'm staying a while."

The night sky was dark and cold. Clouds hid the stars. I scanned the sky for snowflakes, but they'd either given up their search or found a new home.

"No, man, really," he said. "I'm not kidding. You've got to walk away. I was wrong about fucking up the place. That won't help. The thing is to walk away. I know it's cold out here, but it's the only other place."

"No," I said.

"Are you sure?"

"Go home," I said.

"Suit yourself," he said. He turned and headed toward the street. His feet crunched the icy surface, and then I couldn't hear them, and then I was in the house.

Alone.

*Steven LaFond*

# Lone Coyote

I'M ON A BUS TO A SWINGERS CLUB in the middle of the desert. The only other people getting on are native Las Vegans, workers of the strip that man the deep fryers, hustle risqué business cards for escort agencies into unsuspecting hands, and an old man dressed as Gene Simmons who took three minutes to lug his karaoke machine onto the bus.

I'm exhausted. I'm aware I'm not going to get laid tonight. I'm not going for that. Fourteen hours straight of standing on my feet at my company's booth at a tech convention I could care less about has gotten me tired of the strip and its catalog of predictable narratives. *Tomorrow I'm Mrs. Ryan, but not tonight.* No matter what I'm wearing, the men at this convention keep coming up to me and asking if I know where the good cocaine is or "where's the party at?" My childhood friend Jimmy's mother used to say that I looked like trouble. In adulthood, that must have settled into the lines of my face.

Thirty minutes out and the land is dark and flat. Here the real desert begins. The bus rolls past a giant billboard of a woman in a bikini holding an AR-15 next to big Comic Sans letters that say, "Our Shooting Range is 24 Hours." Under the moon, I see a coyote loping through the scrubland next to a construction site. He's hunting by himself. You and me both, I say to him.

The empty landscape almost lulls me into dreamland until the sudden left turn of the bus and its last stop on Jimmy Durante Boulevard. According to my phone's map, that's seven blocks from where I have to walk. But "blocks" don't apply out here in this wasteland that makes me wish for a UFO to land, or to see a bunch of people ten years younger than me dancing around the burning effigy of a rhinoceros while tossing glow sticks at each other. The place I am going, which the sound guy at the hotel (named Rocky) said was BYOB, was also someone's house. In a Walgreens bag I have a plastic bottle of rum and a lock for the locker room. They have a pool, but I probably won't go in unless I practically go blind from the smell of chlorine.

I walk past a grocery store warehouse and the desert chill slides up my arms with a refreshing breeze that reminds me of springtime in Boston. Out here, in the desert, my New England-raised skin glows under the streetlights and I feel like a hungry ghost. There's stirring in the pit of my stomach.

The storage facility that stands on the corner of the street bears the same name as the house I'm headed to, "The Red Rooster." Back home, people meet at places like SIN, or Discreet Pleasures. I'm heartened by the unpretentious name; it's funny and juvenile. A block down the street, I see it standing in proud defiance of the housing developments encroaching on its turf. Red neon on the gutters, Spanish tile roof. The massive house looks like the bordello from Tim Burton's *Beetlejuice*. I'm limping a bit from all this walking, and I contemplate taking a pull from the rum, but who wants to be the guy walking in alone with an open container?

I get to the door. A plastic picture frame is affixed to its face and it contains a list of rules:

NO CELLPHONES, CAMERAS OR RECORDING EQUIPMENT
NO HATS, THIS IS A HOUSE!
NO FIREARMS OR WEAPONS
NO PROSTITUTES!

I want to know what it's like to be their mailman. I take out a handkerchief from my pocket and I rub my neck to make sure I took off all the concealer I wear at work to hide the part of my tattoo that peeks over my collar, a tentacle of the kraken that hugs my chest and back.

I open the door, which feels rude, as it's a house, but there's no bell and the throbbing bass from just inside makes me think no one will hear my knocking anyway. I walk in and the warm, low red light of the thin hallway envelops me and I see the entire left wall is a mirror. A glass case filled with roosters rests against that wall. Taped to the mirror are more rules: a progressive list about consent

I once read on a friend's feminist Tumblr. Underneath that list is a printed out screed against Obamacare.

"Just you?" an old man asks as he appears in a doorway opposite of the mirrored wall. Over his broad shoulders, I see the glare of a 72" flat screen television. Being a single man, I was told my presence here could be unsettling, like a lone coyote circling the yard.

"Yeah," I say, "Rocky sent me."

"Oh," he says, "30 bucks, then."

I pay him 40 and he gives me 20 back. I don't correct him. My skin goose pimples under my rodeo shirt as I shake his hand and walk down the thin hall, which opens up into a large open floor with a dance space to my right and a small bar to my left. The bartender is in her late forties, her bangs hair-sprayed into place a few inches above her head, reminding me of my babysitters from twenty-plus years ago. I hand her my rum, which she offers to mix with a Coke.

The décor, *oh the décor,* reminds me of David Lynch movies, and I feel I've walked into the early parts of the 1980s where people hadn't yet removed the empty indulgent promises of disco from their lives. When Rocky told me it would be like this, I didn't believe him, so I had to check its review on Yelp and sure enough, the place is dated.

Under the multicolored lights, two couples dance to *Pumped Up Kicks*, their hands just shy of what would scandalize their kids were this a wedding reception. The music actually makes me want to move my recently broken foot, knowing full well I may not be able to walk tomorrow if I do. Good. It'll get me a day off.

I slide onto the floor and lose myself in the downbeat, which transitions into Ol' Dirty Bastard's *Baby I Got Your Money* and I just forget who's there, or not there, for a second and dance. It feels nice. Since the car accident, I don't go out anymore. I get up and shave, put makeup on my neck, sigh and stare at my wife's inert Facebook page on my phone, flip through her pictures and then head to work. I can't afford to live in our apartment much longer.

But here, on the floor, I'm losing myself in what makes sense. Occasionally, I open my eyes to make sure that I'm not too close to anyone else. I move my upper body as much as my lower half because, even with rhythm, you can't take the Goth club out of you when you grow up and start wearing color.

The dance floor is getting crowded and a woman has begun this sort of hopping dance near me. That tipsy, jerky hop that shows she's lubricated enough to move but is unsure of the song or the beat. It reminds me of my wife's aunt, who did the same dance at our wedding reception. She's wearing a short black skirt and has a huge tattoo of thorny vines up the side of her leg. Her hair's cut in a bob and the way the flashing lights catch it, I can tell she dyes out her gray. But she's barely got any wrinkles and when we look at each other she waves and laughs.

So I dance with her for a bit. Around the corners of the floor, men and couples stand, holding beers and drinks and watching those few of us out here. We begin dancing a bit closer, and the rum's made me forget the tightness in my foot as she leans in and yells in my ear.

"Careful, kid," she says, "you'll tire yourself out."

But when the song ends, I follow her through saloon doors into a billiard room and there's a giant dude, maybe sixty-two, wearing a Tommy Bahama shirt, playing pool with a woman in a skin-tight silver dress with a spiderweb panel on her midriff that exposes her belly. Her red hair spills over her freckled shoulders as she bends over the table and takes her shot. I try to ignore the predictable jokes about knocking balls around. I take a seat next to my dance partner.

"It's not one of the big nights," she says. "Tuesday in Vegas is like Sunday everywhere else."

"Looks okay," I say.

"I'm Tammy," she says. She points to the big man "That's my husband, Dennis."

I tell her my name. I get introduced to Dennis. He sees my neck tattoo and asks if I've been to prison.

"No," I say. "In spite of myself."

They've been married for thirty years. Tammy doesn't look that old. I'm introduced to their friend in the silver dress, whose name I forget instantly and then to her husband whose mustache fits in with our surroundings. I sink into their conversations about real estate and 1970s road movies. Dennis and the lady in the silver dress keep playing pool. Tammy asks me where I'm from and I just don't bother lying.

"Boston," I say.

"Here for business?" she asks.

"All this week," I say. "Then again in May."

"What do you do?" she asks.

"Convince rich people they need something they don't in order to make their businesses 'best in class.'"

"What's that mean?"

"Absolutely nothing."

Another single male comes into the room and I'm amazed at the way the four of them freeze him out. His face is hungry and hopeful. Rocky, the sound guy at the hotel, he told me to mention him because he and his girlfriend came here. But even though I'm alone, I'm not receiving the level of shade this guy is getting. Even when I peek into the locker-room next to the billiard table and see a couple close to my age heading further into the house wearing only towels.

Tammy has two kids.

"My girl's twenty-eight," she says, "your age."

"I'm not twenty-eight," I say.

"You look it," she says.

"I'm going to get a drink," I say.

I refill my cup and watch the movements on the sparse dance floor. I'm thinking about how my wife and I used to own those spaces. I think she'd find this place fascinating had she been able to make this trip. Had she been able to do anything ever again. It doesn't smell bad. The people are normal. The signs leading to the orgy room are surprisingly subtle. Tammy is waiting for me by the dance floor and reaches a hand out to me.

She wants to dance to AC/DC and the idea of it is so absurd, so agonizingly dated, I do it. It helps me shed the past few days of talking bullshit with contacts and networking with the type of people I wish I had never met. But I'm a good talker and a phenomenal bullshit artist with a degree in art history. There isn't much else I am qualified to do that won't cripple me before I'm fifty. So, I fell into this communications and marketing thing and have found myself selling "solutions," which was better than trying to sponge off what remains of my wife's savings. Especially now that I can't.

On the floor, I tell my first two lies.

"Where's your girlfriend?" Tammy asks.

"With her boyfriend at home," I say.

"You're okay with that?" she asks.

"Dennis is playing pool with your friends," I say.

"Dennis is here," she says.

"We're here," I say. "She's not. But she knows where I am."

For that moment, I'm not smiling anymore and my arms come down to my sides because I realize that the last lie would never be true again.

# BIOGRAPHIES

NATASHA ARNOLD is a third-year student in Old Dominion University's MFA in Creative Writing Program. Her work has been featured in *Oblong Magazine* and *First Stop Fiction*. She currently lives in Norfolk, Virginia.

LANA AUSTIN holds an MFA from George Mason University. Her poems, interviews, and fiction pieces have been featured in *Mid-American Review*, the *Writer's Chronicle*, *Visions International*, and *Cargoes*, among others. Also a journalist, she has written for numerous newspapers and magazines. After living in multiple countries overseas, she currently resides in Alabama with her husband and three children.

JOSHUA BENNETT hails from Yonkers, New York. He is a doctoral candidate in the English Department at Princeton University and has received fellowships from the Bread Loaf Orion Environmental Writers' Conference, the Callaloo Creative Writing Workshop, the Center for the Study of Social Difference at Columbia University, and the Ford Foundation. Winner of the Lucille Clifton Poetry Prize, his work has been published or is forthcoming in *Anti-*, *Blackbird*, *Callaloo*, *Drunken Boat*, *Obsidian*, and elsewhere.

Born in Trinidad, ROGER BONAIR-AGARD is a poet and writer and national slam champion. An author of several books of poems, his most recent, *Bury My Clothes*, was a 2013 National Book Award Finalist. He is cofounder of the louderARTS Project, where he serves as artistic director. He has taught at Fordham University and New School, among others. Over the past decade, he has worked with the youth at Urban Word in New York City, at Volume in Ann Arbor, and with poetry youth organizations in Seattle, San Francisco, and New York. He presently teaches poetry at the Cook Country Temporary Juvenile Detention Center in Chicago.

GRACE BONDY, a senior in Georgia State University's Rhetoric and Composition Program, has always had a deep love for the literary arts. She was born to two bibliophiles, and she would like to thank them for their unconditional love, support, and reassurance, and for always encouraging her to read and write. She would also like to thank Terry Krugman and Jennifer Forsthoefel for being the most inspirational and influential teachers she ever had the honor of learning from, and for going above and beyond the typical call of duty for a student.

KAY MERKEL BORUFF lives in Dallas with her two labs, Dixie Lantzy and Molly Bloom. Her autobiographical novel *Z.O.S.* is a collection of stories set in the "zone of silence." She volunteers at the Veterans Recovery Center and travels with her niece, Rojji.

MARK BROWNLOW lived in Bangkok, Thailand for six years, teaching English and co-hosting a nationally televised quiz show. He received an MFA from Bennington College and has been published in *The McSweeney's Book of Politics and Musicals*, *McSweeney's Internet Tendency*, *Agni*, *Agni Online*, *Carve Magazine*, *Hobart*, *Pindeldyboz*, *The Boston Phoenix Newspaper*, and *Stuff Magazine.* This year, he was a semi-finalist in the Raymond Carver Short Story Contest. He is currently writing a novel based on the events of Black May, the 1992 student uprisings in Bangkok.

WILLIAM E. BURLESON's eclectic writing credits span various genres and styles. Burleson's short stories have appeared in several literary journals and anthologies, including *The Prague Review*, *34thParallel Magazine*, *The Milo Review*, *Recognize*, and *Cosmic Vegetable*, and include *Hunting in the Dark*, a "flash novel." Burleson is currently developing two novels at once, *The Avenue* and *Ahnwee Days.* He won the 2002 Metropolitan State University playwriting contest with his one-act, *Manfinders.com.* He is the author of *Bi America*, and his columns and essays have been published in several local and national publications, such as *Lavender Magazine* in Minneapolis and *Lambda Literary Review*. Burleson lives in Minneapolis, Minnesota, where he works in communications.

BENJAMIN BUSCH is the author of a memoir, *Dust to Dust*, and his essays have appeared in *Harper's*, *The New York Times Magazine*, and NPR's *All Things Considered.* His poetry has appeared in *North American Review*, *Prairie Schooner*, *Five Points*, *The Florida Review*, *Oberon*, and *Michigan Quarterly Review*, among others.

JOSEPH COLONNA lives in New York City, where he is at work on his first novel. He received both his BFA and MFA in creative writing from Columbia University. He is an adjunct professor in English at Fordham University and at The New School.

S. M. DECKER is a current graduate student in the Dartmouth College MALS program. Her poetry appears in the current MALS literary magazine, *The Journal*. She holds a BA in English literature from Fort Lewis College. As an undergraduate, she was active in the FLC literary club, "Scarlet Letters," and published in the college's *Images Magazine*. Her articles have appeared in *The Independent News Magazine* and *Four Corners Free Press*. Via FLC, she attended a life-changing workshop abroad in India, co-taught by Pamela Uschuk and Kate Niles, which helped shape her later work. As a member of Sigma Tau Delta, a national English society, she presented a collection of her poetry titled *Nature of Sin* at the 2006 International Convention in Portland, Oregon. She lives in Vermont with her wife and son.

LYN DI IORIO is a fiction writer, a professor of English, a scholar, and an editor. Her short novel, *Outside the Bones*, won *Foreword Review*'s 2011 Silver Book of the Year Award in the literary fiction category, was Best Debut Novel on the 2011 Latinidad List, and was a finalist for the 2012 John Gardner Fiction Prize, among others. She was also #2 on LatinoStories.com's 2012 Top Ten Latino Authors to Watch (and Read) list. Last year, she published a short satirical story excerpt in The Review of the Americas Society's special issue, *The Americas in New York*. She has published three books of scholarship and has an essay forthcoming in the anthology of essays, *Junot Díaz and the Decolonial Imagination*. She is currently at work on a full-length novel, *The Sound of Falling Darkness*, an excerpt of which was a runner-up for the 2011 Pirate's Alley Faulkner Society Novel-in-Progress Award.

MARGOT DOUAIHY has taught at Marywood University and the QYP Writing Center (Creative Alliance of New Orleans). She is the author of the poetry books *Girls Like You* and *I Would Ruby if I Could*. Her writing has been featured in *Mic, The Madison Review*, *Pittsburgh Post-Gazette*, *Catamaran Literary Reader*, *The Moth Magazine*, *The Common*, and others. Margot is a board member of *Philadelphia Stories Magazine* and is a technology adviser for the NEXT | VIDEO Conference.

GEORGE DREW was born in Mississippi and lives in upstate New York. He is the author of five collections, most recently *The View from Jackass Hill*, winner of the 2010 X.J. Kennedy Poetry Prize, Texas Review Press. His sixth publication, *Fancy's Orphan*, will be published this year, as will his chapbook, *Down & Dirty*. One of Drew's poems recently received an honorable mention for the Allen Ginsberg Poetry Award, and will appear in the *Paterson Literary*

*Review*; another of his poems was the winner of the *St. Petersburg Review* Poetry Contest and will appear in issue 8; and one of his Southern poems was selected for inclusion in the 2015 edition of the anthology *Down to the Dark River: Poems about the Mississippi* by Louisiana Literature Press.

KEVIN FORTUNA lives in Cold Spring, New York. He holds a bachelor's in English literature from Georgetown University. He is the recipient of a Lannan Literary Fellowship, the Quicksall Medal for Writing, a fellowship in fiction at the Prague Summer Writers Workshop, and a full fellowship in fiction at the University of New Orleans, where he received his MFA.

ANNA GOODKIND holds an MFA in fiction writing from the City College of New York. She received the City College Children's Writing Award in 2012, and her short story *Counting* was a finalist in the Hidden River Arts William Van Wert Fiction Competition in 2014. She is also the recipient of the Mary Gordon Prize from Barnard. She is now completing a young adult novel entitled *Cry of the Loon*.

BRUCE GRAHAM's stories have been published in *The Highlander*, *Alfred Hitchcock's Mystery Magazine*, *I Love Cats*, *Lighthouse Digest*, *Eclectica Magazine*, and *WWII Magazine*. His story *The Lots* received honorable mention in the 2013 Art Affair Literary Contest; *Cat Tale* received honorable mention in the 2013 Soul-Making Keats Literary Competition; and *Cross and Double Cross* was awarded first place in the Fiction Division of the 2014 Writers-Editors Network International Writing Competition. His novel, *Haven*, involves winter conditions similar to those experienced in New England this past season.

JODY HADLOCK is a former journalist who became enamored with the story of Diamond Bessie, a well-known prostitute killed in the East Texas town of Jefferson in 1877. She's writing a historical novel based on Bessie's murder and her quest for revenge as an earthbound spirit. Jody lives in Fort Worth, Texas.

KEITH HILL is a New Zealand writer and filmmaker. His debut feature film, "This Is Not A Love Story," won Best Screenplay at Los Angeles' Dances With Films Festival (2003). His poetry includes versions of Mirabai, Kabir and *The Bhagavad Gita*. Three of his nonfiction books, *Striving to Be Human*,

*The God Revolution* and *Practical Spirituality* have won New Zealand's Ashton Wylie Award for writing in the genre of mind, body and spirit.

ALISSA PAIGE JOSEPH's essays and articles have appeared in numerous Jewish periodicals and magazines. A letter of hers was featured in the book *The Bostoner* by Hanoch Teller. She was a member of The Hypothetical Theater Co., where she and fellow members wrote the play *Immigrant Stories*, which was performed on Ellis Island for close to twenty years.

JAMES PATRICK KELLY has won science fiction's Hugo, Nebula and Locus awards and his work has been translated into seventeen languages. A 250,000-word career retrospective of his short fiction, in the Masters Of Science Fiction Series, will be published in January by Centipede Press. He is on the faculty of the Stonecoast Creative Writing MFA program at the University of Southern Maine.

CLARK KNOWLES teaches writing at the University of New Hampshire. He received his MA in fiction writing from the University of New Hampshire, and his MFA in writing from Bennington College. He lives with his family in an old farmhouse in New Hampshire.

STEVEN LAFOND is a writer who lives in Cambridge, MA. His work has appeared in *apt*, *Little Fiction*, *The Drum*, *The Good Men Project*, and elsewhere. He runs the Belt It Out Reading Series in Cambridge, Massachusetts, which is either the most highbrow karaoke night or the drunkest literary singing competition in the area.

MARIANA LIN was born in Taipei, Taiwan, lived in New York City, and currently resides in the San Francisco Bay Area. Her writing has appeared in publications such as *New York* magazine, *The Huffington Post*, *GQ*, *The Washington Post*, and *Picture Magazine*. She was selected as a finalist for the Mississippi Review Prize. She works at Apple as the writer behind the voice of Siri, answering people's daily existential questions around the world.

WULF LOSEE lives and works in the San Francisco Bay Area. His poems have appeared in *Forge*, *Full Moon*, *FRiGG*, *North Coast Literary Review*, *PoeTalk*, and *Rio Grande Review*. His short fiction has been published in *Oak Square*. He won first prize in the 84th and 86th Annual Poets' Dinner Contests and was a finalist in *The New Guard* 2012 Knightville Poetry Contest.

TERRANCE MANNING, JR. holds an MFA from Purdue. Recently, he received first place in *Boulevard*'s Short Fiction Contest for Emerging Writers, the David Nathan Meyerson Prize for Fiction, and *Crab Orchard Review*'s John Guyon Literary Nonfiction Prize. His work appears or is forthcoming in *Boulevard, Witness, Ninth Letter, Southwest Review, Hunger Mountain*, and other magazines, and he has been selected as a finalist in such contests as the *Cincinnati Review* Awards, *Colorado Review*'s Nelligan Prize, and the *American Short Fiction* Short Story Award. He lives and writes in Pittsburgh, Pennsylvania.

ROBERT MCGUILL lives and writes in Colorado. His work has been nominated for four Pushcart Prizes. McGuill is a narrative fiction contest winner, a Best of the Net nominee, and a *Glimmer Train* Stories Contest finalist. His story collection, *The Outskirts of Nowhere*, was selected as a semifinalist in the 2014 Leapfrog Press Fiction Contest.

ZOË MEAGER is from Christchurch, New Zealand, and holds a masters in creative writing from the University of Auckland. In 2013, she won the Commonwealth Writers Short Story Prize, Pacific Region, and her work has since been highly commended in the Momaya Press and Highlands and Islands short story contests. Zoë's work has appeared in various online and print journals.

MATT W. MILLER is the author of the poetry collection *Club Icarus*, selected as winner of the 2012 Vassar Miller Prize in Poetry, as well as *Cameo Diner: Poems*. He is a former Wallace Stegner Fellow in poetry and has published work in *Southwest Review, Harvard Review, Slate, Notre Dame Review, The Briar Cliff Review, The Florida Review*, and other journals. His poem *Ordeal by Water* was selected as the 2015 Trifecta Poem Prize winner by *Iron Horse Review*. He teaches and coaches at Phillips Exeter Academy and lives with his family in New Hampshire.

ABBY E. MURRAY received her MFA from Pacific University and is currently earning her PhD in English from Binghamton University. Her second chapbook, *Quick Draw: Poems from a Soldier's Wife*, was released in 2012 and is based on her husband's deployments to Iraq and Afghanistan. She serves as poetry editor for *Harpur Palate* and director of the Binghamton Poetry Project. Her poems currently appear or are forthcoming in *Rattle, New Ohio Review, Crab Creek Review*, and *River Styx*.

JOSE PADUA's poetry and fiction have appeared in *Bomb*, *Salon.com*, *Beloit Poetry Journal*, *Exquisite Corpse*, *The New Guard*, *Vox Populi*, *Gargoyle*, *Another Chicago Magazine*, *Unbearables*, *Crimes of the Beats, Up is Up, but So Is Down: New York's Downtown Literary Scene, 1974-1992*, and many other journals and anthologies. He has written features and reviews for *Salon*, *The Weeklings*, *The Good Men Project*, *NYPress, Washington City Paper*, the *Brooklyn Rail*, and the *New York Times*. Padua has read his work at the Lollapalooza Festival, CBGBs, the Knitting Factory, the Public Theater, the Living Theater, the Nuyorican Poets' Café, the St. Mark's Poetry Project, the Black Cat Club, the Washington Project for the Arts, and many other venues, and was a featured reader at the 2012 Split This Rock poetry festival. He lives in Front Royal, Virginia with his wife, the poet Heather Davis, and their son and daughter. He and his wife write the blog, Shenandoah Breakdown.

MICAH PERKS is the author of a novel, *We Are Gathered Here* and a memoir, *Pagan Time*. Her short stories and essays have appeared in *Epoch*, *Zyzzyva*, *Tin House*, *The Toast* and *The Rumpus*, among many other journals and anthologies. Her short memoir, *Alone In The Woods: Cheryl Strayed, My Daughter and Me*, was released last December. Some of the material in "Ghost Deer" was taken from her novel-in-progress. She lives with her family in Santa Cruz and co-directs the creative writing program at UCSC.

MARCIA POPP is a retired university professor and the author of three textbooks, two biographies, and the poetry collection *Comfort in Small Rooms*. Individual poems from this collection won the 2008 Robert Cohn Prose Poetry Award, appeared in *Best New Poets 2009,* are included in the online anthology *In the Heydays of His Eyes*, and have been read by Garrison Keillor on *The Writer's Almanac*. Her poems have appeared in *The Bellingham Review*, *The Atlanta Review*, *The New Guard*, *Naugatuck River Review*, *The Mom Egg Review*, and *Memoir.* Other poems have been featured on *The New Guard*'s BANG website, and some are forthcoming in *Aesthetica's 2015 Creative Writing Anthology*.

ADEEBA AFSHAN RANA is a poet and a librarian who writes and reads in Brooklyn, New York. She has been a featured performer with Body Politics at the University of Massachusetts, We Got Issues! at the Apollo Theater in Harlem, Boston Progress, and the louderARTS project in NYC. She is firmly rooted in engagement, inspiring audiences and students towards the art of reading, the craft of writing, and the wonder of inquiry. Adeeba received her MFA in poetry from Stonecoast at the University of Southern Maine, and her Master's in Library Science at Pratt Institute. She is a facilitator at El Puente Academy for Peace and Justice in Brooklyn.

JL SCHNEIDER is a carpenter and an adjunct professor of English at a small community college in upstate New York. His poetry has appeared in *Crazy River, The Taos Review, The Rhode Island Review*, *Slippery Elm*, and *Rolling Stone*, among others.

DON SCHOFIELD's poetry volumes include *In Lands Imagination Favors*, *Before Kodachrome, The Known: Selected Poems, 1981–2000*, *Kindled Terraces: American Poets in Greece*, *Approximately Paradise*, and *Of Dust.* A recipient of the 2010 Criticos Prize (UK), he has also received honors from, among others, the State University of New York, Anhinga Press, *The Southern California Anthology*, and Princeton University, where he was a Stanley J. Seeger Writer-in-Residence. He has been a resident of Greece for many years.

JONATHAN SEGOL's first writing was in the NYC anti-folk music scene and for *Street News* (newspapers sold by homeless people on the subways). Since then, he has also taught writing in various settings: Brooklyn's high school for auto mechanics, a juvenile prison upstate, and currently at Hudson Valley Community College in Troy, NY. He is currently working on a novel about Y2K, chop shops, graffiti, and Coney Island.

HANNAH SILVERSTEIN is an editor and proofreader who holds degrees from Yale and Dartmouth. She attended the 2014 Frost Place Conference on Poetry and has participated in a Vermonter's Week residency at the Vermont Studio Center. She lives in Vermont.

MATTHEW STEPHEN SIROIS is certain that his childhood home in coastal Maine will forever inspire and haunt his prose. At present, he lives in Seattle, Washington, with his wife, his daughter, and their cat. *Follow the Doe* is excerpted from a draft of Matthew's first novel, *Fletcher's Rock.*

JEANIE TOMASKO is the author of *Tricks of Light*, *Sharp as Want*, a poetry/artworks collaboration with Sharon Auberle, an e-chapbook, *If I Confess Before 5:00*, and most recently is the recipient of an Editor's Choice Award from Concrete Wolf Chapbook Series. Her work has been published in *The Midwest Quarterly*, *Right Hand Pointing*, *Rattle*, *Wisconsin People and Ideas*, and *Bird's Thumb*. She works as a home health nurse in Madison, Wisconsin.

BENJAMIN R. TURNER graduated from the University of Southern Maine's Stonecoast program with a master's of fine arts in creative writing. He lives in Maine with his video-editing wife and their increasingly idiosyncratic cats. Ben works as a proofreader and copy editor when not chiseling away on his own projects, trying to remember ghost stories no one has ever told.

SARAH VAN ARSDALE's fourth book of fiction, *In Case of Emergency,* is forthcoming in 2016. Her third novel, *Grand Isle*, was published by SUNY Press in 2012. Her second novel, *Blue*, won the 2002 Peter Taylor Prize for the Novel. Her first novel, *Toward Amnesia*, was published in 1996. Her poetry, book reviews, interviews, and essays have appeared in national publications, including *Guernica*, *Passages North*, *Fiction Writers Review*, *Bookslut*, *Episodic*, and *Oxford American Magazine*. She holds an MFA in poetry from Vermont College and teaches at the Whidbey Writers Workshop Master of Fine Arts in Creative Writing Program and at NYU; she serves on the board of the Ferro-Grumley Award in Fiction and curates BLOOM: The Reading Series at Hudson View Gardens in New York City.

MELISSA J. VARNAVAS is a 2010 graduate of the Solstice MFA Program at Pine Manor College. Her work has appeared in *Margie: The American Journal of Poetry*, *Oberon*, *Blast Furnace*, and *End Times*, among others. Her journalistic endeavors have also earned her numerous awards from the New England Press Association, Suburban Newspapers of America, and the Massachusetts Press Association. She is an active member of the Tin Box Poets, Salem Writers Group, and the Massachusetts Poetry Society, and volunteers for the Massachusetts Poetry Festival. She lives in Beverly, Massachusetts with her husband, Christopher A. Terrell, and their two cats, Katrina and Hugo.

ERICA VEGA is an instructor of English at Elgin Community College in Elgin, Illinois. She holds a BA in English from Northern Illinois University and a master's of fine arts in creative writing (poetry and fiction concentrations) from the University of Southern Maine. Her writing appears in *About Place Journal*, *Cabildo Quarterly*, *elginMuse*, and *The New Guard*, among other places.

ARTRESS BETHANY WHITE earned her master's degree in creative writing from New York University, and a PhD in English from the University of Kentucky. Her poetry has recently appeared in *Mud Season Review*, *Black Renaissance Noire*, and *Harvard Review*, and is forthcoming in *Mom Egg Review* and *Sin Fronteras/Without Borders*. Her poetry earned a 2015 Pushcart nomination, and she was awarded the 2015 Mary Hambidge Distinguished Fellowship to the Hambidge Center for Creative Arts and Science. *Fast Fat Girls in Pink Hot Pants* is her first collection of poetry. She is an associate professor of English at Carson-Newman University and resides in Knoxville, Tennessee.

RENIA WHITE is an MFA candidate in creative writing at Cornell University.

ANNE WITTY lives and writes in Mid-Coast Maine. She works and plays as a museum curator, maritime historian, poet, musician, organic gardener, and sailor of vintage wooden boats. Her poetry has recently appeared in *The Catch*, *Cabildo Quarterly*, and *Stonecoast Lines*. Her research-based non-fiction has been published in *WoodenBoat Magazine*, *North by Degree: New Perspectives on Arctic Exploration*, and *Working the Water*, as well as in various museum publications, exhibitions, catalogues, and websites.

# ACKNOWLEDGMENTS

We'd like to thank a lot of people for their help on this volume. We couldn't have put this book together without the copy editing expertise of Benjamin R. Turner, whose meticulous attention to detail has been a godsend. A huge thanks to our layout designer, Tom Morgan of Blue Design—such a generous friend to *TNG* and an incredibly skilled talent. Thank you to Marilyn Kalish and the Vault Gallery for letting us use your phenomenal painting, "Independence" for our cover art. Thanks to another wonderful artist, Randall Drew, for your cover design and hard work.

Thank you to Portland Maine's wonderful independent bookstore, Longfellow Books. We are very grateful to you for your enduring support of *TNG*. We've had some great readings together. We want to take a moment to remember the late Stuart Gerson, who was always incredibly kind to us and whose enthusiasm for books will never be forgotten. Longfellow's, you have a special spot in our hearts. Thanks to Devaney, Doak and Garrett and Sherman's of Maine, Skylight Books of Los Angeles and McNally Jackson in NYC. A huge hearty thank you to John Fuller of Kinokuniya USA, who has hosted spectacular events in NYC for us and who even gave away free *TNG*s to patrons. Thank you to Chris and Cody of Book Culture in New York City, who have also hosted wonderful *TNG* NYC events.

Thanks to the Kirby Family Foundation for their generous donation, and thanks to Jennifer Hutchins of Creative Portland for your unwavering sponsorship. Thank you to AWP, CLMP, Poets & Writers, NewPages, Duotrope, Every Writer's Resource and Winning Writers for your help and your support and for fostering a sense of literary responsibility in each of your incredible writing communities. Thanks to all of our BANG! authors for keeping TNG fresh and live online, and thanks to our Community Page writers and our social media friends. Thanks to all of our fans and friends, instructors, lecturers, professional contacts, hoteliers, caterers, heads of reading venues, photographers and of course, our attendees of The Writer's Hotel Master Class in Fiction, Nonfiction & Poetry in New York City. Via *The New Guard*, we have been able to open up this teaching and editorial arm, which has brought us a lot of joy.

Last but not least, thank you to all of our talented contest entrants, and thank you, of course, to the outstanding writers whose work is here in this volume. Thank you, all!